Ciba Found

THE EVALUATION
OF SCIENTIFIC
RESEARCH

A Wiley-Interscience Publication

1989

JOHN WILEY & SONS

Chichester · New York · Brisbane · Toronto · Singapore

© Ciba Foundation 1989

Published in 1989 by John Wiley & Sons Ltd, Chichester, UK.
Reprinted October 1990

Suggested series entry for library catalogues:
Ciba Foundation Conference

Ciba Foundation Conference
viii + 276 pages, 23 figures, 32 tables

British Library Cataloguing in Publication Data

Evered, David
 The evaluation of scientific research.
 1. Science. Research
 I. Title   II. Harnett, Sara
 507'.2

 ISBN 0 471 92143 2

Phototypeset by Dobbie Typesetting Ltd, Devon
Printed and bound in Great Britain by
Biddles Ltd, Guildford and King's Lynn

THE EVALUATION
OF SCIENTIFIC
RESEARCH

The Ciba Foundation is an international scientific and educational charity. It was established in 1947 by the Swiss chemical and pharmaceutical company of CIBA Limited — now CIBA-GEIGY Limited. The Foundation operates independently in London under English trust law.

The Ciba Foundation exists to promote international cooperation in biological, medical and chemical research. It organizes about eight international multidisciplinary symposia each year on topics that seem ready for discussion by a small group of research workers. The papers and discussions are published in the Ciba Foundation symposium series. The Foundation also holds many shorter meetings (not published), organized by the Foundation itself or by outside scientific organizations. The staff always welcome suggestions for future meetings.

The Foundation's house at 41 Portland Place, London W1N 4BN, provides facilities for meetings of all kinds. Its Media Resource Service supplies information to journalists on all scientific and technological topics. The library, open seven days a week to any graduate in science or medicine, also provides information on scientific meetings throughout the world and answers general enquiries on biomedical and chemical subjects. Scientists from any part of the world may stay in the house during working visits to London.

Contents

v

Participants

J. Anderson   The Ciba Foundation, 41 Portland Place, London
W1N 4BN, UK

S. Blume   Department of Science Dynamics, University of Amsterdam,
Nieuwe Achtergracht 166, 1018 WV Amsterdam, The Netherlands

T. Braun   Institute of Inorganic & Analytical Chemistry, L. Eötvös
University, PO Box 123, H-1443 Budapest, Hungary

P. Collins   The Royal Society, 6 Carlton House Terrace, London
SW1Y 5AG, UK

B. Dixon   130 Cornwall Road, Ruislip Manor, Middlesex HA4 6AW, UK

E. Garfield   Institute for Scientific Information, 3501 Market Street,
Philadelphia, Pennsylvania 19104, USA

L. Georghiou   Programme of Policy Research in Engineering, Science and
Technology, The University, Manchester M13 9PL, UK

C. T. Hill   Congressional Research Service, Library of Congress,
Washington, DC 20540, USA

P. Hills   The Department of Trade and Industry, Ashdown House,
1 Victoria Street, London SW1, UK

J. Irvine   Science Policy Research Unit, Mantell Building, University of
Sussex, Falmer, Brighton BN1 9RF, UK

F. Kodama   National Institute of Science and Technology Policy, Science
and Technology Agency, 1-11-39, Nagata-cho, Chiyoda-ku, Tokyo, Japan

C. E. Kruytbosch   Science Indicators Group, National Science
Foundation, Washington, DC 20550, USA

J. V. Lake   Agricultural and Food Research Council, Central Office, Wiltshire Court, Farnsby Street, Wiltshire SN1 5AT, UK

T. Luukkonen-Gronow   Academy of Finland, Hämeentie 58, SF-00550 Helsinki, Finland

P. Montigny   Organization for Economic Cooperation and Development, 2 rue André-Pascal, F-7565 Paris Cedex 16, France

M. J. Moravcsik   Institute of Theoretical Science, University of Oregon, Eugene, Oregon 97403, USA

F. Narin   CHI Research/Computer Horizons Inc, 10 White Horse Pike, Haddon Heights, New Jersey 08035, USA

K. Pavitt   Science Policy Research Unit, Mantell Building, University of Sussex, Falmer, Brighton BN1 9RF, UK

Sir David Phillips (*Chairman*)   Laboratory of Molecular Biophysics, Department of Zoology, University of Oxford, The Rex Richards Building, South Parks Road, Oxford OX1 3QU, UK

H. Small   Institute for Scientific Information, 3501 Market Street, Philadelphia, Pennsylvania 19104, USA

A. F. J. van Raan   Science Studies Unit, LISBON-Institute, University of Leiden, Stationsplein 242, 2312 AR Leiden, The Netherlands

S. Wald   Organization for Economic Cooperation and Development, 2 rue André-Pascal, F-75675 Paris Cedex 16, France

A. M. Weinberg   Oak Ridge Associated Universities, Institute for Energy Analysis, PO Box 117, Oak Ridge, Tennessee 37831, USA

Introduction

Sir David Phillips

Laboratory of Molecular Biophysics, Department of Zoology, University of Oxford, The Rex Richards Building, South Parks Road, Oxford OX1 3QU, UK

Let me begin by reminding you that twenty five years ago, throughout the developed world, public support for science was growing at an astonishing rate. In the United Kingdom at that time the annual budget for the research councils grew by some 17 or 18% per annum in real terms, and the concern of the Advisory Council for Science Policy, the Department of Scientific and Industrial Research (DSIR), the research councils, the universities and other agencies was to devise ways of spending that money reasonably. That's not the situation now, as most of us in this room know. Even twenty five years ago there were a few people, and we're lucky in having with us one of them, Dr Weinberg, who recognized that circumstances were bound to change, and in particular that governments would try to define more precisely the purposes for which they invested in scientific research, that they would be concerned with assessing the results of that investment, and that the rapid exponential growth of public support for science could not continue indefinitely. Twenty five years later, these issues are at the forefront of science policy discussions, and I hope and expect that our discussions over the next three days will help us towards a deeper understanding of them.

Before we embark on that discussion it might be useful for me to distinguish between the primary objectives of public support for science and the secondary objectives, which we are likely to spend most of our time considering. The primary objectives, as I see them, are to develop a deeper understanding of the universe and our place in it; to achieve social benefit from that understanding through the development of individual understanding, the promotion of health and welfare and the control of the environment; to further the development of a prosperous economy through the discovery of new knowledge capable of being exploited in wealth creation, and the training of scientists and engineers for roles in shaping that economy; to underpin national defence; and perhaps to further international goodwill and understanding through collaboration in a transnational human experience.

1989 The evaluation of scientific research. Wiley, Chichester (Ciba Foundation Conference) p 1–2

There may be some disagreement about the details of that list, and its order probably isn't the order of priority that most governments would attach to such a list, but I suspect that those are something like the overall aims of most governments in supporting research. We are likely to focus very largely on a part of that, on the generation of new knowledge, for example, and we shall be concerned with such matters as how good, that is to say how worthy of support, are individual scientists or research groups? How fruitful are particular lines of enquiry? How effective are alternative forms of research organizations?

In doing so, I hope that we shall remember that our measures of success at this level may be poor indicators of success in meeting the overall objectives, that there is a risk of distorting the whole scientific enterprise so that it satisfies whatever measures we invent rather than the objectives of the investment, and finally that even as we sit here the nature of the scientific enterprise is changing around us as our understanding develops. That's a slightly cautionary beginning perhaps. Nevertheless I hope we shall remember that it is easy to focus on particular secondary objectives and to lose sight of the primary purposes.

Criteria for evaluation, a generation later

Alvin M. Weinberg

Oak Ridge Associated Universities, Institute for Energy Analysis, PO Box 117, Oak Ridge, Tennessee 37831, USA

Abstract. The debate on criteria of scientific choice is 25 years old. Have the criteria proposed in this debate been useful in the allocation of resources? Judging by the use of such criteria in the National Science Foundation's Proposal Evaluation Criteria, one must answer with a qualified yes. On the other hand, the actual practices of individual peer reviewers probably reflect implicit attitudes towards evaluation rather than explicit *a priori* criteria. Two developments have extended the philosophical context of the criteria debate: a realization that values such as 'utility' and 'unity', which underlie scientific administrative decisions, are not the same as 'truth', the value which underlies scientific practice; and the criterion of embeddedness has been challenged by high-energy physicists who claim unique merit for a criterion of 'closeness to the source of the chain of explanation'. These issues seem to be coming to a practical head in arguments over the superconducting supercollider, the human genome sequencing project and the Strategic Defense Initiative.

1989 The evaluation of scientific research. Wiley, Chichester (Ciba Foundation Conference) p 3–15

Evaluation of scientific research can be either prospective or retrospective. In the first instance one seeks to establish *a priori* criteria for evaluating *proposed* research, in the second instance criteria are sought for evaluating research or research institutions *after* the research has been completed. Philosophical criteria for scientific choice, such as I proposed 25 years ago (Weinberg 1963), conceivably are helpful for both *a priori* and *a posteriori* evaluations, but they were prompted by a drive to evaluate proposals for research, not research already done. (See, however, Martin & Irvine 1981.)

In principle, evaluation of completed research hardly needs elaborate philosophical underpinning. A broad scientific consensus usually forms around the truly important discoveries, and there are qualitative indices, such as citations, to buttress such judgements. *A posteriori* judgements often focus on research performers, whether individuals, groups, or institutions. Track records, however measured, can be used to judge which performer is most deserving. Thus, to use terminology from my paper, 'The philosophy and practice of national science policy', for a 1967 Ciba Foundation Symposium (Weinberg 1968), prospective evaluation involves both scientific and institutional choice, and retrospective evaluation is usually aimed at institutional choice.

Were either approach to choice perfect, the other would be superfluous. Thus if we could identify, on the basis of track record, who the most successful performers have been, we would need only support them, confident that their judgement as to appropriate scientific fields would be better than any other judgement. Or if we knew perfectly in advance which research projects were the most important, we would support only these, whoever the performer. This, of course, is a caricature of the evaluation process. The future of research is largely unknowable, and any *a priori* criteria of scientific choice are intrinsically deficient. On the other hand, support of only successful performers can lead to rigidity and stagnation. New fields that do not interest 'successful performers' always crop up, as do ambitious and able younger scientists.

The philosophical debate on criteria in retrospect

I wrote my paper, 'Criteria for scientific choice' (Weinberg 1963) while I was a member of the President's Scientific Advisory Committee (PSAC). Allocation of resources to competing scientific fields was always of concern to the PSAC and to the Bureau of the Budget. At the time, the two central issues were whether or not to go to the moon, and how much should go for the support of high-energy physics. Thus my criteria were mostly directed toward 'big science'; as for 'little science', I argued that competence of the research performer was the overriding consideration.

My criteria were divided into two categories: internal and external. Internal criteria arose from within the science itself, and were basically criteria of efficiency—how well the proposed research would be performed. Thus one internal criterion was the competence of the performer. Another was whether the science was 'ripe for exploitation'. Internal criteria are necessary criteria for the support of any science, or indeed for any undertaking that demands limited resources. They are criteria of efficiency because, to the degree they are met, money spent on research is likely to produce results.

In little science such criteria of efficiency are generally sufficient as well as necessary. On the other hand, where the required resources are large, internal criteria are insufficient: 'external' criteria, arising from outside the field under consideration, must be considered. External criteria are criteria of utility— that is, they measure the degree to which the given research, if successful, is, in the broadest sense, useful outside the field itself. I identified three such external criteria: technological merit, social merit, and scientific merit. Technological merit measures the degree to which research advances technology; social merit, the degree to which the research helps achieve various social goals, such as better health, better schools, better international relations; and scientific merit, the degree to which the research illuminates the neighbouring scientific fields in which the proposed research is embedded.

Ultimately these criteria of scientific choice involve the concept of 'value' within science. In saying this I distinguish between the 'value' and the 'truth' of a scientific finding. Every valid scientific finding in some sense reveals an aspect of truth; every scientist knows this instinctively. But in the allocation of resources — that is, administration of science — truth alone is insufficient. Not all scientific activities that meet the strictest criteria of scientific truth can be supported; one must judge which activities are the most valuable. Thus the notion of value within science is at the philosophical heart of scientific administration, just as truth is at the heart of the practice of science. So to speak, the philosophy of scientific administration is axiological, and the philosophy of scientific practice is epistemological.

I have returned to these philosophical thoughts in recent years, particularly to elaborate the notion of value in science. My main conclusion is implicit in my previous remarks: that the underlying value in the practice of science is truth: what achieves truth most efficiently is the most valuable. But the underlying value in the administration of science is utility: what is most useful, in addition to being true, is the most valuable. Moreover, in the administration of basic science, usefulness to neighbouring sciences is the main guiding criterion. In other words, those basic scientific activities that impart unity to science are to be preferred to those that do not: *unity* is the ultimate value in the formulation of a grand strategy for basic science.

I have ascribed the description 'fundamental' to basic scientific research that possesses this quality of illuminating (in the sense of unifying) the neighbouring fields in which the activity is embedded. Thus the discovery of the double-helix in DNA is 'fundamental' because it has led to an enormous unification of biology — much more fundamental, say, than the identification of a sequence of amino acids that constitute a particular protein.

High-energy physicists have suggested that my identification of 'fundamental' with implication for other sciences is too narrow. Science progresses along two paths, which Weisskopf (1964) calls extensive science and intensive science. Extensive science deals with configurations of matter, the individual units of which — atom, molecules, cells — are in some sense understood. The basic problem is to understand how such aggregates, whether living or non-living, behave — to explain what are sometimes called emergent properties. Intensive science deals with the very simplest entities, and seeks to characterize these entities. High-energy physics is the paradigm of intensive science; solid state physics, the paradigm of extensive science. Thus Weisskopf criticizes my use of 'fundamental' in that it refers to the extensive dimension, and ignores the intensive dimension of science. In a similar vein, Steven Weinberg (1987) has introduced the notion of 'arrow of explanation' — the constant probing toward the 'source of the chain of explanation', which culminates, inexorably, in the explorations of high-energy physics. In Weisskopf's terms this is the ultimate intensive science. This argument over a somewhat arcane philosophical point — what do we mean when we say a scientific discovery is 'fundamental' — is germane to the current controversy over the support of the superconducting supercollider (SSC), and I shall return to it.

The philosophical debate and practical allocations

To what extent has the philosophical debate influenced the allocation of resources for science, at least in the United States? In a general way, the categories identified in the philosophical debate have provided a language for the practical debate. Although the largest allocations of public funds, even to science, are strongly influenced by politics, I believe the philosophical debate does inform the political debate. Two instances illustrate the point.

The Bromley Report

In 1972, the Physics Survey Committee of the National Academy of Sciences published a three-volume study, *Physics in perspective*, under the chairmanship of Professor D. Allen Bromley of Yale University (Bromley 1972). This study was one of the first to set priorities within a major scientific field. In setting these priorities, the committee devised three general criteria of choice. Two of the general criteria, intrinsic merit and extrinsic merit, were similar to the internal and external criteria I had suggested (Weinberg 1963). These general criteria were subdivided into 14 subcriteria of which five were intrinsic, and nine were extrinsic. The third general criterion was structure. This criterion considered the social structure of physics research, and how this structure would be affected by support of the subfield in question. Examples of issues subsumed in the structural criterion are: the extent to which major new instrumentation is required for progress in the field; the extent to which support of the field is urgently required to maintain viability or to obtain a proper scientific return on major capital investments; the extent to which maintenance of the field is essential to the continued health of the scientific discipline of which it is a part.

The merit of each field was summarized as a 14-component histogram, each component being one of the subcriteria. The weight attached to each component was determined by polling the committee. The committee's assignments of merit are shown in Fig. 1.

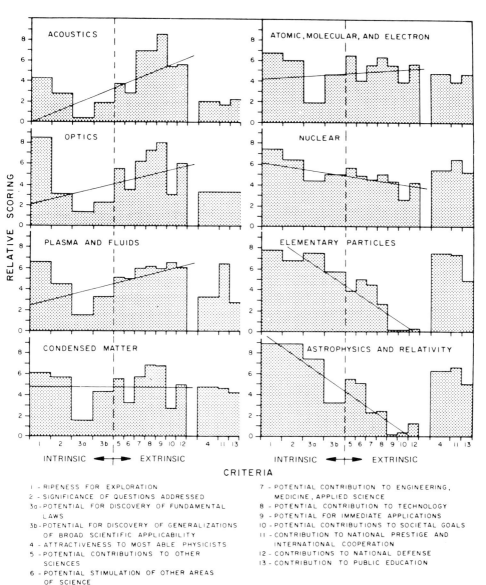

FIG. 1. Histograms of the average jury ratings of the core physics subfields in terms of the intrinsic and extrinsic criteria developed in the Bromley Report (1972). The straight lines superimposed on the histograms provide a characteristic signature for each subfield. Note that these signatures divide naturally into three classes, with emphasis shifting from intrinsic to extrinsic areas as the subfield matures.

TABLE 1   The ten highest scoring programme elements

Programme element	Physics subfield
1 Lasers & masers	Atomic, molecular, and electron
2 National Accelerator	Elementary particle
3 Quantum optics	Condensed matter
4 University groups—elementary particle physics	Elementary particle
5 Stanford Linear Accelerator	Elementary particle
6 Nuclear dynamics	Nuclear
7 Major facilities	Elementary particle
8 Brookhaven Alternating Gradient Synchrotron	Elementary particle
9 Nuclear excitations	Nuclear
10 Heavy ion interactions	Nuclear

Similar 'histograms of merit' were constructed for some 69 'programme elements', a programme element being either a specialized subdivision of a subfield—such as 'semiconductors', a programme element in the condensed matter subfield—or a large facility, such as the National Accelerator Laboratory in the field of elementary particle physics. Finally, the committee produced an overall scoring for the programme elements. The ten highest scoring programme elements and the ten lowest scoring elements are listed in Tables 1 and 2.

The allocations made since the Bromley report appear to conform reasonably well to these recommendations. For example, the National Accelerator

TABLE 2   The ten lowest scoring programme elements

Programme element	Physics subfield
1 Music & architectural acoustics	Acoustics
2 Noise, mechanical shock & vibration	Acoustics
3 Underwater sound	Acoustics
4 Ultrasonics and infrasonics	Acoustics
5 Slow neutron physics	Condensed matter
6 Electroacoustics & acoustics instrumentation	Acoustics
7 Crystallography	Condensed matter
8 Gas discharges	Atomic, molecular, & electron
9 Accelerator development	Elementary particle
10 Metrology	Optics

Laboratory and the Stanford Linear Accelerator Centre have been well-funded (and very productive), and the field of heavy ion interactions has expanded markedly. On the other hand, the 1985 Nobel Prize for Chemistry was awarded to two crystallographers, a field ranked near the bottom!

The National Science Foundation Proposal Evaluation Criteria

The National Science Foundation asks all its peer reviewers to judge proposals according to four 'Proposal Evaluation Criteria'. I reproduce these criteria verbatim from the 1987 edition of the NSF's brochure, *Information for Reviewers*.

(1) Research performance competence — Capability of the investigator(s), the technical soundness of the proposed approach, and the adequacy of the institutional resources available. Please include comments on the proposer's recent research performance.

(2) Intrinsic merit of the research — Likelihood that the research will lead to new discoveries or fundamental advances within its field of science or engineering, or have substantial impact on progress in that field or in other scientific and engineering fields.

(3) Utility or relevance of the research — Likelihood that the research can contribute to the achievement of a goal that is extrinsic or in addition to that of the research field itself, and thereby serve as the basis for new or improved technology or assist in the solution of societal problems.

(4) Effect of the research on the infrastructure of science and engineering — Potential of the proposed research to contribute to better understanding or improvement of the quality, distribution, or effectiveness of the Nation's scientific and engineering research, education, and human resources base.

Criteria 1, 2, and 3 constitute an integral set that should be applied in a balanced way to all research proposals in accordance with the objectives and content of each proposal. Criterion 1, research performance competence, is essential to the evaluation of the quality of every research proposal; all three aspects should be addressed. The relative weight given Criteria 2 and 3 depends on the nature of the proposed research; Criterion 2, intrinsic merit, is emphasized in the evaluation of basic research proposals, while Criterion 3, utility or relevance, is emphasized in the evaluation of applied research proposals. Criterion 4, effect on the infrastructure of science and engineering, permits the evaluation of research proposals in terms of their potential for improving the scientific and engineering enterprise and its educational activities in ways other than those encompassed by the first three criteria.

The first three criteria are essentially the same as the ones proposed in the *Minerva* debate 25 years ago. The fourth criterion in many ways resembles Bromley's 'structure' criterion.

I cannot attest to how seriously peer reviewers take these criteria when they judge research proposals. (I should think a study of this question might be useful.) All I can say is that here is an instance of the institutionalization, if not bureaucratization, of a point of view that emerged from the philosophical debate on criteria for scientific choice. Perhaps this is justification enough for the continuation, and elaboration, of this debate—of which this Ciba Foundation Conference is an important part.

The superconducting supercollider, the human genome project and the Strategic Defense Initiative

Three enormous big science spectaculars are now dominating the debate on science policy in the United States. Two are pure basic research, the superconducting supercollider (SSC) and the human genome (HG) project; the third, the Strategic Defense Initiative (SDI), is applied research. How America decides on these projects will strongly affect the shape of science in the next decade. SSC and HG pit big science against little science, and the outcry against both projects by defenders of little science is of unprecedented intensity. SDI, with its enormous political implications, splits the scientific community along a different fracture plane: those who distrust Soviet intentions generally regard SDI as being technically plausible; those who view the Soviets more benignly regard SDI as a technical fantasy.

With respect to SDI, I shall only offer my own personal view. Because the project is so deeply political, criteria of choice such as I have discussed are hardly relevant; instead one must examine the political contexts on which a decision to deploy will depend in order to decide whether or not to spend the huge sums of money required to learn whether SDI is even feasible. In this I differ from many of my colleagues because I claim that missile defence and arms control are synergistic, not antagonistic. Large reductions in strategic missiles are necessary if strategic defence is to work technically; and a world with a few hundred, rather than 25 000, strategic warheads is at the mercy of the cheater unless defence against a very small clandestine attack exists. This is the message of our book, *Strategic defenses and arms control* (Weinberg & Barkenbus 1987); I refer you to it for further details.

The other two spectaculars, SSC and HG, carry less political impedimenta, but the division in the scientific community is almost as deep. Here I should think the criteria of choice are appropriate—and I suppose my response to Weisskopf in the earlier debate remains relevant. SSC, if not HG, rates extremely highly on internal criteria. From the point of view of high-energy physics, the SSC is a most desirable next step. But the relevance to the rest of science, even physics, is debateable. Why then, must SSC be done in this generation? Progress in the rest of science will hardly be thwarted if SSC is remanded to the next generation.

HG is rather different. Here there is no unanimity as to its merit as judged by internal criteria. Instead, most arguments for HG seem to relate to external criteria; its possible usefulness for advances in genetic medicine, as well as in the technology of gene sequencing.

Frank Press in his 1988 Presidential Address to the US National Academy of Sciences approaches the issues raised by this unseemly scientific controversy by proposing criteria for priorities that are much less philosophical, and perhaps more realistic, than the ones I have discussed. He identifies three categories of projects (Press 1988). In the highest category, Dr Press places measures to maintain the base of science. This means supporting the best scientists, and the flow of young scientists; responding to national crises like AIDS; and exploiting extraordinary breakthroughs, like high critical temperature superconductors. At lower priority he places SSC and HG; if full funding is unavailable, he urges that we authorize these projects now but fund them only as we find money for them. For his third category, Dr Press recognizes that most allocations ultimately are political, and he has the courage to say so. Thus, because the degree of support for such enterprises as national defence, the space station and regional economic development is determined primarily by political, not scientific considerations, they are to be dealt with quite separately from those projects whose worth is measured more in scientific rather than political terms.

Dr Press's advice is realistic rather than philosophical—indeed his criteria are more nearly explicit directions for allocations of funds than they are general criteria in our sense. As such they enjoy the advantage of being directly translatable into government action. Although I would have preferred that these explicit recommendations be set in a context of more general principles for evaluation, I appreciate Dr Press's courage in announcing clearly what he believes are the most important scientific activities.

Dr Press's speech ends with a call to establish priorities '. . . we must . . . be willing . . . to propose priorities across scientific fields, if the times call for it. We can do so in a manner that is knowledgeable, responsible, and useful.' Thus I expect the philosophical debate on scientific priorities and criteria for choice will be a continuing one—and I trust, one which the Ciba Foundation will continue to address as it has in 1967 and now in 1988.

References

Bromley DA 1972 Physics in perspective. National Academy of Sciences, Washington DC

Martin BR, Irvine J 1981 Internal criteria for scientific choice: an evaluation of research in high energy physics using electron accelerators. Minerva 19:408–432

Press F 1988 The dilemma of the Golden Age, Address at 125th Annual Meeting, US National Academy of Sciences, 26 April 1988, Washington DC

Weinberg AM 1963 Criteria for scientific choice. Minerva 1:159–171

Weinberg AM 1968 The philosophy and practice of national science policy. In:
    de Reuck A et al (eds) Decision making in national science policy. Ciba Foundation
    and Science of Science Foundation Symposium. J & A Churchill Ltd, London, p 26–38
Weinberg AM, Barkenbus JN 1987 Strategic defenses and arms control. Paragon House,
    New York
Weinberg S 1987 Newtonianism, reductionism and the art of Congressional Testimony.
    Nature 330:433–437
Weisskopf VF 1964 Two open letters. Physics Today 17:46

DISCUSSION

Moravcsik: Since Alvin Weinberg's first *Minerva* article (Weinberg 1963),
the philosophical basis of this discussion hasn't changed, but there has been an
attempt to apply these ideas to practical problems. Alvin described how in
implementing these assessments one has to work in several dimensions. First,
the situation must be analysed so that one is clear what the dimensions are.
Irvine & Martin's work on the evaluation of institutions in radio astronomy and
high-energy physics illustrates the multidimensional nature of such assessments
(Martin & Irvine 1981, 1983). They emphasized that one is dealing with
composite indicators.

Once we know what the dimensions are, we need good indicators for each
one. Much effort in the last decade has been directed to finding these; it is
agreed, for example, that bibliometric indicators can be used to assess some
activities. The last task is to put together the indicators to obtain a final
judgement. The Bromley Report contained graphs of each 'dimension' of the
analysis and the committee arrived at a single number for each of the fields
(Bromley 1972). This synthesis of different dimensions into one number is
where value judgements are made. To devise a more objective basis for that
process would be a significant contribution to decision making in science. I
don't know if this is possible; little work has been done in that area.

Weinberg: Dr Kruytbosch, how seriously do the National Science Foundation (NSF) peer reviewers take the recommended criteria in their evaluations?

Kruytbosch: When we were putting together the Merit Review Committee
Report in 1987 I talked to programme directors from almost all the NSF
research programmes. In the basic sciences, such as mathematics and chemistry, reviewers use mainly the first two criteria—competence of the resear-
cher(s) and the intrinsic significance of the project. But in many of the newer
programmes, and in engineering, the other criteria are often written into the
programme objectives, and sometimes the review process is specifically established. For example, for those programmes that have dual review processes,
both criteria of contribution to social/economic utility and criteria of contribution to science infrastructure may be written into the programme charter. The

report on merit review stressed the necessity to create review processes specifically tailored to the particular programme objectives.

Weinberg: Is there any evidence that since the criteria have been established peer reviewing has been done any better than before?

Kruytbosch: There's no evidence one way or the other.

Irvine: Three very interesting issues arise from your paper, Dr Weinberg. The first concerns the conflict between the philosophy of science and the philosophy of scientific administration. In most evaluation conferences, one often finds two highly polarized groups: on the one hand, there are the professional evaluators concerned to discuss the technical strengths and weaknesses of different assessment methods; on the other hand, there are those who question the basic legitimacy, viability and validity of the tools used in evaluation. The philosophers and sociologists of science are thus ranged against the scientific evaluators. Dr Loet Leydesdorff of Amsterdam University has undertaken a bibliometric study of the field of quantitative science policy studies (Leydesdorff 1989). He finds three groups: (i) those working in R&D policy who publish in journals such as *Research Policy*; (ii) sociologists of science who use journals like *Social Studies of Science*; and (iii) historians and philosophers of science. Patterns of citation show that there is little interconnection between the intellectual interests of these groups. At the Science Policy Research Unit (SPRU) we belong to the first group and try to use, like engineers, the available techniques for evaluation—e.g. publications as indicators of scientific production and citations as indicators of scientific influence— and have not regarded questioning the meaning of these indicators to be a priority. In fact, we tend to find the long-standing debates on the meaning of citations rather arid.

The second issue concerns planning and priority setting in science. We are preparing a review for the Dutch government of longer-term foresight in nine industrial countries. You alluded to what is probably the biggest barrier to acceptance of priority setting—the notion that planning is invariably equated with bureaucratic inflexibility. It is only when one can show that planning is possible without bureaucratic control of science that researchers will consider discussing the subject. Important questions here are: How much planning should be done? What should be the role of the scientific community? And at what level should planning take place; is it possible to identify priorities at the aggregate national level and still allow scientists sufficient freedom to set lower level priorities through peer review?

This relates to the third issue, the current concern in the USA with priority setting. The discussion about priorities for big science has just come to the fore, while we in Europe had such a debate ten years ago. As a result, there has been a general trend in the UK to decrease funding of big science and increase support for smaller science specialties. Similar debates have taken place in other European countries and, as you are learning, a tremendous amount of politics is involved. This is illustrated by our experience publishing a review in *Physics Today* of the comparative scientific performance of the major world high-energy physics centres. The first part of the paper demonstrated that there had been a tremendous decline in the relative standing of the US laboratories. We then went on to assess the prospects for high-energy physics and showed that the superconducting supercollider (SSC) was not regarded by high-energy physicists as a particularly promising option. However, this part of our paper did not pass the peer review system operated by the American Physical Society. In the end, we had no option other than to agree to publication of a shortened version of the paper (Irvine et al 1986). This had the opposite impact to that we originally intended: the data documenting the serious decline in US high-energy physics were used to make the case for the pressing need for the SSC! What is causing this debate on priorities in the USA at the moment? Previously there has always been the view that pluralism is necessary in research support, and that any form of coordinated priority setting should be avoided. Is the reason for this change in philosophy the fact that you are now in a rather poor economic situation? Are you perhaps in the same position as the UK 10 or 15 years ago—having to cope with decline of empire and the need to adjust to one's real economic situation? Or is the explanation purely a newfound desire to plan?

Weinberg: I suspect it is the extraordinary budget stringency. The Gramm-Rudman Act, which set a firm limit to government spending, was an attempt to deal with the huge budget deficit in the USA. This is forcing us to deal with the issue of priorities much more explicitly than in the past. As long as the budget increased by 17% per year, science administration was very easy. It becomes difficult when the budget is constant or diminishing. I think that is the primary reason. The second reason is that it is unprecedented for a single scientific activity to demand $6000 million.

Moravcsik: I agree. My estimate is that the SSC will cost something like $10 billion—the official estimate is $4.4 billion and I am adding the usual kind of factor that occurs in these situations. Furthermore, after the machine is built, I would estimate from past experience that 10% of the construction costs will be needed as running costs per year. Let's say it's a billion dollars a year for as long as the laboratory functions. This is between 5 and 10% of the money spent annually in the United States on basic scientific research. It is certainly an unprecedented amount for one particular scientific project. Many people do not believe the claim of the proponents of the SSC that this money will come from some source outside the present science budget, and that added to the sharpness of the debate.

Luukkonen-Gronow: How rational can decision making on strategic choices be? This discussion of differentiation of evaluation criteria implies a high degree of rationality. Mike Moravcsik also seemed to imply that this enterprise could be very rational. What were the effects of the Bromley Report on the allocation of funds among the physics fields? Was it only an academic exercise or did these evaluations play a role in strategic decisions?

Weinberg: How rational can any political decision making process be made? What the philosophical debate supplies is perhaps a more rational language in which the political debate is conducted. I quite agree that it's not like Einstein's theory of relativity or quantum mechanics where you can come to a conclusion with which everybody agrees. I am pleased if the philosophical debate supplies a language for the political debate, but I recognize always that it is the political debate that finally triumphs. The Bromley Report was only one of a dozen reports that the US National Academy of Sciences put out in different fields of science. These reports did serve to inform the programme directors in the National Science Foundation, the President's Scientific Advisory Committee, and those working in the funding agencies. I think the Fermi Accelerator had already been decided at the time of the Bromley Report, so I can't point to any allocations that resulted from the report. It is interesting that the final line-up that the report gave did more or less coincide with how the money was spent.

References

Bromley DA 1972 Physics in perspective. National Academy of Sciences, Washington DC

Irvine J, Martin BR, Skea JF, Peacock T, Minchin N, Cronk D 1986 The shifting international balance of power in experimental particle physics. Physics Today 39:211–223

Leydesdorff L 1989 The relations between qualitative theory and scientometric methods in science and technology studies: introduction to the theme issue. Scientometrics 15(5–6): in press

Martin BR, Irvine J 1981 Internal criteria for scientific choice: an evaluation of the research performance of electron high-energy physics accelerators. Minerva 19:408–432

Martin BR, Irvine J 1983 Assessing basic research: some partial indicators of scientific progress in radio astronomy. Research Policy 12:61–90

Weinberg AM 1963 Criteria for scientific choice. Minerva 1:159–171

Organization of evaluation

L. G. Georghiou

Programme of Policy Research in Engineering, Science and Technology, Mathematics Building, The University, Manchester M13 9PL, UK

Abstract. Most discussions of evaluation concern methods and the results of their application. This paper argues that methods represent only part of a larger process and that the organization of that process is critical to the outcome of evaluations. The organization of evaluation includes the issues of what is being evaluated, by whom, by which criteria, for whom and to what purpose. Four precursors should be articulated in advance of an evaluation. The *scope* of an evaluation addresses the type of research to be evaluated, its boundaries and the timing of the exercise. *Criteria* provide the basis for the issues to be investigated. The *purpose* needs to be clear to all concerned and the *organization* involves selection of evaluators, the operating procedures and decisions on the level of resources to be made available. The critical element is the interface between the evaluation and the wider policy making process. These issues are discussed in the context of two examples of evaluations carried out by PREST (Programme of Policy Research in Engineering, Science and Technology). The first is a real-time programme evaluation, addressing the Alvey Programme for Advanced Information Technology and the second an institutional evaluation, of the British Museum (Natural History).

1989 The evaluation of scientific research. Wiley, Chichester (Ciba Foundation Conference) p 16–31

The growth of research evaluation both as an academic discipline and as part of the policy environment has taken place against a background of declining or even negative growth rates in the resources available for science. At the same time, the expansion of the 'new technologies' has focused attention upon the exploitability of science and increasingly has led scientific managers to use this argument to justify their resources. Inevitably, competition for resources has intensified both within and outside the scientific system. Externally, value-for-money has to be demonstrated both in terms of efficiency and of impact so that science can compete with other demands upon public funds. Internally, demand for resources has outstripped supply and has made selectivity and concentration the only viable strategies if standards are to be maintained. The traditional mechanisms for allocation and reward systems in the scientific industry, all stemming from peer review, have been unable to provide the information necessary to sustain these competitive processes and it is in this context that evaluation has emerged into the policy arena.

In this paper, I shall not discuss in any detail the methods by which evaluators extract and process information about research. Instead, I shall concentrate on the way evaluation itself fits into the system, examining its connections to those being evaluated and to the audience for its outputs. Evaluation is a social process and the way in which it is organized is critical to its outcome. The organization of evaluation includes the issues of what is being evaluated, by whom, by which criteria, for whom and to what purpose.

Firstly, I shall discuss what I have previously termed the 'precursors' of evaluation (Gibbons & Georghiou 1987). The precursors provide a framework for evaluations against which methods and techniques may subsequently be employed. Secondly, I shall consider two examples of evaluations in the light of these precursors and in the context of the interface between evaluation and the wider policy-making process. Evaluation approaches, however elegant, cannot be justified as intellectual activities in their own right; they must be seen in the context of how they are applied and what effect they achieve. The examples, which my unit, Programme of Policy Research in Engineering, Science and Technology (PREST), has been carrying out, are an evaluation of a programme, the Alvey Programme for Advanced Information Technology and an institution, the British Museum (Natural History).

Definition phase of an evaluation

In the initial stages of an evaluation, the task ahead needs to be defined. This definition can be categorized in terms of the purpose of the evaluation, its scope and the criteria to be applied.

Purpose of evaluation

Three main groups of actors are involved in evaluations:

those being evaluated;
those performing the evaluation;
and the audience for the evaluation.

An evaluation may be initiated by any of these groups but the nature of the exercise which emerges is affected by its *purpose*. The audience for evaluations generally includes the organization which sponsors the institution or programme. When an evaluation is initiated by the sponsor, the requirement of accountability for resources may be the predominant motive. Often an evaluation of this type has a strong institutional framework and its performance is a routine activity. In contrast, sponsors may also institute *ad hoc* evaluations which are essentially problem-solving. For example, evaluators may be asked to consider whether the mission of an institution is still relevant or to investigate an area prior to reorganization.

Evaluations instituted by those who become the subject of the evaluation may take place as a result of an actual or anticipated external requirement or where an organization wishes to produce evidence cataloguing its achievements and justifying its activities. In other cases, those responsible for the programme or institution seek to use the evaluation as a management tool, measuring performance and seeking ways of improving it. These motivations may be combined.

Where the initiative comes from the evaluators themselves the evaluation is generally a more academic exercise, perhaps to develop new methodologies or simply as a research activity in science policy or science studies.

Scope of evaluation

Once an evaluation is decided upon, it is as well to clarify the *scope*, a term which embraces a number of features including the type of research, the level of the evaluation and the time-frame which it addresses.

In most cases the criteria applied and the methods used are different, at least in emphasis, according to whether the research is basic or applied. This may be a problem as the scope of many evaluations, particularly those of institutions, may encompass research from several parts of the basic–applied science spectrum. Establishing comparability may be difficult in these circumstances. Institutions and programmes may also span different disciplines which demand their own performance criteria.

The level of evaluation is concerned with whether it is individuals, projects, programmes, institutions or even whole fields of science which are to be evaluated. Clearly this has methodological implications as, for example, the performance of a programme can be more than simply the sum of the performances of its constituent projects. The defined level also has a practical impact upon the execution of evaluations, because individuals or project representatives will have different attitudes to questioning if they believe that they have been picked out for specific evaluation rather than being asked for information on the broader thrust of the programme.

The time-frame of an evaluation refers to when the evaluation is carried out in relation to the research being evaluated. In general terms there is a tension between maximizing the amount of information available, which increases during and after the programme, and delivering results early enough to have a significant impact upon the current or successor programme. For institutional evaluation there may be no clearly defined beginning or end to the research activities, which leaves the evaluators to decide which combination of past and present performance fairly represents the research.

Criteria for evaluation

Though expressed in many different ways, evaluation criteria may usually be grouped in three broad categories:

those addressing the quality and originality of the scientific and technological content;
those addressing the strategic goals of a programme;
and those concerned with the operational implementation.

The weighting given to these is dependent upon the scope and purpose. In practice, generic lists of criteria are featured far more prominently in *ex ante* project selection than in *ex post* evaluations. In the latter category, it is usually necessary to articulate the criteria into a set of more detailed and specific evaluation issues. An evaluation issue does not have a theoretical grounding; it is defined as an item upon which evaluation is required to gather information or form a judgement. A frequent difficulty when establishing criteria and their concomitant issues is explaining to those being evaluated that the evaluation cannot be constrained within the actual or perceived objectives pertaining when the research began. For example, a programme of long-term research may, as a result of policy changes, come to be assessed in terms of its achievements in commercial exploitation. Researchers complain bitterly in such circumstances that the goal-posts have been moved and that hence the question is unfair. It is here that pre-definition of the scope of the evaluation, and in particular the level, is important. An evaluation may conclude that a programme is inconsistent with current policy objectives but it must not project its conclusions down to the level of projects or individuals whose duty was to fulfil the programme objectives as *originally* defined.

Implementation of an evaluation

Once the definition of the scope, purpose and criteria for an evaluation is complete, the next task is to organize its implementation. Early practical decisions include setting the budget for the evaluation and selecting the evaluators. The cost of an evaluation is made up of both direct and indirect components. Direct costs include those personnel involved in evaluation and associated travel and overhead costs. Use of 'unpaid' evaluators, as in some peer reviews, merely transfers the cost to the evaluators' normal employers. The indirect costs of the more interactive forms of evaluation may be greater, consisting of the time spent in servicing the evaluation (through interviews etc.) and any associated disruption. It should be remembered, though, that being interviewed or serving on a review panel also yields benefits to the subject. What the cost of evaluations should be is often debated. The UK House of Lords Select Committee on Science and Technology (1987) recommended a figure of 1% of the R&D budget but clearly this should vary according to the degree of interest in the results, which itself depends on the scale and significance of the research in question.

Choice of evaluators

The choice of who is to carry out the evaluation is also significant. Where peer review is used, considerable skill is required in blending the required characteristics of objectivity and sufficient knowledge of the subject and its practitioners. This problem becomes important where the number of actors is small, either because the research groups are aggregated (as in capital-intensive science) or because the national community is relatively small. Use of foreign evaluators is one solution adopted by some countries.

Peer review processes address scientific merit and occasionally offer views on operational implementation. They do not often address issues of impact or the achievement of strategic goals. These tend to be the preserve of professional evaluators. This group may be within the organization being evaluated or may be independent. Again the trade-off is between familiarity and perceived objectivity.

Use of resources

Within the constraints of cost and personnel, the implementation of an evaluation requires priorities to be established. Evaluators can rarely afford all the information which could be collected and sometimes lower grade information is adequate even when more detailed approaches are possible. The most frequent choice in this respect is whether to carry out personal interviews, telephone interviews or a postal survey. Depth is achievable from the first approach and breadth from the last. A well-constructed evaluation will allocate resources appropriately according to the importance of the interviewee.

In a real-time evaluation, for example that of the Alvey programme, the logistic problems are greater. The evaluation has, during the programme, to address a full range of issues. In the *ex post* case these may be organized according to the evaluator's convenience and maybe pursued in parallel. In real-time evaluation there is a requirement for early and continual feedback. Experience has indicated that a predominantly serial mode of organization is optimal, addressing a small number of issues in some detail and reporting on them prior to undertaking further topics.

This may be underpinned by a parallel programme of evaluation activity aimed at collecting longer-term information. The greatest potential problem with the serial form of organization is that issues or topics will only be treated at one stage of the programme and subsequent developments in those areas will be ignored. In the Alvey evaluation this difficulty was minimized by relating the topics under study at a particular time to the life cycle of the programme. Hence, early evaluation reports addressed formulation of strategy, selection of proposals and arrangements for intellectual property rights whereas those scheduled for the end of the programme concerned technology transfer and exploitation.

External involvement

Perhaps the final aspect to be addressed outside the area of techniques is that of whom to approach for information in the course of the evaluation. It is not an overstatement to say that if you can identify the users of research outputs then you are more than halfway to completing an evaluation. The users may be other scientists, industrial companies, regulators, government departments or even the public at large. Peer review and associated bibliometric methods seek to identify scientific users of research. Going beyond this community is usually more difficult as the ways in which research results enter the economy are frequently indirect and difficult to attribute. Much research, for example that aimed at improving the environment, benefits a large number of users to a small degree. The more tenuous the link, the more difficult it becomes to identify specific users and then to obtain informed views from them relevant to the evaluation. Identification of users, in concert with the points made above about evaluation resources and criteria, yield a close pointer to the appropriate methods and techniques to be applied.

Evaluation and its interfaces: two case studies

In this section, two evaluations are described with some indication of how they fit into the framework outlined above. Emphasis is also given to the arrangements for interaction with those being evaluated and for dissemination of results. A summary is given in Table 1.

An institutional evaluation: the Natural History Museum

This exercise took one year to complete with a multidisciplinary team of five persons (three biologists and two economists, all with evaluation experience) contributing a total of 1.5 person-years of effort. The initiative for the evaluation came from the management of the museum. Traditionally a leading international centre for taxonomic research, the museum employs over 200 scientific staff who

TABLE 1 Organizational aspects of the evaluations

	British Museum (Natural History)	Alvey Programme for Advanced Information Technology
Initiative	Evaluated organization	Evaluated organization
Motive	Defensive management information	Management information
Type of research	Basic	Strategic
Level	Institution (and departments)	Programme (and sub-programmes)
Time-frame	Point-in-time	Real-time
Criteria	Scientific merit Impact Implementation	Impact Implementation
Cost	1.5 person-years (over 1 year)	36 person-years (over 6 years)
Proportion of research budget	1/800	1/350
Type of evaluators	External professional academic	External professional academic (2 teams)
Research users	Other scientists Commercial users	Exploiting companies
Interface	Liaison Officer Steering Committee (including Director and Sponsors)	Liaison Officer Steering Committee (including Director) Working Group Workshop

combine research with curation of 67 million reference items of animals, plants, minerals and meteorites. In recent years it has experienced severe budgetary problems and has responded by introducing admission charges for the public and seeking external funding. The evaluation was motivated by a desire to demonstrate the impact of the museum's work and to inform the management as an aid to decision making and increasing revenue. The museum persuaded its sponsoring government department to co-fund the evaluation and join it on a Steering Committee for the exercise. Most of the research in the museum was basic but the main questions were to the extent to which taxonomy underpinned other areas of science, and, primarily through identification of specimens, provided the basis for commercial activities. The evaluation was pitched mainly at the level of the five museum departments, headed by Keepers, and interviews were carried out with 51 Section Heads within these.

Among the interview objectives was a desire to map the orientation of the researchers (what criteria they applied to their work) and to enlist their help in identifying the users of their work. Results from the interviews were checked in plenary meetings with other scientific staff. These meetings were also used to explain the evaluation and to give feedback. An early problem, which delayed the whole exercise, was the need to convince the trade unions in the museum that the evaluation was not a direct threat to their members and would not be used for individual assessment. By a series of meetings and careful explanation, acceptance of the exercise was achieved and there were no instances of non-cooperation.

Through the interviews it was established that research visitors to the museum and members of a selection of learned societies represented the main external scientific users. Surveys were undertaken of samples of these groups. 308 members (out of 600 forms distributed) and 89 visitors responded to the surveys which explored the nature of their use of the museum's research and their rating of it. At an institutional level, scientific organizations such as research councils were invited to comment and detailed replies were received. Other activities included use of bibliometric indicators to assess the extent to which the museum's work was cited outside taxonomic journals, and other output indicators such as numbers of inquiries and loans. Telephone interviews were undertaken with commercial users of the museum to investigate the market and pricing.

Interface with the museum was through the Director's assistant who provided a large amount of briefing, dealt with queries and commented on findings as they emerged. The Steering Committee discussed an interim report and made some suggestions and considered the final report. At the time of writing the report is being considered by the Museum Trustees and the sponsoring government department, which changed during the course of the evaluation from the Advisory Board for the Research Councils (responsible for scientific research) to the Office of Arts and Libraries (responsible for museums).

It is too early to assess the impact of the evaluation. Some of the recommendations were overtaken by events; for example, the museum implemented a policy of increased selectivity between areas of research as the report was being drafted. At this stage it seems clear that the report is being taken seriously and will not be ignored.

Real-time evaluation: the Alvey Programme

The Alvey Programme for Advanced Information Technology is a five-year national initiative aimed at promoting advanced information technology (IT) through collaborative research. Such collaboration is between firms and between firms and universities. Firms receive 50 per cent contributions to their research from the programme and universities get normal research council funding. The programme was sponsored by three government departments and managed by a directorate established for the purpose.

The evaluation was initiated by the Director who felt that its position as the UK's largest research programme and the significant structural innovations merited detailed evaluation. After a tendering process it was decided to divide the evaluation into first three and later two components. PREST is evaluating structural and organizational features of the programme and the Science Policy Research Unit is looking at the impact on the UK economy. As already noted, the evaluation is unusual in that it has taken place in real-time.

The evaluation is a large-scale exercise (approximately six person-years per annum) because of the large-scale of the programme itself. The designation of the programme content as strategic research has led to some problems of goal-post shifting. As originally conceived, the objective was to support 'pre-competitive underpinning research' in enabling technologies. Many projects the programme sponsored aimed to improve techniques and processes. Policy changes have now led to expectations of demonstrated benefits from exploitable products. These are being produced but the evaluators have found themselves in the position of having to defend the programme against its critics by pointing out the wider benefits and at the same time having to explain that these cannot be quantified for well-accepted methodological reasons (the problems of attribution and timing of benefits).

It has always been agreed that the evaluation is at programme level, or, for some issues, its technical sub-programmes. Projects are subject to a separate monitoring system. Nevertheless, many of the evaluation interviews and surveys inevitably are at project level. Project participants are the main group of users of the results as these firms are expected to exploit the results. Interviews have ranged well beyond this group to senior management, foreign competitors and many other connected bodies. There has been full access to documentation but the large volume of material has proved a problem. Also, on many occasions it was necessary to assemble original information on items that had not been covered by the directorate (for example, some financial data on projects) but which was subsequently used by them.

The interface with the directorate has been with the Director of Administration and one of his staff. Twice a year, a Steering Committee, including the Director, discusses evaluation findings and forward plans. A quarterly Working Group covers administrative aspects of the evaluation, while a quarterly workshop is run by the Department of Trade and Industry's Economics Branch to discuss reports and methodological aspects. Reports are widely circulated for comment by the subjects of the evaluation before they are finished. Following the removal of confidential material, they are then made publicly available. A summary is provided in a regular column in the Programme Newsletter. A more rapid form of feedback takes place at an informal level between evaluators and the directorate, with an interchange of information and occasional requests for opinions on specific subjects. Results were pulled together for a formal interim report halfway through the programme (Georghiou et al 1988).

The evaluation was intended primarily to influence future programmes and it is apparent that some features of Alvey's successor have been affected. One of the evaluators was asked to make the economic case for the research component of the successor programme, and elements of the way in which the programme is harmonized with the EEC's ESPRIT programme (a similar, but larger, collaborative programme) were first suggested in evaluation reports. These large-scale policy influences are difficult to attribute as they often affect the climate of thinking rather than specific matters at a more mundane level. Several real-time changes resulted from evaluation reports, including altered proposal-processing procedures and monitoring procedures. One interesting feature is that turnover in the administration has meant that the evaluators have now been in place longer than any of the programme staff and form the corporate memory.

Conclusions

As with research itself, it is difficult to identify an end-point for the effects of an evaluation and even harder to assess its additionality (what changes would have taken place if there had been no evaluation). What does seem clear, both on the basis of personal experience and of wider observations, is that the impact evaluations have is strongly dependent upon the organizational context in which they are made. Evaluations need to preserve their independence but they can communicate their results into the system without adopting a public adversarial stance if the system has mechanisms for absorbing and responding to the results.

There is no recipe that can be followed precisely in the establishment of an evaluation but there are substantial benefits to be gained if, in the early stages, clarity is established in the purpose, scope and criteria of an evaluation and this is communicated to those being evaluated and those who constitute the audience for the evaluation.

Lest this position be misinterpreted, good organization should not be confused with more organization. Evaluators are still at their best operating as guerillas in the system rather than regulars, taking advantage of speed, flexibility and the element of surprise.

Acknowledgements

The author would like to acknowledge his colleagues involved in evaluation work in PREST, and the Alvey Directorate and the British Museum (Natural History) for sponsoring the evaluations referred to in the text. However, the views in this paper and any errors are solely those of the author. Finally, thanks are due to Wendy Walker for typing the text.

References

Georghiou LG, Guy K, Cameron HM, Hobday M, Ray T, Duncombe R 1988 Evaluation of the Alvey Programme—interim report. HMSO, London
Gibbons M, Georghiou LG 1987 Evaluation of research—a selection of current practices. OECD, Paris
House of Lords Select Committee on Science and Technology 1987 Report on civil research and development. HMSO, London

DISCUSSION

Hill: Did you learn anything useful about the operation and goals of the museum from talking to the trade unions, or was it simply a matter of doing an adequate sales job to capture their cooperation?

Georghiou: Most members of the trade union committee were very helpful and they were an important source of information. They were also the dominant speakers during the plenary meetings we conducted with all the staff. We felt that it was important, as the exercise was so sensitive, that everybody should have an opportunity to talk. The management were not present at these plenary meetings.

Hill: How did your evaluation at the museum differ from the approach that a 'management consulting' firm might use for a similar task? Were you influenced by how they operate? What would any scientific evaluation group contribute that such a firm might not offer and *vice versa*?

Georghiou: There were elements of consultancy type activity, particularly at the commercial end of the museum exercise, but we placed enormous stress upon what I call the orientation of the museum's researchers. We put most of our effort, the first six months, into interviews in the museum that were designed to locate the motives, attitudes and outside contacts of the museum staff and to discover where they placed themselves in the scientific community. Only when we understood that framework did we feel that we could make sense of the indicators and survey questions. Those could have been quite trivial if we had presented them alone.

Dixon: How do those of you who are evaluators see yourselves? I have wondered about this over the last five or ten years as the evaluation game has grown. A director of research who commisions an evaluation obviously wants good news. So there is pressure on you to produce helpful results. Equally, an outside client, from a research council perhaps, might be looking for bad news. How rational is the process? If, for example, you have an impression that research institute A rates rather poorly with research institutes C & D, you might do a straight comparison. But if that gave the 'wrong' result, you could resort to international measures, or look at data showing how much institute A had improved over the last ten years. There are many different methodologies that can be applied. Do you see yourselves almost as physicians—from whom patients want an accurate diagnosis and prognosis, whether good or bad? Or do you see yourselves rather as attorneys? A lawyer may turn down a brief or at least discuss with the client the sort of arguments that he is going to deploy. To which of the two models do you adhere?

Georghiou: Of the two, it would be far closer to the first. It's essential to approach an evaluation with as much integrity as you can muster and stick to your conclusions regardless. The evidence largely speaks for itself, because professional evaluators, unlike members of peer review committees or visiting groups, do not approach the task with prior expertise and opinions in that area. Evaluators tend to start with fairly open minds and form opinions as they proceed with the interviews. In the Alvey evaluation we have had a few fairly bitter internal reactions to criticisms, although never at the level of the Director. We have been mainly criticized for being too favourable. Late in 1987 we went through a period of high political risk; we had to speak out and say that the programme was doing better than the policy makers wanted because they wanted to cut down the size of the successor programme.

Irvine: Bernard Dixon's question is extremely important because it highlights the need to clarify the organization of evaluations. It can be dangerous for evaluators to report directly to a client being evaluated, as Dr Georghiou did with the Department of Trade and Industry (in the Alvey Programme), because this can lead to a variety of political pressures. Instead, it is good practice to use an 'authorizing committee' (as is normal in Japan) or an independent panel of senior researchers who are responsible for the evaluation. The professional evaluators do the tasks agreed by the authorizing or assessment committee and provide the systematic inputs required to make informed decisions.

When professional evaluators have too close a relationship to the agency they are assessing, it is easy for them to slip into the sort of situation that Dr Georghiou found himself in where he was publicly defending in newspapers the success of the Alvey Programme. This was in response to a National Audit Office evaluation which concluded that the impact of Alvey had not been as high as expected, a somewhat different result to Dr Georghiou's assessment. By becoming personally involved, it is easy to leave oneself open to accusations of bias. The problem is, in my view, systemic and could have been avoided by the existence of an independent cross-departmental committee to evaluate the programme. This committee would defend the results of the evaluation and the evaluator would not become involved. Evaluation nowadays is often implicitly linked to the process of defending R&D budgets, and it is difficult to avoid being drawn into legitimization and politics. Professional evaluation groups therefore need to ensure at the outset of a study that they have adequate organizational defence against such pressures.

Georghiou: I agree with the principle of reporting to an independent committee but you misunderstood my earlier remarks. The point was that we avoided getting drawn into legitimization and politics by sticking to our findings. The National Audit Office report leaned heavily on our earlier work but drew some exaggerated conclusions.

Montigny: John Irvine has raised an important topic. Dr Georghiou, you emphasize the first phase of the evaluation— the definition phase. When I do evaluations I have what I call a negotiation phase, involving the three groups you mentioned—the evaluators, those being evaluated and the audience. If we have enough time to negotiate the purpose, scope and criteria, we can expect to produce an evaluation with a strong impact, both on the scientific community, that is the programme or institution, and also at the political level, for example on those responsible for funding.

van Raan: In our group we are using bibliometric methods to assess research. Because we do research on evaluation, we need to interact with the people who are evaluated. The chairman of one of the larger institutes in Leiden asked us, for 'advertisement purposes', to update our Leiden indicators work. We discussed the preliminary results with him and he said that the results for a particular, important research group were not 'beautiful' enough. The number of publications was increasing, but the short-term impact of the group, as measured by citations, was decreasing. The chairman asked if we could improve the picture and he remarked that we had measured short-term impact. In his opinion, the impact on the longer term could give a better picture of the group's work. We investigated this and, indeed, a different picture came out (see van Raan, this volume). Thus in evaluation research there must be discussion between the people developing indicators and the 'customers' about what are the important indicators of research performance and why.

Blume: Some of what has been said has made me wonder whether 'evaluation' really differs from management consultancy. There's no reason why it should be different, except that the evaluation of science is sometimes regarded as part of a larger activity which claims to be an academic field. John Irvine made the point that evaluation sits uneasily between the demands made of it by potential users and an academic peer group doing historical, sociological and other studies, with whom affinity is claimed. Evaluators who claim to be doing something other than management consultancy have some responsibilities to this academic peer group; if we wish evaluation to fit into an academic field called 'science studies', evaluative studies should not only look for the approval of a committee (John's idea of an authorizing committee is a nice one), but a scientific community must also validate the work.

Moreover, the activity of programme evaluation isn't new. In the field of social policy, it has been done on a large scale for 30 years. With all the attempts to develop policy rationally, such as the introduction of Programme Analysis and Review, PPBS (planning, programming and budgeting systems) and cost–benefit analysis, one is driven to pretend that one has a value-neutral discourse for making decisions; that is what everybody wants and many of us have an interest in pretending that that is what we can offer. But, looking at accounts of these methods we know now that it's impossible to escape certain built-in value assumptions. This was true of cost–benefit analysis and it is true in research evaluation. By virtue of the sanctioning process of the scientific community, the academic connections and embedding of evaluative activity ought to give rise to a willingness to explore the assumptions that go into evaluations. It is these broader intellectual, critical and ethical responsibilities which ought to differentiate academic evaluative activity from management consultancy.

Weinberg: As the former director of a small institute which was evaluated two or three years after its formation, I look at the matter from the other side of the fence! I was pleased that Tony van Raan introduced the idea that taking a snapshot of what's going on in the first two or three years might give an entirely wrong impression of what the overall impact has been. In my experience at least, directors generally look at the activity and purpose of their institutions from a longer-range point of view than do those who are giving them the money. The people who provide funding generally have to ask for money year-by-year; the continuity of outlook resides in the institution, rather than in the agency. At least, that's the way it is in the USA. Therefore, Dr Georghiou, do you make a point of documenting in full the aspirations, the claims of success and the admissions of failure from the management of the institution that you are evaluating?

Georghiou: That is probably the central activity. The Alvey Programme was newly founded, so there wasn't this historical dimension, although it was relevant for some of the institutions they were sponsoring. But with the museum, we tried to take a very long perspective. In the bibliometric analysis this was essential—palaeontologists cite papers written in the last century! Research done at that time is still relevant because of the geological time-scale involved. We accepted that much of that kind of work is done with a 20-year time horizon; that doesn't mean it shouldn't be done.

Lake: I would like to turn from snapshot evaluations to the continuing evaluation that's needed at intervals through the life of a programme. The Alvey Programme was defined for this purpose as a six-year operation, but taxonomy in the British Museum certainly goes on for tens of years and is likely to go on for hundreds. And yet the museum underwent simply a snapshot evaluation. You specified the questions 'how far does taxonomy underpin other areas of science?' and 'is it undervalued?'. How does one organize evaluation at regular intervals through the life of an organization such as the British Museum? A visiting group, operating, say, every four years, has two tasks that, in the jargon of evaluators, we could distinguish as *ex ante* and *ex post* or, as the Cabinet Office will have it, appraisal beforehand and evaluation afterwards, which I quite like because it uses English! What organizational method is appropriate to a visitation on a regular basis? You can still have guerillas rather than establishment regulars but there seem to be at least two components. When you do the evaluation, the *ex post* part, what you are looking at is never completed—you are looking at what's been done since you last came. Likewise, for the *ex ante* part you can set a four-year target, but one cannot solve a taxonomic issue in four years; one can just make progress.

Georghiou: The museum does have a visiting group system but the management felt that was insufficient. It has all the classic peer review, visiting group problems: good comments are made strictly within a discipline and in a time of cutbacks the group sees its main function as being to protect that discipline against the others in the museum.

Your general point is a very good one. The guerilla operation is normally brought in during times of change, but if you can repeat the evaluations from time to time, not too often or they became disruptive (perhaps every five years for an institution like the British Museum), you can establish some longitudinal results which should be more valid than the horizontal ones you achieve in the single exercise.

Pavitt: I'd like to comment on what we define as evaluation. Much of the work described during this conference is at another level, addressing issues that don't relate to specific institutions or laboratories, but rather to broader questions—such as those in our discussion of Dr Weinberg's paper—of comparisons amongst fields, amongst countries and amongst technological sectors. In this context, there is another form of 'public good' quantitative analysis, of the sort supported by the Advisory Board for the Research Councils and the Economic and Social Research Council. Such analysis is of papers, patents and R&D activities at a broader level, not aimed at specific institutions, but having a real influence on the perceptions of decision makers. This area of research needs support so that we achieve more general understanding of the way in which resources for science and technology evolve and interact.

Kodama: We have heard that research evaluation is a social process. That means it depends on the culture. For example, in Japan we've discussed extensively the importance of research evaluation, but without any success. I have led a three-year study by the Science and Technology Agency of research evaluation in a national research institute. My conclusion is that unless there is mobility research evaluation is meaningless. Lack of mobility means researchers have to continue to work in the same organization, even if they receive a bad score. Therefore researchers are not happy about evaluation. The lack of mobility also means that the research community is homogeneous and people know each other well. Everyone is aware of who is the best scientist, but it is never explicitly stated. The function of evaluations is to make everything explicit. These factors make it difficult for research directors to implement evaluations.

Reference

van Raan AFJ 1989 Evaluation of research groups. In: The evaluation of scientific research. Wiley, Chichester (Ciba Foundation Conference) p 169–187

An alternative quantitative approach to the assessment of national performance in basic research

*T. Braun, W. Glänzel and A. Schubert

*Information Science and Scientometrics Research Unit (ISSRU), Library of the Hungarian Academy of Sciences, P.O. Box 7, 1361 Budapest and *Institute of Inorganic and Analytical Chemistry, L. Eötvös University, P.O. Box 123, 1443 Budapest, Hungary*

Abstract. The national performance in basic research of the Federal Republic of Germany, France, Japan, the United Kingdom and the United States of America is assessed by their publication productivity and citation impact in all sciences and some individual fields and subfields. A new scientometric indicators, the 'relative citation rate' (RCR), is computed for these five countries and is presented with data on its statistical reliability. A two-dimensional approach, using 'relational charts', was devised to further refine the RCR indicators. The assessment has been applied to the aggregated publication output of the five countries for the 1981–1985 period. It is shown that the citation impact of the US is greater than that of the other countries in all sciences, and in the fields and subfields studied. The UK and the FRG publications have the next greatest impact, there being no statistically significant differences between their research performances, and France and Japan are in a third group, France being in a slightly better position. This approach failed to reveal any weakness in the UK research performance, in the period examined, in all sciences, or in the science fields and subfields considered.

1989 The evaluation of scientific research. Wiley, Chichester (Ciba Foundation Conference) p 32–49

The many quantitative studies of national performance in basic scientific research encompass national growth or decline as it affects the strength or weakness of that country's performance during the 1973–1984 period (Garfield 1987, Irvine et al 1985, Martin et al 1984, 1987, Smith et al 1986). These studies presented a pessimistic view of the health of basic science in some countries. Although a 'declinistic' approach is not without some historical antecedents in West European science studies (Nye 1984), it has also been shown that the investment in basic and related research by some industrialized countries has decreased relative to their main competitors (Irvine & Martin 1986).

We have studied (Braun et al 1985, 1987a, b, c, 1988a, b, c) the contributions of different countries to world science between 1981 and 1985 using the same basic bibliometric or scientometric tool but a different methodology (Braun et al 1985, Schubert & Glänzel 1983, Schubert & Braun 1986, Schubert et al 1988) from that used for the 1973–1984 period (Irvine et al 1985, Martin et al 1984, 1987, Smith et al 1986). In this study, we use this approach with our own version of the *Science Citation Index* database to compare the functional effectiveness of basic research in some top-performing countries.

Data sources and processing

The SCI database (on magnetic tapes) of the Institute for Scientific Information (ISI), Philadelphia, was used as a source of raw data. The procedure for cleaning up and refining the data has been described previously (Braun et al 1985, 1987a). For this analysis, both the number of publications and the number of citations have been considered for a cumulative five year period, 1981–1985. Thus the effective citation period varies from zero to five years.

Methodology

The following scientometric indicators (Braun et al 1985) were computed from the database:

(a) Number of publications;

(b) Percentage of publications cited;

(c) Expected citation rate per publication. The mean citation rate per paper published in the period 1981–1985 was calculated for each journal. The product of the number of papers in a given subject field and from a given country and the mean citation rate was then calculated for each journal, and the results were summed;

(d) Observed citation rate per publication. The mean number of citations recorded in the database between 1981 and 1985 to the papers published in that period were counted for each country and subject field. The indicator obtained provides a complex measure of medium-range citation impact for a large population of papers;

(e) Relative citation rate (RCR) (Schubert & Braun 1986)—the ratio of observed to expected citations. This indicator assesses the relative contribution of scientists from a particular country to the average citation rate (citation impact) of the journals in which they publish. The relative citation rate has a value of unity if the publications in question are cited at the average rate, values between zero and one indicate a lower-than-average citation rate, and values greater than one indicate that the publications of the given country have a greater citation impact than the average for the respective journals. In other words, when applied to the assessment of national performance, this indicator measures each country's

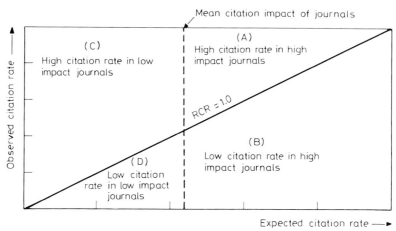

FIG. 1.   Relational chart of relative citation rate (RCR) zoning.

contribution relative to the mean citation impacts of the publication channels (journals) they use. The RCR enables direct comparison and even linear ranking of citation impact of publications in different fields. However, because, even within a single field, countries may use publication channels of varying quality, comparisons based on the RCR values alone might be misleading. A two-dimensional relational chart displaying both observed and expected citation rates is usually more informative. These are diagrams with identical scaled axes and display the 'main diagonal' (the straight line, $x = y$) and the vertical boundary between 'low' and 'high' impact journals, marked by the mean citation impact of the journals considered for analysis (Fig. 1). Points in this diagram may be considered to belong to a 'higher class' or 'lower class' depending on which zone (A–D) they are in. In this sense, the RCR can also be viewed as an indicator of the publication strategy of the country in question, giving information on the quality of the publication channels used by scientists in that country.

Statistical reliability of the RCR indicators

The theoretical background of statistical reliability of citation rates was outlined by Schubert & Glänzel (1983). The reasoning is based on the postulate of a negative binomial distribution of citations giving the following error formula:

$$\Delta RCR = \sqrt{RCR.Q/N}$$

where N is the number of the country's publications in the given field and time period, and Q is the solution of the equation

$$\log Q/(Q-1) = -\log (1-f)/X$$

in which f is the fraction of cited publications, and X the mean observed citation rate for papers from a given country, subject field, and time period. The test statistic as to whether an RCR value differs significantly from 1.00 is defined as

$$t_{RCR} = (RCR - 1)/\Delta RCR$$

This statistic is distributed according to Student's t-distribution, which, in large samples, can be approximated to a standard normal distribution. For example, if $|t| > 2$, the indicator does not differ significantly from 1.00 at a significance level (p) of 0.95. For two given relative citation rates the test statistic

$$t = (RCR_1 - RCR_2)/\sqrt{(RCR_1 - 1)^2/t_1^2 + (RCR_2 - 1)^2/t_2^2}$$

is a random variable of approximately standard normal distribution. Table 1 indicates the appropriate value of test statistic (t) for different significance levels (p).

TABLE 1 Values of t statistic for given significance levels

p	t	p	t
0.5	0.6745	0.9	1.6449
0.6	0.8416	0.95	1.9600
0.7	1.0864	0.99	2.5785
0.8	1.2816	0.999	3.2905

Results

This analysis has been applied to the publication performance and citation impact of a group of five countries—the USA, the UK, Japan, France, and the Federal Republic of Germany. The data and results refer to their performance in all science as well as separately in physics, chemistry, physics of condensed matter and genetics and heredity. Thus we have an insight into the general performance of the respective countries in all sciences, in two major science fields and also in a physics and a biology subfield.

The results are presented in Tables 2–6. Table 7(a–e) presents the test statistic (t) matrices to indicate the reliability of pairwise intercomparison of the relative citation rates of papers from the five countries.

Discussion

All sciences

The RCR data in Tables 2 and 7a reveal the leading position of the FRG followed by the US and the UK with no significant differences in the RCR performances

TABLE 2 Scientometric indicators for all sciences

Country	Number of publications 1981–1985	Publications cited 1981–1985 (%)	Expected citation rate per publication	Observed citation rate per publication	Relative citation rate (RCR)	
					Indicator value	Test statistic (t)
FRG	121 557	55.43	2.73	2.95	1.08	9.08
US	751 635	59.23	3.90	4.11	1.05	12.43
UK	183 109	57.32	3.05	3.20	1.05	6.77
France	97 676	53.35	2.74	2.65	0.97	3.69
Japan	139 645	56.36	2.77	2.49	0.90	14.97

TABLE 3 Scientometric indicators for physics

Country	Number of publications 1981–1985	Publications cited 1981–1985 (%)	Expected citation rate per publication	Observed citation rate per publication	Relative citation rate (RCR) Indicator value	Relative citation rate (RCR) Test statistic (t)
US	134 937	63.52	4.45	4.83	1.09	10.42
UK	26 470	61.00	3.03	3.25	1.07	3.59
FRG	24 521	64.40	3.61	3.92	1.09	4.15
France	20 772	60.59	3.38	3.35	0.99	−0.11
Japan	26 761	59.72	3.12	2.76	0.88	−8.81

TABLE 4 Scientometric indicators for chemistry

Country	Number of publications 1981–1985	Publications cited 1981–1985 (%)	Expected citation rate per publication	Observed citation rate per publication	Relative citation rate (RCR)	
					Indicator value	Test statistic (t)
US	59 596	65.66	3.82	4.08	1.07	5.04
UK	16 943	65.92	3.02	3.24	1.07	3.52
FRG	19 506	64.99	2.97	3.15	1.06	3.20
France	12 828	61.33	2.85	2.73	0.96	−1.90
Japan	29 348	61.06	2.63	2.56	0.98	−1.83

TABLE 5 Scientometric indicators for physics of condensed matter

Country	Number of publications 1981–1985	Publications cited 1981–1985 (%)	Expected citation rate per publication	Observed citation rate per publication	Relative citation rate (RCR)	
					Indicator value	Test statistic (t)
US	8743	73.93	4.92	5.80	1.18	4.55
UK	2103	71.75	3.40	4.04	1.19	2.91
FRG	3484	70.49	3.82	4.36	1.14	2.65
France	2367	66.12	3.48	3.85	1.11	1.66
Japan	2182	65.35	3.19	3.08	0.97	-0.63

TABLE 6 Scientometric indicators for genetics and heredity

Country	Number of publications 1981–1985	Publications cited 1981–1985 (%)	Expected citation rate per publication	Observed citation rate per publication	Relative citation rate (RCR) Indicator value	Test statistic (t)
US	8183	70.37	4.52	4.94	1.09	2.51
UK	2139	66.76	3.84	4.02	1.05	0.72
FRG	1267	73.95	4.67	5.21	1.12	1.23
France	1104	67.21	4.18	4.29	1.03	0.27
Japan	1466	63.51	3.92	3.51	0.90	−1.43

TABLE 7   Relative citation rate test statistics matrices

(a) All sciences

	FRG	FRA	JPN	US	UK
FRG	0.00				
FRA	−9.00	0.00			
JPN	−16.18	−5.78	0.00		
US	−2.94	8.55	19.30	0.00	
UK	−2.72	7.12	15.03	−0.29	0.00

(b) Physics

	FRG	FRA	JPN	US	UK
FRG	0.00				
FRA	−3.01	0.00			
JPN	−8.52	−5.07	0.00		
US	1.04	4.83	13.20	0.00	
UK	−0.72	2.46	8.35	−2.08	0.00

(c) Chemistry

	FRG	FRA	JPN	US	UK
FRG	0.00				
FRA	−3.54	0.00			
JPN	−3.66	0.62	0.00		
US	0.22	4.24	4.80	0.00	
UK	0.41	3.80	3.94	0.26	0.00

(d) Physics of condensed matter

	FRG	FRA	JPN	US	UK
FRG	0.00				
FRA	−0.43	0.00			
JPN	−2.33	−1.68	0.00		
US	0.56	0.98	3.23	0.00	
UK	0.55	0.91	2.65	0.11	0.00

(e) Genetics and heredity

	FRG	FRA	JPN	US	UK
FRG	0.00				
FRA	−0.66	0.00			
JPN	−1.85	−1.08	0.00		
US	−0.20	0.66	2.43	0.00	
UK	−0.58	0.18	1.54	−0.60	0.00

of the last two. France and Japan follow in that order. The picture becomes considerably more diversified when the two-dimensional approach of Fig. 2a is taken into account. When we combine the linear ranking and the relational chart approach, it becomes clear that although the papers published by authors from the FRG are highly cited when related to the expected citation rate of papers in the journals in which they are published, those journals belong to a lower impact (below world expected citation rate) journal group. It is interesting to see that the expected citation rate of the papers from France and Japan is very near to that of those from the FRG (Fig. 2a), although their observed citation rate situates them near to, or in, zone D. Fig. 2a also shows that the US and the UK are in the highest impact zone (A), with the US in a stronger position. In other words, the West German scientists publish high average impact papers in lower average impact journals whereas British authors' papers appear in high average quality journals and have there a high average impact. The papers from US authors show the most privileged position on all the relational charts in Fig. 2.

Physics

Tables 3 and 7b show that the RCR performance of the US gives it the leading position, followed by the FRG without significant differences between their RCR values. The UK follows in rank, with its RCR indicator significantly lower than that of the US but without differing significantly from that of the FRG. France's RCR value surpasses significantly that of Japan. The relational chart in Fig. 2b shows only the US and the FRG in zone A, but reveals that the US papers were published in 'higher class' physics journals.

Chemistry

Tables 4 and 7c show that, according to the RCR indicator, the US, the UK and the FRG lead the ranking without significant differences between the three, followed by Japan and France ranked together in second position. The two-dimensional approach in Fig. 2c confirms this by showing the same three countries in zone A, but it accentuates a privileged US position within the zone.

Physics of condensed matter

(Tables 5 and 7d). The RCR ranking and the two-dimensional chart (Fig. 2d) show a situation similar to that in chemistry with the sole difference of France advancing to zone A.

Genetics and heredity

Tables 6 and 7e show a quite homogeneous RCR performance of the five countries with the only significant differences between those of the US and Japan. However, Fig. 2e gives a more disparate picture with the US, the FRG, the UK, and France in the outstanding (A) zone, and Japan alone in zone B.

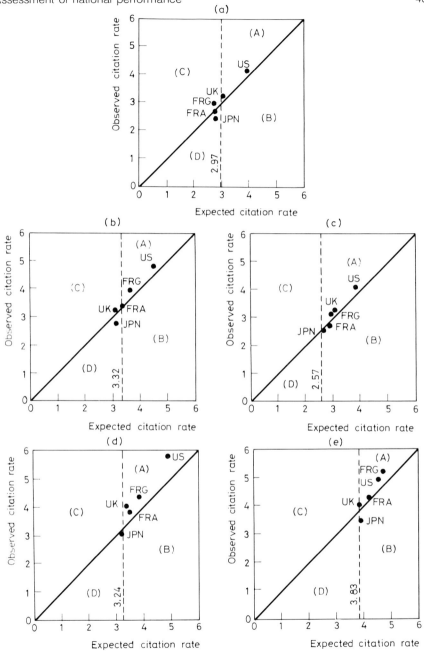

FIG. 2.   Relational charts: (a) All sciences; (b) Physics; (c) Chemistry; (d) Physics of condensed matter; (e) Genetics and heredity.

Although there are not significant differences between their RCR values, the FRG appears somewhat ahead of the US in the average impact of the journals used for publication of their genetics and heredity papers.

Conclusions

The only unambiguous conclusion of using the RCR indicator together with the relational charts for assessing national performance is that the US holds the leading position in basic research in all science fields considered together and also in the four fields and subfields examined. The ranking of the other four countries is more complicated. The UK and the FRG seem to follow in the rank without clear and discernable differences between their research performances, and France and Japan form a third group, France being in a slightly stronger position. Chemistry shows up as perhaps the most equalized field as far as the top national research performances are concerned. Additionally, we haven't felt that the UK research performance in the fields and subfields considered and the period examined was falling behind any of the five countries examined, with the exception of the US. It should be emphasized, however, that the results refer only to those aspects of national research performances that are reflected in publication productivity and citation impact.

References

Braun T, Glänzel W, Schubert A 1985 Scientometric indicators. A 32-country comparative evaluation of publishing performance and citation impact. World Scientific, Singapore & Philadelphia

Braun T, Bujdosó E, Schubert A 1987a Literature of analytical chemistry. A scientometric evaluation. CRC Press, Boca Raton

Braun T, Glänzel W, Schubert A 1987b One more version of the facts and figures on publication output and relative citation impact of 107 countries, 1978–1980. Scientometrics 11:9–15

Braun T, Glänzel W, Schubert A 1987c One more version of the facts and figures on publication output and relative citation impact in the life sciences and chemistry, 1978–1980. Scientometrics 11:127–140

Braun T, Glänzel W, Schubert A 1987d One more version of the facts and figures on publication output and relative citation impact in physics and mathematics, 1978–1980. Scientometrics 12:3–16

Braun T, Glänzel W, Schubert A 1988a The newest version of the facts and figures on publication output and relative citation impact of 100 countries, 1981–1985. Scientometrics 13:181–189

Braun T, Glänzel W, Schubert A 1988b The newest version of the facts and figures on publication output and relative citation impact in the life sciences and chemistry, 1981–1985. Scientometrics 14:3–17

Braun T, Glänzel W, Schubert A 1988c The newest version of the facts and figures on publication output and relative citation impact in physics, engineering and mathematics, 1981–1985. Scientometrics 14: in press

Garfield E 1987 Is Japanese science a Juggernaut? Current Contents (Life Science) (46) November 16:3–9
Irvine J, Martin BR 1986 Is Britain spending enough on science? Nature (Lond) 323:591–594
Irvine J, Martin BR, Peacock T, Turner R 1985 Charting the decline in British science. Nature (Lond) 316:587–590
Martin B, Irvine J, Turner R 1984 The writing on the wall for British science. New Scientist 104:25–29
Martin BR, Irvine J, Narin F, Steritt C 1987 The continuing decline of British science. Nature (Lond) 330:123–126
Nye MJ 1984 Scientific decline. Is quantitative evaluation enough? ISIS 75:697–708
Schubert A, Glänzel W 1983 Statistical reliability of comparisons based on citation impact of scientific publications. Scientometrics 5:59–74
Schubert A, Braun T 1986 Relative indicators and relational charts for comparative assessment of publication output and citation impact. Scientometrics 9:283–293
Schubert A, Glänzel W, Braun T 1988 Against absolute methods. Relative scientometric indicators and relational charts as evaluation tools. In: van Raan AFJ (ed) Handbook of quantitative studies of science and technology, Elsevier, Amsterdam, in press
Smith DC, Collins PMD, Hicks DM, Wyatt S 1986 National performance in basic research. Nature (Lond) 323:681–684

DISCUSSION

Garfield: At the Institute for Scientific Information (ISI) we have received complaints from smaller countries, especially in the third world, because we are reducing the coverage of journals in the *Science Citation Index* (SCI) database for economic reasons. What would be the effect of reintroducing more low impact journals?

Braun: I don't think it would affect the big countries much, but it could seriously affect the results for smaller less-developed countries.

Garfield: Downward?

Braun: I think it would be downwards, but I don't know. I have the results for about 100 countries and 128 fields and subfields. The USA falls in zone A in 100 of the 128 subfields. Second is the UK, which is in zone A in 51 subfields. Third is The Netherlands, in zone A in 37 subfields. This is a selection of countries that published at least 100 papers in the subfield in question between 1981 and 1985. If the number of papers is lower than 100 the indicator does not give a reliable result. I don't think it is feasible for ISI to include more journals in the database, but for the practitioner the solution is to increase the assessment period from five years to ten. Then you have a population of papers and citations that gives reliable indicators.

We also have results for the less-developed countries. To study these you cannot use the confidence level of 0.95 for the indicator, but have to go to a

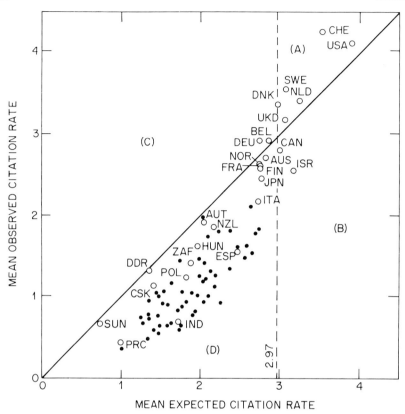

FIG. 1. Relational chart of relative citation rate zoning for all science fields combined, 1981–1985. Open circles, countries publishing more than 100 papers; filled circles, countries publishing less than 100 papers.

lower confidence level for intercomparison. We were surprised by the results for both the 1981–1985 and 1978–1980 periods. The relational chart shown in Fig. 1 shows the positions of all countries that published a statistically significant population of papers in the 1981–1985 period (open circles). Countries lacking a significant population of papers and citations in that period are shown by the filled circles. As well as the USA and the UK, Switzerland (CHE) is very highly placed in zone A, as are The Netherlands, Sweden and Denmark. This is a striking result. Small, developed European countries appear, when using this specific impact indicator to surpass the big countries.

Narin: There are some interesting and particularly clever aspects of this approach. However, the language problem is important, as some of Eugene Garfield's earlier papers and some of our work pointed out. There's a large difference between the citation rates for papers published in English and for journals that are primarily in English and those for German or French papers. These may vary by a factor of two or more, and the phenomenon is field dependent; in physics and mathematics, the language bias is less important than in descriptive fields such as clinical medicine. By referring your data to the journal itself you implicitly take into account some of the language bias, because if a country publishes a large fraction of its papers in German you essentially compare that country to the German language journals. What you are seeing, to a partial degree, is that the countries in the upper right (zone A) are the smaller ones that publish primarily in English language journals, such as Sweden, Switzerland and The Netherlands. But the Canadian results, for example, may be kept down by the Canadian papers which are published in French and are probably cited half as frequently as those Canadian papers that are published in English.

Moravcsik: To what extent is the result for Switzerland influenced by CERN, which counts as Swiss although it is a big international laboratory?

Braun: These are overall figures and we didn't make that distinction, but it could be done; one can refine the database. This is true also for what Francis Narin said. We know there is a language bias in this evaluation and also in the five-country intercomparison, because there are only two English-speaking countries among the five. This is an issue; here is the science world reflected in one database, but even with this database, we need to know that we can select the proper conditions. We wanted to show that this indicator is available and reliable and that the data can be refined. With our database we can disaggregate the data as we wish. We can even change the definition of a journal: we can aggregate other packages of papers to use as a reference base for comparison. The result will be the same, whether you use the journal or another package of papers selected by yourselves or a group of specialists.

Irvine: You emphasize very precise statistical techniques such as significance tests. I am not sure, however, that the quality of the data warrants treating the statistics in this way. A number of problems exist in large-scale bibliometric databases of the sort used in your study. Francis Narin has raised the language question and I agree that this is very important. A second problem concerns the classification of papers into fields and subfields. It is extremely difficult to do this accurately. Did you individually classify all papers by field, or was it on the basis of the journals in which they appeared? If you used a journal classification scheme, there are likely to be severe technical limitations and I would urge you to highlight them in greater detail.

A third problem relates to how the publications are counted. We have compared the CHI database with other databases and it is quite clear that fractional counting is strongly preferable in international comparisons of research output. If a researcher from one country produces a paper jointly with someone from another, it should be counted as half to each country. The alternative procedure of 'whole counting', which you used, is likely to have technical limitations. In a recent notorious case, a Dutch researcher failed to appreciate that England, Scotland, Wales and Ireland are separate countries in the ISI database, and as a result collaborative papers from these four countries were counted two or three times. He consequently came to what has now been shown to be an erroneous conclusion about British science. Are you sure that your analysis is not beset with similar technical difficulties?

Several other problems can also arise in cross-national comparisons of bibliometric indicators. In particular, there is the question of what constitutes a paper. In your use of the ISI database, do you include all publications or do you exclude, for example, obituaries in journals? My strong preference is only to take into account articles, review papers and notes. One reason is that English language journals constitute quite a large fraction of the SCI database and there is inevitably a tendency for British researchers to undertake more book reviews or to contribute more obituaries. Unless one removes such non-research publications, a significant amount of bias can be introduced.

Braun: In a short presentation it is not possible to discuss all the details of refining the data. All the data and responses to most of your questions are discussed in Braun et al (1985, 1987). As far as fractional or non-fractional counting is concerned, for the same set of 1981–1985 papers we have used three different types of counting—fractional counting, first author counting and total author counting. In your approach, using the percentage share method, this type of counting is important, but in the type of indicator we are using and for the aggregate of the data, it is less important. Using different types of allocation has some effect, but it does not give you different rankings.

Anderson: At the Ciba Foundation we have used a method of analysis which is similar to Professor Braun's relative citation rate technique. In many respects, it is a very attractive approach to evaluation, because average journal citation rates offer a nice reference standard which is indirectly set by the appropriate scientific community. But we are worried about the validity of using mean citation rates as reference standards. The frequency distributions of citations are usually skewed. The degree of skewness varies considerably from journal to journal, from discipline to discipline and even from nation to nation. So it is a little suspect to compare the mean of a skewed observed distribution with the mean of an expected distribution, which one may expect to be less skewed. In my paper (this volume), I present data that show the sort of errors that this can cause.

Braun: We have worked for twelve years with the SCI database, trying to refine it and to extract reliable data, and although our data are not highly sophisticated, I think we have reached an acceptable level of sophistication. Using differences between means or differences between percentage shares are rough methods; both can be used, but we believe, although we can't state which is best, that our method offers another useful approach.

Anderson: How useful is your approach for measuring performance over time? Policy makers are usually most interested in how national performance is changing with time. You showed a relatively strong position for UK science, but this was only at a single point in time. In contrast, a study that John Irvine and I have been involved with (Anderson et al 1988) has confirmed that since 1981 UK science has declined considerably on the basis of its percentage share of world publications.

Braun: As I mentioned, we used an aggregation of the three years 1978, 1979 and 1980 and compared the rankings of that three-year period with a second ranking of the five years 1981–1985. The data appeared quite robust; the top countries remained stable. I have to stress the leading position of the USA, but our data also show that the UK is still very strong when we use an aggregated population of papers and citations and a longer period. We didn't see any decline of science in the UK between the 1978–1980 period and 1981–1985 period. This is, of course, a relative statement.

References

Anderson J 1989 The evaluation of research training. In: The evaluation of scientific research. Wiley, Chichester (Ciba Foundation Conference) p 93–119

Anderson J, Collins PMD, Irvine J et al 1988 On-line approaches to measuring national scientific output—a cautionary tale. Science and Public Policy 15(3):153–161

Braun T, Glänzel W, Schubert A 1985 Scientometric indicators. A 32 country comparative evaluation of publishing performance and citation impact. World Scientific, Singapore & Philadelphia

Braun T, Bujdosó E, Schubert A 1987 Literature of analytical chemistry: a scientometric evaluation. CRC Press, Boca Raton

Technology and
its links with science:
measurement and policy implications

Keith Pavitt

Science Policy Research Unit, University of Sussex, Brighton BN1 9RF, UK

Abstract. Technological activities are major determinants of a country's economic welfare. As in other Organization for Economic Cooperation and Development (OECD) countries, those in the UK are located mainly in business firms. The core activities are development and production engineering, rather than research. Conventional R&D statistics greatly underestimate technological activities in small firms and the effects of technological change in traditional industries (including non-manufacturing) through the purchase of materials and machinery embodying new technology.

The relatively slow growth of funding for R&D by British firms results not from a less favourable economic climate, but from an unwillingness or inability of British firms to increase the share of their profits spent on R&D at the same rate as their competitors in other countries. The international technological competitiveness of the British aerospace and chemicals (especially fine chemicals) industries is relatively strong, whilst that of the electronics and automobile industries has declined drastically. This is reflected in trade performance and can be attributed to a small number of large firms.

Specific and pragmatic technological knowledge is substantially different from generalisable scientific knowledge. The contribution of science to technology varies widely amongst sectors, the highest being in biotechnology and chemicals, and the lowest in mechanical engineering. However, this captures only part of the contribution of university research to technological practice which also includes postgraduate training for researchers, and technological intelligence networks (mostly informal) between firms and university laboratories. This means: (a) Britain cannot live off other countries' science without its own; (b) the scope of indicators of impacts of science need to be broadened to include training and networks, as well as direct knowledge transfer; (c) the UK problem is not too much science, but too little technology.

1989 The evaluation of scientific research. Wiley, Chichester (Ciba Foundation Conference) p 50–68

Most of this symposium is concerned with indicators of scientific activity. A major justification advanced for society's large-scale support of science is its supposed contribution to technical advance, and therefore to improvements in economic and social well-being. Thanks largely to advances in the quality of statistical indicators of technological activities, the links between technological activities and economic efficiency are now empirically well-established (Soete 1981, Fagerberg 1987, 1988). In this paper I shall use a variety of indicators to describe the nature and composition of technological activities in the UK, and to identify promising subjects for future research. Then I shall explore the nature of the links between science and technology, and discuss the implications for the future development of indicators and for policy.

Main characteristics of British technological activities

R&D statistics and other measures show that Britain's technological activities are similar to those of most other Organization for Economic Cooperation and Development (OECD) countries in the following characteristics: location and type of technological activity; and distribution amongst sectors and amongst firms in different size categories.

Location

As in all advanced Western industrialised countries, British R&D activities are located mainly in business firms (61% of the total in 1983), with supporting activities in higher education (14%) and government laboratories (22%). Notwithstanding the predictions and prescriptions of two Nobel Prize-winning economists (Stigler 1951, Arrow 1962) and the practice of centrally planned countries in Eastern Europe, independent contract and cooperative laboratories still account for a very small proportion of total business R&D expenditure in the UK and elsewhere in the OECD.

Nature of technological activities

This reflects the nature of the activities that produce technology. In Britain and other OECD countries, well over half the 'R&D' activities performed in business are in fact 'D'—undertaken with the purpose of designing, building and testing specific prototypes (for products) or pilot plants (for processes). Furthermore, studies in Canada, Israel and the USA have shown that R&D expenditure statistics cover only part of the total costs of an innovation (Kamin et al 1982). In particular, they do not measure production engineering (PE) activities for the design of manufacturing systems, or marketing for the launching of product innovations. According to these studies, the breakdown of these expenditures averages out as follows: research, 10–20%; development, 30–40%; production engineering (excluding normal investment), 30–40%; marketing 10–20%.

This combination of activities reflects the essentially pragmatic nature of most technological knowledge. Although a useful input, theory is rarely sufficiently robust to predict the performance of a technological artefact under operating conditions, and to eliminate, with a high enough degree of certainty, the costly and time-consuming construction and testing of prototypes and pilot plant. Even the most science-based and science-dependent of all technologies—pharmaceuticals and pesticides—has been described in *The Economist* (1987a) as 'a highly empirical business', involving the development and screening of a vast range of synthetic compounds, the full range of biological effects of which cannot be completely predicted from knowledge of their molecular structure. The problem is even more severe in the design and development of complex machinery and production systems, involving multiple objectives and multiple constraints, and the combination of a variety of technologies and materials. In this context, the essence of engineering skill and the engineering profession is the ability to make things work by drawing upon and combining knowledge from a variety of sources.

The sectoral distribution of technological activity

As in other OECD countries, UK business enterprise R&D is heavily concentrated in manufacturing, with just five sectors—chemicals, mechanical engineering, electrical and electronics (including instrumentation), automobiles and aerospace—accounting for 80% or more of total expenditure. Broadly similar sectoral patterns emerge from the distribution of patenting, and of significant innovations. Other industries benefit from the impact of the technological advances in these active industries through a dense network of inter-industry purchases and sales of equipment, materials and components. As Table 1 shows, there are similar intersectoral flows in the USA, with non-manufacturing sectors benefiting considerably from embodied technology purchased from elsewhere. In the UK, the proportion of significant innovations used outside manufacturing has been increasing steadily since 1945, the proportion originating in chemicals and electronics being particularly high.

One shortcoming of the above measures of technology produced and used is their almost exclusive concern with hardware technology, so that the apparent primacy of the manufacturing sector is almost a matter of definition. With the growing importance of software technology, organizations providing services will become increasingly important loci of complex computer equipment, and of the consequent development of software technology (Barras 1986, Coopers & Lybrand 1987, OECD 1985). Although reliable statistics are not yet available, we should anticipate relatively more technology in software and services in future. This will present a new stimulus and challenge for the development of indicators of technological activity.

TABLE 1 Comparison of sectoral patterns of technology production and use in the UK (1970-79) and the USA (1974)

	% of all technology produced		% of all technology used	
	UK	USA	UK	USA
Core Sectors	68.3	62.8	18.3	18.8
Secondary Sectors	20.6	23.9	16.4	12.7
Other Manufacturing	8.3	12.0	26.0	11.4
Non-Manufacturing	2.9	1.3	39.4	57.1

Core Sectors include chemicals, machinery, mechanical engineering, instruments and electronics. Secondary Sectors include metals, electrical engineering, shipbuilding/offshore engineering, vehicles, building materials, rubber and plastic goods. Other Manufacturing includes food, aerospace, textiles, paper, printing. Non-Manufacturing includes agriculture, mining, construction, utilities, transport, business, R&D, other services, health care, defence, other government services, final consumers.

In the US study (Scherer 1982), the measure of technology produced and used was a combination of R&D expenditures (for producer sectors) and sectors of applications of patents resulting from the R&D (in user sectors). In the UK study (Robson et al 1988), the measure was the number of significant innovations produced and used in the sectors.

Reproduced with permission from Robson et al (1988).

The size distribution of innovating firms

As in most other OECD countries, R&D statistics broken down according to firm size suggest that innovative activities in the UK are heavily concentrated in large firms. However, two recent Science Policy Research Unit (SPRU) studies have produced evidence that this is only partially correct. The larger firms, as a group, undertake a greater proportion of British technological activity in terms of R&D expenditure than their relative share of significant innovations, or of British patenting in the USA: the top 100 firms account for about 90% of R&D expenditure compared to about 60% of innovations or patents (Patel & Pavitt 1987). At the other end of the spectrum, Table 2 shows that firms in the UK with fewer than 1000 employees account for only about 3% of the total business R&D budget, but for 30% or more of significant innovations. The latter proportion is consistent with that found in US studies using similar direct measures of innovative output.

These discrepancies can be explained by the nature of technological activities in small firms which typically do not have specialized and separately accountable R&D departments. Rather, they have design offices with engineers and others involved part-time in technological activities. Whilst R&D was the source of about 80% of the knowledge inputs into innovations made by firms with more than 50 000 employees, it accounted for only about 40% in firms with between 100 and 499 employees, compared to 49% from design, production engineering and operating staff (Pavitt et al 1988).

TABLE 2   The size distribution of innovating firms: results of various surveys

Source	Country	Measure used	Period	*0–999*	*1000–9999*	*>10 000*
				Distribution of innovative activity (%) according to numbers of employees		
Science Policy Research Unit	UK	Number of identified innovations	1945–54	28.7	30.8	40.5
			1955–64	30.9	26.5	42.6
			1965–74	32.2	23.4	44.6
			1975–83	38.8	15.8	45.4
UK Government	UK	R&D expenditures	1975	3.3	16.4	80.3
Feinman & Fuentevilla (1976)	USA	Number of identified innovations	1953–59	42.2	25.6	32.2
			1960–66	44.1	19.3	36.6
			1967–73	38.3	16.0	45.7
Kleinman (1975)	USA	Number of identified innovations	1963–74	30.5	17.7	51.1
National Science Foundation	USA	R&D expenditures	1974	4.5	11.6	83.9

Reproduced with permission from Pavitt (1988).

The volume of technological activities

In spite of structural similarities between Britain's technological activities and those of other OECD countries, there are also some differences. Fig. 1 shows that the 1950s put Britain's technology in an untypical and flattering light, compared to Germany before World War II and both Germany and Japan since then. Table 3 demonstrates that, since the late 1960s, firm-funded R&D in Britain has grown more slowly than in most major OECD countries, and that by the 1980s it lagged well behind that of its main competitors. This relatively low rate of increase of firm-funded R&D in Britain cannot be attributed to either an unfavourable economic climate or to slow change in the mix of output towards more R&D-intensive product groups. The main problem has been the inability or unwillingness of firms in Britain to commit an increasing share of profits or output to R&D at the same rate as their main foreign competitors (Patel & Pavitt 1987).

Sectors, firms and strategies

Firms' strategies have been highly variable and have had major effects on the sectoral pattern of Britain's technological competitiveness. Table 4 summarizes

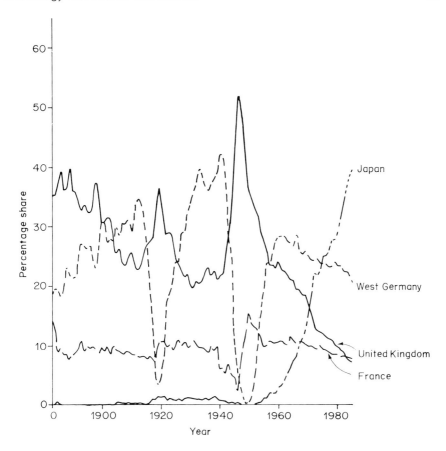

FIG. 1.   Shares of foreign patenting in the United States of America, 1883–1985.
Source, OTAF (1977) and data subsequently supplied to the Science Policy Research
Unit.

patterns and trends in British technological competitiveness in 32 sectors, on
the basis of their 'Revealed Technology Advantage' (RTA)—the ratio of
Britain's share of US patenting in a sector, to its share of US patenting in all
sectors. As such, the RTA is the measure of the technological position of a British
sector in the world, relative to the British average, with a ratio greater than
unity reflecting strength, and one less than unity weakness.

From the data in Table 4, it can be argued that the UK remains relatively
strong technologically in aerospace and has become so in many chemical-related
sectors, but has declined in electronics (especially semiconductors and computers)
and automobiles. This pattern is confirmed even more starkly in an analysis

TABLE 3   Industry-financed R&D: 1983

Country	Distribution (%)	Proportion of value-added (%)	Per capita ($)	Growth rate per annum (1967–83) (%)
United Kingdom	5.03	1.22	49.5	1.08
Belgium	1.15	1.33	64.9	6.53
France	5.67	1.15	57.7	5.80
West Germany	10.79	1.86	96.4	5.64
Italy	2.58	0.60	25.0	5.12
Netherlands	1.42	1.18	54.9	2.01
Sweden	1.67	2.18	109.4	6.59
Switzerland	1.61	n.a.[a]	136.8	1.80
Japan	25.30	2.12	116.0	10.80
United States	44.40	1.50	105.0	4.10

[a]n.a., not available.
Reproduced with permission from Patel & Pavitt (1987).

TABLE 4   Sectoral patterns of revealed technological advantage (RTA) of the UK

	High (RTA > 1.1)	Medium (RTA < 1.1 and > 0.9)	Low (RTA < 0.9)
Increasing	Drugs Food and tobacco Mining machinery Chemical processes	Agricultural Chemicals	Miscellaneous metal products
Stable	Bleaching, dyeing etc Plastic and rubber Aircraft Non-electrical machinery	Telecommunications Instruments Inorganic chemicals Specialised non-electrical machinery Non-metallic minerals Organic chemicals Other transport Chemical apparatus	Textiles, clothing etc. Image and sound equipment Electrical devices Assembling and material-handling apparatus Photography and photocopying
Decreasing	Power plants	Road vehicles Metallurgical and other mineral processes	General electrical machinery Metallurgical and metal-working equipment Semiconductors Calculators and computers Hydrocarbons and mineral oils Nuclear reactors and systems

A sector is defined to be increasing in strength if the RTA has increased by more than 20% from the period 1969–72 to 1981–84 and is defined to be decreasing if the RTA has declined by more than 20%. High, medium and low refer to the value of the RTA Index in 1981–84.
Reproduced with permission from Patel & Pavitt (1987).

of fast-growing fields of US patenting, and is reflected in trends in Britain's international trading performance.

Between the early 1960s and the early 1980s, Britain's sectoral pattern of technological strengths and weaknesses was more unstable than those in France, West Germany, Japan and the USA, in the sense that Britain's sectoral RTAs in the two periods 1969–72 and 1981–84 were less closely correlated than those in the other countries. These changes reflect both government policies and the decisions of specific large firms and other organizations, responsible for 20% or more of US patenting, mainly within the aerospace, chemicals, and electrical/electronics sectors (see Table 5). The following changes are of

TABLE 5   Firms with 20% or more of all UK patenting in the USA in specific sectors

Firm	Period				
	1969–72			1981–84	
	No.	Sector		No.	Sector
Beecham	0			1	Drugs
Lucas	2	Road vehicles Power plant		2	Road vehicles Power plant
Rolls-Royce	1	Power plant		1	Power plant
British Aerospace	1	Aircraft		1	Aircraft
ICI	4	Plastic & rubber Agricultural chemicals Organic chemicals Bleaching & dyeing		4	Plastic & rubber Agricultural chemicals Organic chemicals Hydrocarbons
CIBA-GEIGY	1	Photo & photocopying		2	Photo & photocopying Bleaching & dyeing
UK Atomic Energy Authority	1	Nuclear reactors		1	Nuclear reactors
National Nuclear Corporation	0			1	Nuclear reactors
Unilever	1	Food, drink		0	
Fisons	1	Agricultural chemicals		0	
GEC	2	Image & sound Semiconductors		0	
Philips	1	Semiconductors		0	
BP	1	Hydrocarbons		0	
Kodak	1	Photo & Photocopying		0	
Total sectors	17			13	

Source; SPRU Database on US Patenting.

particular interest (for more detail, sources and methods, see Patel & Pavitt 1987):

(a) Within the energy sector, the strengthening of coal-mining machinery associated with the National Coal Board, and the relative decline of nuclear energy;

(b) The differing effects of government defence R&D on aerospace and on electronics. In the former, the maintenance of British technological competitiveness has been associated with the continuing dominance of British patenting in the USA by Rolls-Royce and British Aerospace, and an increasing contribution of firms themselves to their total R&D expenditures. In electronics, declining technological competitiveness in semiconductors and computers has been associated with a precipitous drop in the contribution of the major British firm (GEC) to US patenting in these key areas, and with increasing reliance on governmental R&D funding during the 1970s.

(c) ICI maintained its strong position in most chemical-related sectors, whilst shifting resources towards fine chemicals — pharmaceuticals and agricultural chemicals — where there were other even more dynamic new (if otherwise large) entrants, namely, Beecham, Smith-Kline-French and Shell.

(d) Lucas was the main UK source of patenting in automobile technology. Unlike their counterparts in Germany and Japan, British-based automobile manufacturers made negligible contributions both to automobile technology, and more generally to manufacturing technology.

Promising areas for future research

There is, of course, no single perfect measure of technological activities; improvements in calibration, together with the combined use of more than one indicator, will continue to be important in the future. In addition, rapid improvements in access to, and understanding of, US patent statistics as measures of technological activities are opening up three important and challenging areas of research.

The determinants of international differences in the volume and sectoral distribution of technological activities: in particular, the relative effects of the general economic and institutional environment, of sector-specific inducement mechanisms, and of the technological strategies of large firms. What, for example, is the significance, in technologically more dynamic Germany, of the greater concentration and sectoral stability of the technological activities of the top five firms, compared to their British counterparts (Patel & Pavitt 1988)?

Technological activities at the level of the firm: their volume, composition, stability, and effects on competitive performance over time.

The links between scientific and technological activities: a better understanding of the complex and variegated links between scientific and technological activities, that we shall now begin to explore in the third and final part of this paper.

Science and technology

Historical perspective

Analysis of the links between science and technology goes back a long time. In Chapter 1 of *The Wealth of Nations*, Adam Smith identifies 'philosophers or men of speculation' as one of the three major sources of technology, together with both producers and users of machinery—a categorization that still has relevance today. In the 1830s, Alexis de Tocqueville predicted a rosy and growing future for science in the modernizing society that he observed in the USA. Its application would create considerable opportunities for profit, so that business demand would grow for applied scientists and for the institutions that trained them. Basic research, unconstrained by preoccupations of immediate application, would be necessary if profitable opportunities for application were not to dry up. Events since then have on the whole confirmed de Tocqueville's prediction: the relative contribution of science to technology has been increasing.

Industrial science

With the growth of industrial R&D departments in the 20th century, and their large-scale recruitment of university trained scientists, some social scientists have questioned the usefulness of distinguishing between the content of science and of technology. It has been suggested that the analytical tools of the sociology of science can readily be transferred to technology (Pinch & Bijker 1984, 1986). Two distinguished economists, Partha Dasgupta and Paul David (1986), have argued that the contents of science and of technology have become indistinguishable, and they cite molecular biology, biochemistry and solid-state physics as examples. By doing so, they may have fallen into a trap, common in studies of science and technology policy, of generalizing from the particular in what are in fact very heterogeneous activities. This was understandable when science and technology policy studies were mainly of particular cases, but has become less so with the development of science and technology indicators. These indicators show not only that the content of science is in general different from that of technology, but that the nature and extent of interaction between the two varies considerably across sectors.

Intersectoral differences

This field of analysis has been pioneered largely by Francis Narin and his colleagues in the USA (Carpenter 1983, Carpenter et al 1981, Narin 1982, Narin & Noma 1985). Their main conclusions are that technology builds largely on technology, but that the rate of interaction with science varies considerably amongst scientific fields and amongst technologies. Between biotechnology patents and biomedical research, the links are at present very strong, with the former using scientific results just as up-to-date as the latter. A recent case study of a development in monoclonal antibodies comes to a similar conclusion (Mackenzie et al 1988). In this type of sector, at least, the assumption that science and technology are close may be correct.

However, biotechnology may be the limiting case, because a comprehensive survey of citation patterns shows enormous variations amongst technologies in 'science dependence', as measured by the frequency of patent citations to journal papers. On average, a pharmaceutical patent cited journals thirty-six times more frequently than a patent in transportation. Chemical and biochemical patents are the most frequent in their citations of journals, the majority of which relate to basic research. Electronics and electrical patents are the next most frequent, but with a higher proportion of citations in journals reporting the results of applied research and engineering. Machinery patents have most of their citations to applied engineering, whilst instrumentation patents cite over the whole range of journals. As might be expected, chemical patents refer mainly to journals in chemistry, biology and medicine; electrical and electronics patents to journals in physics and engineering; and mechanical patents to those in engineering.

Training and networks

Similar differences amongst industrial sectors and scientific fields emerge from a recent survey of 650 directors of industrial R&D in the USA (Nelson 1986, Levin et al 1984), where a higher proportion of biochemical and chemical knowledge emerging from academic research was expected to find direct applications than of knowledge from other disciplines. However, across a wide range of industries, the perceived value of universities was less for the content of their research than for the training that it gave to future industrial researchers. This pattern is reflected in a SPRU study of British radio astronomy, which concluded that the main economic benefits of such research have been the skills that it has given in computing and electronics, and the abilities to define complex problems, to communicate effectively and to work in a team (Irvine & Martin 1980).

Another important benefit of such postgraduate training emerges from studies of the information sources used by technical problem-solvers in firms (Gibbons & Johnston 1974, Rothwell et al 1974, Allen 1977). In nearly all cases, the sources of such information are varied. What the university trained scientist or engineer brings to technical problem solving is not just substantive and methodological skills, but also the rich and informal network of professional contacts who can be called upon to help to solve problems: science and engineering graduates involved in problem solving are part of a larger intelligence system involving their former teachers and colleagues.

Implications for policy and the development of indicators

Given these characteristics, the relations between the differentiated and interrelated systems of science and technology are bound to be of concern to policy makers at a number of levels. For Britain, they point to the following conclusions.

First, the arguments that Britain could usefully carry a smaller 'burden' of the world's freely available scientific knowledge begins to look threadbare and wrongheaded. As we have seen, the world's basic research cannot be applied by users without costs, comprising those to firms of employing graduate scientists and engineers, and those to governments of providing the academic infrastructure, including postgraduate training and research. If a government decides to run down the infrastructure, industrial firms will have to provide it themselves or, as has been hinted by the former chairman of ICI (*Economist* 1987b), they will move their core activities to places where an adequate infrastructure is provided.

Second, any policy must recognize that the nature of the complementarities between science and technology varies considerably amongst sectors of application, in terms of the direct usefulness of academic research results, and of the relative importance attached to such results and to training. In addition to direct transfers of knowledge, any evaluation of the 'science base' for industry should include academic engineering, research training, and an assessment of the effectiveness of informal networks between academic research and places of application. These networks can probably best be traced and assessed through the employment patterns of scientists and engineers outside academia. In the short term this will be difficult to do, given the poor state into which British statistics on scientists and engineers have fallen since the late 1960s. In the meantime, we should be asking ourselves whether research funded by the research councils is sufficiently linked to postgraduate training, since such links are essential for the formation of these informal networks (Select Committee on Science and Technology 1986).

Third, we should be aware that the complementarities between the science and technology systems mean that the efficiency of the whole does not necessarily result from making the science system more like the technology system. There has been considerable pressure in the past few years to make the British science system more applied in its objectives. As we have seen, de Tocqueville rightly predicted a growing division of labour and interdependence between basic research and training, on the one hand, and technological activities on the other. He also predicted that neglect of the former would eventually destroy the latter.

Finally, we should be aware that some British science has been very relevant to application. In a paper commissioned by the Department of Industry, Narin & Olivastro (1987) identify the most frequently cited US patents of British origin in the period from 1975 to 1982. Because frequency of citation in other patents turns out to be a pretty good indicator of an invention's usefulness, it is relevant to note that the top British patent by far, with nearly 100 citations, was not granted to a British firm, but to the National Research Development Corporation (now called The British Technology Group), and resulted from publicly funded research by the Agricultural Research Council into synthetic pyrethrin insecticides (G. Barclay & M. Fottit, British Technology Group, personal communication 1987, D. Davies, personal communication 1980). It is also relevant that the second most frequently cited British patent was for work on liquid crystal materials and devices carried out at Hull University (Select Committee on Science and Technology 1983).

British-based firms have been active in converting these examples of relevant science into commercial technology. Unfortunately, there is more general evidence that the practical relevance of British science is often better perceived by foreign firms. There are, to my knowledge, at least two cases on the Sussex campus where foreign firms have been more active in the commercial exploitation of the University's academic research than British firms. And the Medical Research Council has gone on record to regret the lack of prominence of British firms, compared to their foreign counterparts, in exploiting the results of the Council's research in the fields of scientific instrumentation and specialized patient care (Select Committee on Science and Technology 1983). In other words, the British problem should be seen not as 'too much science' but as 'too little technology'.

Acknowledgements

This paper is based on research undertaken as part of the programme of the Economic and Social Research Council-funded Designated Research Centre on Science, Technology and Energy Policy, established at the Science Policy Research Unit. I am grateful for help in its preparation from Mohamed Ahmed, Richard Nelson, Geoffrey Oldham and Pari Patel.

References

Allen T 1977 Managing the flow of technology. MIT Press, Cambridge, Massachusetts

Arrow K 1962 Economic welfare and the allocation of resources for invention. In: Nelson R (ed) The rate and direction of inventive activity. Princeton University Press, New Jersey

Barras R 1986 Towards a theory of innovation in services. Research Policy 15(4):161–173

Carpenter M 1983 Patent citations as indicators of scientific and technological linkages. Annual meeting of the American Association for the Advancement of Science

Carpenter M, Narin F, Woolf P 1981 Citation rates to technologically important patents. World Patent Information 3(4):160–163

Coopers & Lybrand Associates 1987 Computing services industry, 1986–96 — a decade of opportunity. Department of Trade and Industry, London

Dasgupta P, David P 1986 Information disclosure and the economics of science and technology. In: Feiwel G (ed) Essays in honour of K. Arrow. Macmillan, Basingstoke/New York

The Economist 1987a In search of a cure. 7th February

The Economist 1987b Britain's university challenge. 18th April

Fagerberg J 1987 A technology gap approach to why growth rates differ. Research Policy 16(2–4):87–99

Fagerberg J 1988 International competitiveness. Economic Journal 98(391):355–374

Feinman S, Fuentevilla W 1976 Indicators of international trends in technological innovation. Report for the National Science Foundation, Gellman Research Associates, Jenkintown, USA

Gibbons M, Johnston R 1974 The roles of science in technological innovation. Research Policy 3(3):220–243

Irvine J, Martin B 1980 The economic effects of big science: the case of radio-astronomy. In: Proceedings of the international colloquium on economic effects of space and other advanced technologies, Strasborg, 28–30 April. European Space Agency, Paris

Kamin J, Bijaoui I, Horesh R 1982 Some determinants of cost distribution in the process of technological innovation. Research Policy 11(2):83–94

Kleinman H 1975 Indicators of the output of new technological products from industry. Report to the National Science Foundation, National Technical Information Service, US Department of Commerce

Levin R, Klevorick A, Nelson R, Winter S 1984 Survey research on R&D appropriability and technological opportunity. Part I: Appropriability. Yale University, New Haven

Mackenzie M, Cambrosio A, Keating P 1988 The commercial application of a scientific discovery; the case of the hybridoma technique. Research Policy 17(3):155–170

Narin F 1982 Assessment of the linkages between patents and fundamental research. Workshop on patents and innovation statistics, OECD

Narin F, Noma E 1985 Is technology becoming science? Scientometrics 7(3–6):369–381

Narin F, Olivastro D 1987 Identifying areas of strength and excellence in UK technology. CHI Research

Nelson R 1986 Institutions supporting technical advance in industry, American Economic Review 76(2):186–189

OECD 1985 Software; an emerging industry, Paris

Office of Technology Assessment and Forecast (OTAF) 1977 Technology assessment and forecast: 7th Report. US Department of Commerce

Patel P, Pavitt K 1987 The elements of British technological competitiveness. National Institute Economic Review 4(122):72–83

Patel P, Pavitt K 1988 The technological activities in FR Germany and the UK: differences and determinants. DRC Discussion Paper No 58, SPRU, Sussex

Pavitt K 1988 The size and structure of British technology activities: what we do and do not know. Scientometrics 14(3-4):315-346

Pavitt K, Robson M, Townsend J 1988 A fresh look at the size distribution of innovating firms. In: Arcangeli F, David P, Dosi G (eds) The diffusion of new technology: modern patterns in introducing and adopting innovations. Oxford University Press, Oxford

Pinch T, Bijker W 1984 The social construction of facts and artefacts: or how the sociology of science and the sociology of technology might benefit each other. Social Studies of Science 14(3):399-441

Pinch T, Bijker W 1986 Science, relativism and the new sociology of technology: reply to Russell. Social Studies of Science 16(2):347-360

Robson M, Townsend J, Pavitt K 1988 Sectoral patterns of production and use of innovations in the UK, 1945-83. Research Policy 17(1):1-14

Rothwell R et al 1974 SAPPHO Updated — project SAPPHO Phase 2. Research Policy 3(3):258-291

Scherer F 1982 Inter-industry technology flows in the United States. Research Policy, 11(4):227-245

Select Committee on Science and Technology 1983 Engineering research and development, (House of Lords), Vols I, II & III. HMSO, London

Select Committee on Science and Technology 1986 Civil Research and Development, (Evidence submitted to the House of Lords Select Committee, D. Hague), Vols. I, II and III. HMSO, London

Smith A 1985 edition The wealth of Nations. G. Routledge and Sons, London

Soete L 1981 A general test of technological gap trade theory. Weltwirtschaftliches Archiv 117:638-660

Stigler G 1951 The division of labour is limited by the extent of the market. Journal of Political Economy 59:185-193

de Tocqueville A 1963 edition De la democratie en amerique (abridged edition). Union Generale d'Editions

DISCUSSION

Hill: The assertion that basic research has secondary spill-over benefits of research training and background knowledge creation seems to me to be on very shaky ground. One must look at alternative pathways to the same goals; are there better ways of getting there? I would argue, without any data in support, that typical basic research training (and radio astronomy would not be typical for reasons that you alluded to) ill-prepares one for service in industrial research because it emphasizes individual contributions, not team approaches, and in-depth investigation in narrow areas, rather than the breadth of acquaintance with a diversity of technical specialities that is necessary to make progress in industry. I find it hard to understand the counter-argument that basic research is good training; my own experience would tell me it's poor training for industrial service. I would suggest (and this has been discussed recently in the USA for industrial research training) that masters level training in a diverse set of fields that are complementary to an industrial sector provides a better general background than the narrow and highly specialized research training that is provided at the doctoral level.

Pavitt: You may be right and you may be wrong; it's an empirical question. I am impressed that enlightened industrial research directors say that the business of universities is to do good basic research and let others do the applying. In evaluating the importance of science–technology links, or academic–business links, one must also look beyond direct, useful knowledge transfer.

Phillips: But isn't it sector dependent? The leaders of the chemical industry assure me that the most important products of the academic system are the people that they recruit, and they don't particularly mind what they do during the training.

Moravcsik: Many of the technology-intensive basic research fields are also big science fields in which team cooperation is important. Many people obtaining degrees in experimental high-energy physics, for example, find it easy to get jobs in industry because they are geared towards big operations.

Kruytbosch: In our studies of industry–university relationships (National Science Board 1982, Peters & Fusfeld 1982), most of the companies we surveyed said that the first thing that they looked for in giving support to universities was to have access to the best and brightest students and professors. Whether or not the training of these students could have been improved is still an open question.

Irvine: In a study of the employment profiles of radio astronomy postgraduates, we found that a large proportion were working in areas strongly related to their research field; such as helping run the police national computer, developing automatic fingerprint recognition systems, and designing antennae for telecommunications receivers (Martin & Irvine 1981). Similarly, a parallel study of postgraduates in high-energy physics showed that specific use was being made of skills developed during research training (for example, in computing software).

The advertisements in popular scientific journals such as *New Scientist* demonstrate that many companies are actively recruiting research skills within defined specialties. Companies moving into new research areas know that one way rapidly to develop a basic capacity (e.g. in superconductivity) is to recruit doctoral and postdoctoral staff with relevant expertise. Consequently, in many science-based industrial sectors there are quite strong links between the disciplinary skills of researchers and the type of work they undertake in R&D laboratories. It may therefore be dangerous to assume that companies can recruit research staff solely on the basis that they are 'the best and brightest'.

On a slightly different issue, Keith, you presented a large amount of empirical data and made claims for associations between various factors such as R&D expenditure and economic performance. As far as I understand, these are only correlations and yet you impute causal relationships. On what basis have the links been established? Do you, for example, have a theoretical model to test using the various data sets?

Pavitt: I have a theoretical model, but you know from problems of statistical inference that there is no completely satisfactory answer to that question. It is easier to use case studies to demonstrate causalities: Apple Computers would be an example. But economists, politicians or sceptical bankers will still ask whether we can generalize from the particular. We therefore need more aggregate studies that impute causality in a theoretical model.

Weinberg: You outline various criteria and policies that one sees in countries that were successful in their technological development. It seems to me that the climate of entrepreneurship might also be important. Have you considered adding another dimension to the four on your list—the amount of money that is available for technical entrepreneurship? That's one quality that the USA has.

Pavitt: It depends what you mean by climate of entrepreneurship, and it's even ambiguous in the way you speak about it. If you define it as the willingness of firms and individuals to spend money on R&D and technological develop-ments, there is clear variance amongst countries. Top is Switzerland, second Sweden, third Japan, fourth Germany and then the USA. I think this is the proper measure. However, another definition of the 'climate of entrep-reneurship' is that money is provided generously to allow small firms to develop new technologies; here, the United States is supposed to have a lead. My own personal view is that so many small firms exist in the USA because the big ones are not capable of being entrepreneurial. This goes against the conventional wisdom, but the impression I have is that although the Germans and the Japanese don't fit in with the Anglo-Saxon or Yankie idea of entrepreneurship, they have a more impressive record in terms of technological dynamism over a long period.

Weinberg: Is there clear statistical evidence of this, not so much with respect to the amount of money that's available for R&D *per se*, but rather the amount of money that's available for starting new companies?

Pavitt: That's the point I was making. The country, the USA, that supposed-ly has the greatest record for starting new companies, is not doing very well by most long-term measures of technological dynamism. The large Japanese firms and the heavily concentrated concerns in Germany and Sweden seem to be doing better.

Kruytbosch: One of the most common ways that large US firms innovate is by buying up or buying into small high-technology businesses and investing in them. That's another way of looking at it.

Pavitt: That's true. But small businesses are often started by dissatisfied engineers leaving the large firms.

Narin: I want to disagree with your model of West Germany as a picture of dynamism. From the work we have done, particularly comparing the UK and the West German performance, I think the pattern in Germany is much more of strength in the old technologies, rather than in the newer technologies. Germany is strong in the older chemical areas, such as separation, and weak or declining in biotechnology, electronics and communications. The system there is not a model of how to get dynamic, innovative research or industry. In fact, it shows how to hold onto old, high quality but relatively mundane work for a long time. The Germans are quite vulnerable over the next 10–20 years to the effects of the more dynamic British pharmaceutical industry and the Japanese electronics and communication industries.

Hill: Lewis Branscomb (Director, Public Policy Program, Kennedy School of Government, Harvard) recently suggested in a semi-public forum that venture capital had destroyed the American semiconductor industry. Keith, you seem to be observing the centrality of a small number of large, integrated, technically based corporations. In the USA the perception is beginning to re-emerge that some of our major companies are failing to perform as well as we would like, or perhaps as they used to. Therefore the public policy problem is to stimulate those large corporations so that they can compete effectively with Japanese companies.

That raises what may be heresy in the UK–US context; can one build a technology policy on a 'hands-off', free market model when there are only a few large, identifiable individual actors? What meaning does free market have in that context? The answer is not state control or socialism, but we need to search for other mechanisms of positive intervention in those kinds of institutions. In the USA, we haven't been able to hold that debate for the last seven years and neither have you in the UK. Meanwhile, the Japanese have been able to get on with it, and we are going to have a real struggle over the next decade to put that system back together.

Pavitt: That's a good point.

Blume: Some of the difficulty in conceptualizing the relations between science and technology arises from the tendency in most work to look at research as purely a problem-solving activity. This is partly a methodological artefact. The tendency has been to ask how science has been used to solve certain problems in innovation. I am convinced that science and research contribute in other ways as well. One concept missing from your paper was that the users of different kinds of technological products are different, and stand in different sorts of relationships to those technologies. For example, in my work on medical technology, the users are sophisticated consumers and research does more than help solve the technical problems of production; it establishes a use for the technology. It is through clinical research and investigation of what a diagnostic instrument can achieve that uses are established and the market is constituted. Moreover, research is socially and cognitively organized. When research is seen as other than pure problem solving, there's a tendency to imply that science is made up of disciplines that are almost as traditional as rhetoric and geometry. However, much science is in technical fields such as optoelectronics and biotechnology. The crystallization of these as technical fields of research has profound importance for innovation processes, partly because users and producers are involved with each other intellectually as well as through market relationships.

Pavitt: I agree.

Georghiou: You gave us a convincing review of the techniques and methods you would use for measuring these impacts at the national level. Do you think they could be scaled down to measure the impact of a research programme on the economy, and if not how would you do that?

Pavitt: I don't think you can do it for an Alvey-type sectoral activity.

References

Martin BR, Irvine J 1981 Spin-off from basic science: the case of radio astronomy. Physics in Technology 12:204–212

National Science Board 1982 University–industry research relationships: myths, realities and potentials. (NSB 82-1) National Science Foundation, Washington DC, p 19

Peters L, Fusfeld H 1982 Current US university–industry research connections. In: University–industry research relationships: selected studies (NSB 82-2). National Science Foundation, Washington DC, p 35

The role and effectiveness of peer review

Carlos E. Kruytbosch*

Science Indicators Group, National Science Foundation, Washington DC 20550, USA

Abstract. Peer review in science can be defined as the advice about proposed actions solicited by decision makers from experts in relevant technical areas. The term peer review is used in several contexts, but in this paper it refers to the review and selection of research projects. Peer review is both a social process (a set of practices) and a social ideology (a set of ideals). The practices have become more formalized in recent decades as a corollary of the increasing professionalization of science and the bureaucratization of its support structures that has accompanied growth in public funds allocated to it. Acceptance of the tenets of peer review as an ideology has been critical in maintaining a distance between political issues and concerns for technical excellence in the arrangements for disbursing public funds for basic science. (In what other area of government funding are major sums disbursed on the advice of often anonymous advisers?) Stringencies in public finance have put pressures on R&D budgets to justify returns. This has led both to greater emphasis on evaluation (especially in Europe) and to attempts to broaden both the concept and practice of peer review to include a variety of non-technical, socioeconomic objectives. In the USA this has been termed 'merit review'. This paper traces the development of these issues in the experience of the National Science Foundation (NSF). Questions of effectiveness are addressed with data from a 1986 survey of proposers to NSF research grant programmes.

1989 The evaluation of scientific research. Wiley, Chichester (Ciba Foundation Conference) p 69–85

Peer review can be defined as advice about proposed actions solicited by decision makers from recognized experts in relevant technical areas. In recent decades the term peer review has come primarily to refer to advice on research project selection for financial support (or access to research facilities), and to manuscript selection for journal publication. It is also sometimes used to refer to the process for assessing and judging cases of alleged professional misconduct, and to the *post hoc* evaluation of completed research. The thrust of my remarks will be

---

*The views presented here are those of the author alone and do not necessarily represent any policies or positions of the National Science Foundation.

towards review and selection of research projects, based primarily on the experience of the National Science Foundation (NSF) in the USA.

Peer review is both a social institution (a set of practices) and an ideology (a statement of a set of ideals). It seems fair to say that the practice of review by peers came first, as an extension of scientific cooperation. Past accounts of scientific activity reveal the eagerness of investigators to establish their priority and to have their work critiqued and recognized by those capable of appreciating it (Merton 1957).

Formalization of the process came first with the growth of scientific societies and the need to regulate the process of scientific conflict and controversy in their meetings and journals. It was greatly accelerated with the professionalization of research in universities and industrial laboratories around the beginning of the 20th century. In the USA the great foundations that began supporting research, especially in medical areas, used informal peer review, and most eventually developed scientific advisory panels (see Abir-Am 1982, 1984, Fuerst 1984, Bartels 1984, Olby 1984, Yoxen 1984).

The advent of major public (Federal) support for basic research after World War II with the creation of the National Institutes of Health (NIH) and the NSF saw the emergence of bureaucratic formalization of the peer review process. The NIH developed a two-tier system of review. Study panels assess proposals for scientific excellence and institute-level reviews judge the mission relevance of the projects. The process was spelled out in formal structural requirements. Interestingly, the process of peer review for the selection of projects is not mentioned in the statutes of the NSF (England 1982).

At that time, peer review as an ideology became critical as a way of maintaining distance between political issues and concerns for technical excellence in the arrangements for disbursement of funds for basic research. That funds would only be allocated to technically excellent projects was guaranteed by a rigorous, competitive review and selection process conducted and overseen by the scientists themselves. This assurance paved the way for the establishment of the National Science Foundation. It was also necessary conceptually to sever the connection between the research efforts to be funded and their eventual potential applications, or else it was feared that the process would be overwhelmed by interest groups jostling for their priorities. This was accomplished by Bush (1945) who established the term 'basic research' as part of a conceptual continuum followed by 'applied research' and 'development'. The original NSF Act authorized only 'basic scientific research' but was amended in 1968 to authorize support of 'applied' research. (It is interesting to note that the full report consisted of 40 pages by Bush and about 140 pages of appendix reports by four advisory committees. In Bush's portion, the term 'basic research' is used almost exclusively. In the appendix reports the term 'basic research' is almost never used — the favourite terms are 'pure' research or science.)

The 'long debate' (England 1982), about who would control the allocations and how, lasted for nearly five years, from 1945 to 1950. The scientists feared Federal control, while many Administration and Congressional officials feared loss of control to the scientists. The eventual compromise resulted in the unique structure of the NSF in the Federal system. The National Science Board (NSB), the NSF's governing body, was to act as an 'insulating' mechanism, being composed of three staggered sets of six-year Presidential appointees requiring approval by the US Senate.

Evolution of peer review at the NSF

Unlike the more codified and centralized system at the NIH, the aphorism 'let 1000 flowers bloom' characterized the evolution of peer review at the NSF. Each Division, and often each programme, developed its own version of proposal review and project selection (see General Accounting Office 1981). There was, and is, no central office for peer review at the NSF. One consequence of this is a relatively poor quality of information about system operations. For example, even now there are no data on the critical question of reviewer response rates to answer worrisome questions about whether the willingness to review is declining, as has been suggested (National Science Foundation Advisory Committee on Merit Review 1986). General NSB policies and NSF regulations specified the general criteria to be used in review, and set forth the types of exceptions to the requirement to review. Several main types of review emerged:

(a) *Ad hoc* mail reviews. These are primarily used in the physical science programmes. A unique set of reviewers is chosen for each proposal by the programme officer. The review is conducted by mail, and the reviewer has no interaction with others reviewing the same proposal. The review is anonymous; the names of reviewers and the ratings they give the proposal remain confidential information. However, since 1976 the NSF has routinely returned 'anonymized' versions of reviewer comments to the proposer. This communication is generally viewed as important and educational.

(b) Standing panel review. This is primarily used in the biological, behavioural and social science programmes. Panels of 5–15 publicly announced members with appointments (made by the programme officers) of one to three years meet for a couple of days two to three times a year. In one variant, one or two outside *ad hoc* mail reviews are solicited for each proposal in a batch. In another variant, *ad hoc* reviews are only solicited when there is deemed to be inadequate expertise in the existing panel for a particular proposal. Most panels designate one or more lead reviewers who make a presentation and lead the discussion on a proposal. The group discussion on the proposal is summarized and returned to the proposer when the final go/no-go decision is made.

(c) *Ad hoc* panel review. This has primarily been used for special programmes or projects, and was used extensively in the NSF Science Education Directorate. They are likely to be used where non-scientific criteria (e.g. geographical, institutional or disciplinary distributions, or relevance to particular kinds of social utility or infrastructure goals) are included in the programme aims. Again, variations are the rule. The Engineering Research Centers Program has a two-tier review process; an initial screening on technical grounds (peer review), and a second screening including broader goals and purposes of the proposed centres. Together the two procedures are termed 'merit review').

(d) Inter- or multidisciplinary proposal review. It is widely felt that interdisciplinary proposals are often prone to 'fall between the cracks' (Porter & Rossini 1985). Where interdisciplinary aspects of an investigation appear to be coalescing, a separate programme can be set up. For example, at the NSF a new 'Chemistry of Life Processes' programme is a cooperative effort between the Chemistry and Biological Sciences Divisions. In this programme, proposals were initially reviewed in a two-step process. The relevant disciplinary programmes conducted mail reviews. The results of these were fed into a final discussion by an *ad hoc* interdisciplinary panel. In its second or third year of operation the panel was scrapped, and the programme now supports only those highly rated proposals that both sets of Divisional reviews agree upon.

Major issues in peer review at the NSF: 1975–1985

Three sets of issues tended to reoccur during this period, although to varying degrees of importance: fairness, efficiency and planning.

In 1974/75 some members of the US Congress became concerned about the direction of some of the NSF's science education curriculum development projects. Being conservative, they generally disapproved of Federal involvement in the content of education, which they felt was a matter reserved by the US Constitution to the States. An anthropology curriculum, Man: A Course of Study (MACOS), was singled out for criticism. Amid much publicity about the revelations of Eskimo customs of infanticide, gerontocide, and wife-lending, the critics declared the cultural relativism of the course an unsuitable perspective for US school children. In this climate, the US House of Representatives accepted an amendment to the NSF's 1976 budget bill which would have given the legislators an opportunity to pass judgement on *all* NSF grants individually. 'Happily for the Foundation—and for science—the spectacle of the United States Congress sitting as a board of review on the some 15 000 grants annually approved by the Foundation was quickly dissipated by the refusal of the Senate to go along with the Bauman amendment.' (Lomask 1976).

Despite this set-back, and still suspicious of the existence of 'old boy networks' which would exclude proposals from non-members, the House directed the NSF to supply it with the names of NSF reviewers. The NSF's response was to provide an alphabetical listing of over 100 000 names and institutional affiliations of NSF reviewers. A Congressional wag dubbed it the 'Hong Kong telephone book'. Further negotiation the following year resulted in provision of listings of reviewers at the Divisional level. Thus, the essential principle of anonymity of reviewers on particular proposals was maintained.

The turmoil about science education was exacerbated by the discovery that there had been some irregularities in the proposal review and recommendation process in a major (more than $1 million) curriculum project to develop an Individualized Science Instruction System (ISIS). Negative reviews had been omitted in the review analysis presented by the programme to the National Science Board. This revelation led to a Congressional directive for the NSB to study the NSF management of the peer review process. The Congress desired to know the effects of the system on the success rates of proposals from different regions (geographical distribution), major or minor institutions, and young or senior investigators. It also directed a study of the hypothesis that the peer review process tends to stifle unorthodox science.

The NSF undertook both internal and extramural studies of these issues. The internal investigations generally found no patterns of discrimination by institutional prestige; though the non-doctoral institutions submitted a tiny proportion of all proposals, their success rates were only slightly below the mean. Again, the success rates did not vary much by seniority of the investigator. The study of innovation showed that the NSF's share of all major advances in several fields was roughly in proportion to its share of total funding of the field. This was taken as evidence against the conservative hypothesis (National Science Board 1977).

On the management issues, the NSF made a number of changes including: a commitment to always return 'anonymized' copies of the comments of *ad hoc* mail reviewers to all proposers; institution of an appeals process which would review not the content of the award/decline decision, but whether the process had been fully and fairly followed; and a commitment to widen the search for competent reviewers from outside the research universities.

The NSF also commissioned the National Academy of Sciences to investigate these issues using evidence from a sample of 1000 grant files in six programmes. Lengthy methodological disputes within the Academy committee delayed the appearance of their report until 1978, but it generally confirmed the findings of the internal studies (Cole et al 1978). The study of the case files themselves yielded a new finding of a very high correlation between the decision to award and the ratings given by reviewers. NSF programme managers were clearly taking the advice of their reviewers seriously.

Phase Two of the Academy studies involved a 'blinded review' experiment in which the identities of the proposers of applications which had already been reviewed and awarded or declined by the NSF were altered. The proposals were reviewed again by new reviewers. The results—not published until 1981—showed significant differences in the new rankings from the original NSF reviewer scores (Cole & Cole 1981). One newspaper report of the study likened the NSF review process to 'tossing a coin'. The fact that, remarkably, there was virtually no Congressional reaction to these provocative findings which would have been gasoline on the fire only a few years before, suggests that peer review as an ideology was finally (if sceptically) accepted by Congress. It was time to move on to other issues.

Congress had turned its attention from the inputs to the outputs of research projects. In 1980 the Senate Committee on Appropriations directed the NSF to, 'secure an independent third party to develop a methodology for post-performance evaluation of scientific research endeavors' (US Senate 1980). The National Academy of Sciences produced an interesting study (National Academy of Sciences 1982) and its recommendations for another procedural change were accepted by the NSF. Now proposers to the NSF are required to include descriptions of prior NSF-supported work in their proposals, and reviewers are requested to consider this record in arriving at their ratings.

In the early 1980s, issues from the debate about Federal funding for academic research facilities led to new questions about peer review. This began with an NSF award to a university for a research ship. The award was challenged in part on the grounds that other declined proposals had received higher technical ratings from reviewers. The NSF argued that its well-publicized national plan for the academic research fleet required a particular distribution of ships with different capabilities along the several US coasts. The winning proposal best fitted this plan and met all the procurement requirements, despite having a lower technical rating. Subsequently, an investigation by the Congressional watchdog agency, the General Accounting Office, upheld this judgment (General Accounting Office 1982).

Also at this time, the academic research community began to push for Federal recognition of its needs for renewal of outdated and inadequate research facilities. The title of one book was, 'Crumbling Academe' (Kaiser 1984)! Scepticism was apparent in the Office of Management and Budget about the claimed magnitude of the need for facilities, and many officials held the view that support for science buildings on campuses was not an appropriate Federal role. A preliminary study by a Federal Interagency Committee looked at existing construction plans for science and engineering facilities at a sample of research universities, and estimated a need of $1.3 billion per year over the next five years (Interagency Steering Committee on Academic Research 1984, see also National Science Foundation 1986). As the debate proceeded, it became apparent that in the contemporary budgetary climate there was little chance for any major Federal facilities programme. Some universities began to look to their

Congressional Representatives for assistance, and in the time-honoured fashion for allocating Federal funds for public works in their districts, Senators and Representatives began to sponsor 'floor amendments', earmarking funds from Federal R&D agency appropriations for specified facilities in their districts. This practice has continued and the total amounts involved have reached several hundred million dollars annually.

This development was seen to be a major breach in the ideological and institutional aspects of peer review. The 'pork-barrel' allocations, made without review of any kind, threatened to skew the priorities of the R&D agencies funding academic research, because ultimately the funds had to come from the zero-sum budgetary pool of funds for science. The reluctance of the R&D agencies to fully support the urgent academic demands for facilities programmes stemmed in part from their perception that Congress might well require them to initiate such programmes, but instruct them to 'swallow' the costs (i.e. give them no new funds) and thus disrupt their regular research programme priorities.

The debate pitted the elite research universities (represented in the Association of American Universities) against some of the lesser institutions, led by the President of Boston University, Dr John Silber, an unashamed recipient of 'floor amendment' funds. He argued that 'have-not' institutions will not be able to develop their capacity to do scientific research if they cannot acquire facilities. Regular peer review would permanently exclude his kind of institution from the research game. A number of Congressmen supported this view. These issues were discussed in a National Science Board Committee report which recommended a thorough investigation of the problems and options in this delicate area. The NSF Director promptly appointed a national Advisory Committee on Merit Review, charged with looking at the whole spectrum of issues in project review and recommendation procedures in Federal agencies, with special attention to the various issues in the funding of facilities.

This group's final report (National Science Foundation Advisory Committee on Merit Review 1986) described the different types of review and selection methods in terms of their *appropriateness to different kinds of goals*. It documented the emergence at the NSF of concerns beyond pure/basic research, and the accompanying changes in the methods of project review and selection. All the emergent modes included a rigorous component of technical review, as well as the application of other relevant criteria. These 'peer-review-plus' modes were dubbed 'merit review'. Predictably, at first the report stimulated some alarmed responses from people in the scientific community who believed that peer review was being replaced by some loosely defined, administratively controlled process. While it embodies no reduction in the primary requirement for technical (peer) review, the concept of merit review has served to *extend* the traditional ideology of peer review to cover circumstances in which technical review by itself is inadequate.

On the issue of the 'floor amendments', the report stated that the basic problem was that the need for facilities could only be met in the long run by Federal involvement. But until that time, Congress should set up its own 'process for obtaining independent technical assessment of proposed academic facilities projects prior to including the items in agency budgets' (National Science Foundation Advisory Committee on Merit Review 1986). Not surprisingly, this was the one Committee recommendation not accepted by the NSF Director.

The Congress was apparently responsive to the flood of criticism about floor amendments, and in the spring of 1988 the House Committee on Agriculture devised a new approach to the problem. The Committee directed that nearly $100 million be added to the budget for the US Department of Agriculture (USDA) for construction of six biotechnology research centres at specified universities. The cost of the centres varied from $3 to $30 million each. The Committee's action broke new ground in requiring the USDA Cooperative Research Service (CRS) to conduct technical, managerial and planning feasibility studies at each site. These studies would be reported to the Secretary of Agriculture, who in turn would transmit them, without recommendation, to the Committee. Should the studies reveal flaws or deficiencies in the proposed centres, it was understood that the appropriation for that item would be altered or eliminated. At the time of writing (June 1988), interdisciplinary site visit teams of leading scientists were involved in the process of review. It remains to be seen whether this process will become a new mode of providing funds for academic research facilities which uses technical peer review to validate (or reject) political choices.

The view from within the research community

The history recounted above is largely the record of external suspicion of the integrity of peer review. In this the political forces were frequently activated by individual or institutional 'have-nots' within the scientific community who believed the game was rigged against them. Evidence from a recent survey (National Science Foundation 1988) of individual researchers whose proposals were reviewed by NSF during the financial year 1985 suggests that there is still a significant pool of dissatisfaction with the process. Overall, 38 percent of the respondents indicated dissatisfaction or moderate dissatisfaction with the review process. Of course, perception of the system varied according to how it had worked for them. Table 1 shows the distribution of these perceptions among six 'experience classes'.

The most cited five reasons for dissatisfaction (92% of dissatisfied respondents wrote in remarks) were, in order of frequency:

(1) reviewers or panelists not expert in the field, poorly chosen, poorly qualified (18%);

TABLE 1 **Satisfaction with the NSF review process, by experience class**

Experience class[a]	Satisfied (percent)	Neutral (percent)	Dissatisfied (percent)	Percent in class
Consistent declinee	27	16	57	28
One-time declinee	35	21	44	13
Frequent declinee	40	16	44	14
Frequent awardee	61	11	28	26
Consistent awardee	83	5	12	13
One-time awardee	87	7	6	5

[a]The experience classes characterize experience with the NSF over the previous five years. Consistent declinee, at least two proposals submitted, all declined; One-time declinee, one proposal submitted and declined; Frequent declinee, at least three proposals submitted, only one of which was awarded; Frequent awardee, one of two proposals awarded, or two or more awarded of three or more proposals (but not all); Consistent awardee, either received as many awards as proposals submitted, or received five or more awards in five years; One-time awardee, one proposal submitted and awarded. These findings are very similar to the results of a survey of NSF applicants and reviewers conducted in 1975 (Hensler 1976).
Data taken from National Science Foundation, Program Evaluation Staff (1988).

(2) reviews perfunctory, cursory non-substantive (17%);
(3) reviews were conflicting (12%);
(4) 'cronyism', politics, 'old boys network' (12%);
(5) decision unclear or inconsistent with reviews (10%).

Nine other categories of remarks received 7% or less of the total. While the Consistent declinees were three times as likely to respond to this question than others, the rank order of reasons given by awardees and declinees was about the same. The awardees tended to indicate dissatisfaction with the 'slowness' of the process; the declinees were slightly more likely to cite politics or cronyism.

Seventy-five percent of all the applicants said they had served as a reviewer or panelist for NSF during the past five years. The proportion of One-time declinees (44%) and Consistent declinees (62%) who had served fell significantly below this average, but the Frequent declinees (83%) outdid the One-time awardees (80%) in participating in the work of the agency. Needless to say, 97 percent of the Consistent awardees had served as reviewers during the period. These data stress how important it is for seekers of research support to participate across a wide range of review and proposal activities.

Conclusion

It seems fair to say that peer review as an ideology, having survived a number of concerted attacks over the past 40 years, remains firmly in place as a keystone of the US system of Federal funding of academic R&D. Furthermore, it has apparently been successfully modified (at least as of 1988) and extended (and renamed) to include both technical and non-technical concerns within its purview. As a response to criticism from outside and inside science, many changes have been incorporated to improve accountability, effectiveness and participation.

Every national system of research support, while providing primarily for work targeted at national needs, must also provide some (usually less than 10%) support for creative exploration of fundamental problems. Basic/pure research can be viewed as an essential overhead cost of national R&D (see Betz et al 1980). Peer review arrangements (while, like democracy, imperfect) constitute the only effective system yet devised to allocate funds among competing proposals for basic research.

Since 1985 I have been connected with designing, reviewing or assessing the introduction of new competitive peer review arrangements for the support of basic research in such disparate political entities as Bulgaria, Texas, China and Malaysia. The common theme in each case is the perception that political and bureaucratic decision making concerning allocation of research resources, while essential in large measure, must be leavened by funds competitively allocated on the basis of technical merit. Such a process is believed to provide the opportunity for new ideas and innovations to surface and thus to stimulate the technical and economic environment.

References

Abir-Am P 1982 The discourse of physical power and biological knowledge in the 1930s: a reappraisal of the Rockefeller Foundation's 'policy' in molecular biology. Social Studies of Science 12:341–382

Abir-Am P 1984 Beyond deterministic sociology and apologetic history: reassessing the impact of research policy upon new scientific disciplines. Social Studies of Science 14:252–264

Bartels D 1984 The Rockefeller Foundation's funding policy for molecular biology: success or failure? Social Studies of Science 14:238–243

Betz F, Blankenship LV, Kruytbosch C, Mason R 1980 Allocating R&D resources in the public sector. In: Dean BV, Goldhar JL (eds) Management of research and innovation. North-Holland Publishing Company, Amsterdam, p 235–252

Bush V 1945 Science the endless frontier

Cole S, Rubin L, Cole JR 1978 Peer review in the National Science Foundation, phase one of a study. National Academy of Sciences, Washington DC

Cole JR, Cole S 1981 Peer review in the National Science Foundation, phase two of a study. National Academy of Sciences, Washington, DC

England JM 1982 A patron for pure science. The National Science Foundation's formative years, 1945–57. (NSF 82–24). National Science Foundation, Washington DC, p 165–166

Fuerst JA 1984 The definition of molecular biology and the definition of policy: the role of the Rockefeller Foundation's policy for molecular biology.

General Accounting Office 1981 Better accountability procedures needed in NSF and NIH research grant systems. (PAD-81-29). General Accounting Office, Washington DC

General Accounting Office 1982 NSF's award of two research vessels met requirements. (GAO/PAD-82-14). General Accounting Office, Washington DC

Hensler DR 1976 Perceptions of the National Science Foundation peer review process: a report on a survey of NSF reviewers and applicants. Prepared for the Committee on Peer Review, National Science Board and the Committee on Science and Technology, US House of Representatives, Washington DC, p 35

Interagency Steering Committee on Academic Research, with the assistance of the NSF Task Group on Academic Research Facilities 1984 Adequacy of academic research facilities. Washington DC

Kaiser H 1984 Crumbling Academe. Association of Governing Boards of Universities, Washington DC

Lomask M 1976 A minor miracle: an informal history of the National Science Foundation. (NSF 76-18). National Science Foundation, Washington DC, p 257–259

Merton RK 1957 Priorities in scientific discovery: a chapter in the sociology of science. American Sociological Review 22:635–659

NIH Grants Peer Review Study Team 1976 Grants peer review: report to the Director, NIH, Phase I. NIH, Washington DC

National Academy of Sciences 1982 The quality of research in science: methods for postperformance evaluation in the National Science Foundation. National Academy Press, Washington DC

National Science Board 1977 Report of the National Science Board to the Subcommittee on Science, Research and Technology of the Committee on Science and Technology, US House of Representatives, regarding peer review procedures at the National Science Foundation. (NSB 77-468). National Science Board, Washington DC

National Science Foundation 1986 Science and engineering research facilities at doctorate-granting institutions. National Science Foundation, Washington DC

National Science Foundation Advisory Committee on Merit Review 1986 Final Report. (NSF 86-93). National Science Foundation, Washington DC

National Science Foundation, Program Evaluation Staff 1988 Proposal review at NSF: perceptions of principal investigators. (NSF 88-4). National Science Foundation, Washington DC

Olby R 1984 The sheriff and the cowboys or Weaver's support of Astbury and Pauling. Social Studies of Science 14:244–247

Porter AL, Rossini FA 1985 Peer review of interdisciplinary research. Science, Technology and Human Values 10:33–38

US Senate, Department of Housing and Urban Development — Independent Agencies Appropriations Bill 1980. 96th Congress, 1st Session. Report No. 96-258. US Government Printing Office, Washington DC

Yoxen EJ 1984 Scepticism about the centrality of technology transfer in the Rockefeller Foundation Programme in molecular biology. Social Studies of Science 14:248–251

DISCUSSION

Luukkonen-Gronow: You said that in the USA requests for support for science facilities had gone to Congress without any peer review. How were the needs assessed? In the Nordic countries the research councils have enlisted panels of foreign experts primarily to assess the performance of particular projects but also, among other things, to advise on instrumentation require-ments. It appears that experts from within a research field tend to stress the great urgency of the needs of that field and to support all the requests. Who then is to decide which needs should be met? This is done by the science policy community, made up of such people as the members of advisory committees, who represent a broad range of fields, and the bureaucrats in ministries. Criteria other than scientific ones may be most decisive in the end. This is an intrinsic problem with peer review.

Kruytbosch: I agree with you. One consequence is an immediate demand for data. When academic research facilities and instrumentation are in question how do we know that the universities haven't got perfectly good little Volk-swagens and yet are now asking for Cadillacs? From the legislator's point of view, academic science is an interest group no different from milk producers, wheat farmers or broccoli seed raisers, all of whom want more resources. Therefore there was much activity to generate data demonstrating the urgent needs of academic science for facilities, instrumentation and targeted training programmes. Some data showed very large needs for academic research facili-ties; other data showed that these needs were mostly being met without Federal involvement. So you could pick your studies. There wasn't enough political steam generated to persuade the Office of Management and Budget (OMB), or even the Congress, to put several hundred million dollars into a facilities programme. Therefore the alternative piecemeal 'pork-barrel' approach was used.

Small: There are significant forms of research evaluation that are not in-cluded in the scope of our discussion. Examples are the peer review of articles for publication and tenure or promotion decisions. For all these, we can talk about the idealized criteria of intrinsic or extrinsic value. However, if we were to study the process of decision making followed by the individual evaluator, we might be surprised to see the use of criteria that we consider to be biased or totally subjective and arbitrary. This highlights the need for research into the evaluation process, not producing an idealized set of prescriptions, but rather as a study of what really goes on.

Some time ago I looked at reviewers' reports on scientific papers which were later published. There was a great variety of reasons that people gave for rejecting or accepting papers: particularly accusations that this work has been done before, so why do it again; or 'he forgot to refer to my paper or somebody else's paper in his proposal or in his paper'. There's a well-known book in cognitive psychology called 'Judgement under uncertainty' by Kahneman et al (1982). Evaluation is a perfect example of that type of activity, operating on very incomplete and insufficient cues. It could be studied using a different approach to the one we have been discussing.

Kruytbosch: I think that's an excellent idea, but don't come to me for money because my budget has been cut in half!

Irvine: I would also agree that those issues are important and merit further research. Dr Harry Collins of Bath University is undertaking a detailed study of the peer review process, and this has involved attending meetings of grant-awarding committees within the Science and Engineering Research Council.

Garfield: There is a related point about the use of the *Science Citation Index* (SCI). This conference is devoted to its use in providing science indicators. But nothing has been said about its highly relevant use for information retrieval, particularly for the identification of suitable people to review papers and proposals. Those research scientists who know how to use the SCI correctly use it for direct retrieval of subject information, and also to find experts in the field. However, a significant percentage of scientists have never used the SCI for any purpose.

Kruytbosch: The hard copies (paper version) of the SCI are used to locate potential reviewers in many of the research programmes at the NSF, particularly in social science programmes.

Garfield: Perhaps the people that you use as experts go to their own libraries to use the SCI, but generally it is not used for the explicit purpose of identifying experts. At a conference on 'Scientific data audit policies and quality assurance' (University of Maryland, 8–10 May, 1988), the possibility of creating a qualification termed 'Certified Public Scientist' was discussed. Those awarded this title would have demonstrated that they were qualified to use all these retrieval and evaluative techniques.

In another connection, Manfred Kochen (1987) published an interesting paper in the *Journal of Documentation* exploring how well we acknowledge our intellectual debts. In the future, qualified reviewers would have to certify that the appropriate references have been cited. This is quite similar to the role of patent examiners.

Irvine: At the Netherlands Foundation for Technical Science (STW), Dr Le Pair has constructed a detailed database of national experts in engineering and applied physics fields. This includes an assessment of the quality of their previous reviews of proposals and their track record in research (e.g. details of publication output and citation records). This information is used in selecting reviewers and provides a model that might usefully be adopted elsewhere.

Lake: We might think about the role of peer review in the context of the evolutionary development of science. For evolutionary development you have first to encourage a wide diversity of research initiatives. I was prompted by Carlos Kruytbosch's use of the aphorism 'let a thousand flowers bloom' in connection with the review process. How do we stimulate the blooming of a thousand flowers in terms of scientific initiatives and ideas? You spoke about the 'disgruntees' who perhaps were people with novel ideas that were unacceptable to the established community. How do we achieve diversity in science and then apply a strong selection pressure, not only at the outset to fund promising ideas, but later to add funding to success as it appears in the ordinary evolutionary process and to take funding away where there's failure? We seem to be addressing just the initial appraisal.

Kruytbosch: The second part was included in the requirement for the proposers to provide a record of what has been done with the past funds. It is widely believed (but unproved) that the peer review system tends to operate against the encouragement of diversity. At one stage in my NSF career I had the job of answering letters from certain disgruntees and all of them felt that they had the best idea since sliced bread. I couldn't judge those ideas but I did try to look at the history of their involvement with the NSF programmes. There were all kinds of reasons for them not to be funded.

Erich Bloch, Director of the NSF, has been concerned with encouraging diversity. The NSF Engineering Directorate is experimenting with giving small awards (up to 10% of a programme manager's budget can be spent in this manner) without peer review, but with *post hoc* review of the results. The plan is to give a quick response to somebody who has an innovative research idea. We don't yet know how effective this approach is.

Irvine: One feature of your paper, Carlos (and a characteristic of most other studies of peer review), is a lack of emphasis on the role of programme officers. Many criticisms of peer review relate not to the system itself but to the activities of programme officers (for example, in their selection of reviewers with insufficient knowledge or from opposing research traditions). My experience in social science leads me to believe that some programme officers become too committed to advocating particular lines of research and may therefore influence decisions through their choice of reviewers. The legitimate role of programme officers and how they should operate in the peer review system merit further investigation.

Kruytbosch: I agree that this is an important and insufficiently studied topic. But in the USA the social science programmes have standing review panels, and papers are evaluated by whoever happens to be on the panel at that time; it can't be fixed. Although most reviews in the physical and chemical sciences are by *ad hoc* mail reviewers selected by individual programme officers, there do not appear to be any more complaints in these fields. Every three years each programme is quite intensively reviewed by an outside visiting committee; the allocation of awards is compared with proposals and the committee looks to see whether there's a fair balance. So programme officials are working in glasshouses where their past actions will be evaluated and any strong biases will be revealed. Also, between a quarter and a third of the programme officers at the NSF are 'rotators' who are there for two years and then return to their universities. This is an excellent system for bringing in new blood, but it does tend to hinder the institution of rational management practices.

Collins: Programme officials are always with us and, by and large, probably do an honest job. As we have heard, they have their own constraints; they themselves are under review and have to demonstrate competence. It is not a matter necessarily of competence or of honesty; it's a matter of credibility, of being visibly competent rather than just being competent.

Garfield: You might learn something from jury selection; one is trying to find those people who have the fewest built-in biases. It's not easy because it is claimed that experts are needed to judge the proposal. However, this says something about the way proposals are written. They ought to be more comprehensible to a broader base of people.

Dixon: What is the NSF's policy on the use of overseas reviewers? Has there been a comparison of the quality of reviews by overseas and domestic experts? Several scientists have told me that it is easier to say exactly what they feel about a proposal or paper from another country. I think this problem might have been exacerbated in recent years as research funds have become tighter. One researcher summed it up by saying that he now felt unhappy about advising against a proposal in the UK because he didn't want to promote the loss of research funds. Also, some of the strongest criticism I have seen of scientific methods was in a series of booklets produced in Finland by international panels who were invited to look at various areas of science. Inorganic chemistry received a very critical report that might have been impossible if domestic reviewers had been used.

Kruytbosch: In 1987 the State of Texas allocated $60 million for two competitively peer-reviewed research programmes at Texas universities. It was decided early on that the review process should not involve in-state reviewers. This provided insulation from all kinds of troubles within the State.

The policy of the NSF about overseas reviewers is to solicit the opinion of the best people, wherever they are.

Luukkonen-Gronow: Bernard Dixon is talking about the *ex post* assessment of research fields. As I mentioned, in the Nordic countries foreign experts are called upon by the research councils to make such assessments more objective. Nevertheless, it is not necessarily true that foreign experts are more outspoken. Evaluation reports submitted to research councils vary. Some are very diplomatic and difficult to interpret. This depends on the characters of the reviewers. In addition, for research fields in which there is extensive cooperation between researchers in different countries, there cannot be an objective outside group; the researchers have frequent contact with each other and may have similar reservations about being outspoken as experts from the same country. The more international science becomes, the more difficult it is to get objective peer review.

Collins: Some of the problems with peer review are particularly important if there is only one source of funding and matter less if there are many sources. It is important in a system under pressure to maintain the plurality of sources. This is increasingly a problem in the UK.

Braun: How far can the system of competitive peer review be directly applied to countries that are not big enough to satisfy the requirements for openness and competitiveness to procure a correct decision?

Kruytbosch: There are at least three examples. One is the National Natural Science Foundation of China, initiated in 1986, which has developed such a competitive peer review system. Malaysia has just started a system, as has Bulgaria. Each country is doing it differently, adapting the system to the institutional conditions in their countries. The theme common to them all (including Texas) is to provide an alternative, competitive source of funds for innovative research.

Braun: These systems are not reversible. I was asked to review a PhD thesis from a small university in a less- developed country. After a while I was flooded by dissertations from the same university and from neighbouring universities, and I had to give up. There is also a question of quality. I feel very honoured when I am asked to review a paper for *Nature*, let's say, but I don't feel so honoured when I am asked to do the same for some obscure journal. This poses the problem of size; everything seems to be easy in the big countries, for example the USA, but gets complicated when you are working on a smaller scale.

Moravcsik: Many of the scientifically small countries are also the so-called developing countries. I think the developing countries should be encouraged to use an international peer review system. This is difficult for a number of reasons. Prestigious, strictly non-governmental organizations could do a lot in alleviating the fears and misconceptions about international peer review that scientists in these countries have.

Weinberg: Dr Kruytbosch, does the NSF reimburse peer reviewers? Is there a correlation between the amount of compensation and the seriousness of the review?

Kruytbosch: If they come to town for a panel they get $100 a day plus expenses. Mail reviewers receive no compensation.

Weinberg: Has the NSF considered changing that? If you raised the sum, the person might feel guilty if he didn't give a serious review.

Kruytbosch: The question of the seriousness of reviews has been emphasized by the survey of proposers to the NSF discussed in my paper. The Merit Review Committee recommended that programme officers should pay attention to this issue. But providing compensation for over 125000 reviews annually would cost a lot. It is not being considered at the present time.

Hill: You have given a fair view, as we would see it from the US Congress, of how peer assessment works in the NSF. However, the National Science Foundation budget is about 3% of US Federal R&D expenditure, and the other 97% is allocated by quite different methods. We don't know which method works best. The NSF method works well for the NSF, but one shouldn't feel obliged to explain why one uses some other method.

References

Kahneman D, Slovic P, Tversky A (eds) 1982 Judgement under uncertainty: heuristics and biases. Cambridge University Press, Cambridge
Kochen M 1987 How well do we acknowledge intellectual debts? Journal of Documentation 43:54–64

General discussion I

Science and surprise: evaluation and uncertainty

Kodama: Dr Weinberg (this volume) described criteria for the evaluation of science within or across disciplines, but it is generally acknowledged that it is difficult to make policy decisions across disciplines, especially in basic science. At a conference organized by the Engineering Academy of Japan in April 1988, Professor John Pierce of Stanford University gave a paper entitled 'Science and surprise'. He said that the purpose of science is to surprise people. Good science surprises; that is, it argues against previous common assumptions. But technological development is fundamentally different; it is done to avoid surprise. The concept of surprise might provide a new type of criterion in our assessment of research. Many science administrators complain about the cost of high-energy physics, but it is argued that the research is seeking a fundamental truth. One cannot easily decide between a project in high-energy physics which costs a great deal, and a biotechnology project. Perhaps the criterion of surprise would enable us to discriminate in some way.

Hill: Ex ante judgements are also the ones that concern us most in the USA at the moment; should we fund the supercollider, should we fund the new magnetic fusion device? I am perturbed by the absence in most of the discussion of something Professor Kodama is alluding to—the consideration of uncertainty in our ability to make the judgements that peer reviewers, merit reviewers and politicians all make in this system. Henry Small suggested earlier that we should take advantage of the work in the last decade on making judgements under uncertainty. This has been developed in a different arena, that of risk analysis and risk management for environmental health and safety and occupational hazards. We have learned in this field not to trust in our ability to do the kinds of things that we claim to be able to do in an *ex ante* way using peer review, whether it's looking at individual investigator projects or at engineering research centres. We know a lot less about how to do that in an unbiased way than we seem to think we do.

The National Science Foundation (NSF) should fund studies of the uncertainties in peer review. For example, the NSF rarely uses more than three peer reviewers on a small project; the tyranny of small numbers certainly applies in that case. We don't know whether three is a representative sample of scientific opinion, but we act as if it were and usually accept a 2:1 or unanimous vote. That is probably meaningless in terms of the distribution of prior judgements in the community, let alone of the potential for surprise. So I would plead for greater explicit consideration of uncertainty. The caveats will all disappear by the time the research gets into the half-page report that I write for a Member of Congress, but they still need to be addressed in some way.

Weinberg: On the matter of decision and uncertainty, as in all that we are talking about here, I don't think we should expect too much! Tversky & Kahneman (1974) were mainly concerned with the social psychology of decisions made under uncertainty. They emphasized that when people try to make decisions in situations of great uncertainty they resort to 'heuristics', or rules of thumb, with which they are comfortable, but which do not necessarily lead to the best decision. Tversky & Kahneman pointed out that often these heuristics lead to decisions about the risks faced which are quite wrong in terms of the quantitative assessment of the real risk.

This is relevant to Professor Kodama's point about the importance of the element of surprise in science. The difficulty always is that surprise, by its very nature, is fundamentally uncertain. Who would have recognized that in 1985 we should find superconductors with critical temperatures around 70K?— possibly only Berndt Matthias, who died about five years before this discovery was made. Was there any way of anticipating that we should be spending more money on research in superconductors along the lines of Matthias rather than along the more traditional lines opened up by the Bardeen-Cooper-Schriffler theory?

We shouldn't expect too much from this sort of exercise. Programme managers, research directors and perhaps some practising scientists may acquire instincts which are shaped and coloured by this broader philosophical, even statistical, debate, but we should not expect miracles.

Hills: As one who has, directly or indirectly, to advise people within government where they should place their money, and bearing in mind that they should do this on a rational basis, I find our discussion encouraging but also depressing. It's encouraging in that there is a great deal of activity and thought in the field of evaluation. It's depressing in that it doesn't seem to be producing any very clear answers, but it is a mistake to expect easy solutions.

Much of our discussion has been rather unfocused because we have been talking about very different kinds of research for which different kinds of evaluation are appropriate. Sir David Phillips introduced the meeting by outlining the primary purposes of science. Understanding the universe was the first one, and evaluation of research with that aim is very different from evaluation of research aimed at one of the other purposes, wealth creation. If one accepts the primary purposes, one has to address each of them individually and not expect a single answer. An evaluation will only be effective when several techniques are applied to a category of research. One hopes they will provide similar answers. If they don't, I suppose you go on until they do.

We should remember that our audience will not be convinced by sophisticated statistical techniques that are not obviously directly relevant in all cases. I think the techniques often are relevant, but they are not sufficiently convincing on their own. We need lots of techniques and we shall have to deploy different sets of them for each kind of science. Perhaps the purpose of this conference is to convince, on the one hand, the policy makers that evaluation can produce something useful and, on the other hand, those who are being evaluated that they needn't be frightened of it.

Collins: As a community of technicians in the business of evaluation we can learn from our collective experience, but the ability to do a decent evaluation depends very largely on getting a decent question in the first place. That is developed by interplay between the immediate customer and the immediate contractor but also among the community of customers. The learning has to happen on both sides.

Blume: Some of us would say that we are not technicians doing evaluations. Those of us who feel ourselves also to be part of the scientific community are more concerned with understanding how science works, and what the scope and the possibilities might be of any kind of policy influence on the production of scientific and technical knowledge. I think it's an important distinction. I see myself to be in the business of understanding how the scientific community evaluates what it does, and what influence society can have on those processes and on the kind of knowledge that is produced. Understanding how evaluation works is important (as illustrated by Kruytbosch, this volume) and, though necessarily related, it is different from producing evaluations that can be immediately used.

Montigny: We should make a clear distinction between two forms of evaluation of research. The first is the evaluation of the actors in research—the scientists themselves—where the evaluation is to assess the quality of their work. The scientific community has always had a set of practices through which it evaluates its members. In a report written with Robert Chabbal for the European Commission I have described a second form of evaluation—the evaluation of the operator (Chabbal 1987). By 'operator' we mean all the structures set up by government to carry out a scientific process. An operator can be a policy, a programme or an institution, and its evaluation is not by the same method, or for the same clients, as peer review. To evaluate actors we must understand the structure, functions and aims of the community. To evaluate an operator we must know about its impact and its effectiveness.

van Raan: The interaction between the evaluators and those evaluated is still crucial. I was asked to advise the Ministry of Education and Sciences of The

Netherlands on how to use bibliometrics in the technical sciences. They wanted to make a national survey on chemical engineering, electrical engineering and electronics, and mechanical engineering. We obtained interesting preliminary results using bibliometrics. Next we had to discuss these results with those working in these areas in the universities of technology. The discussions about the quality of research performance in their field highlighted a wide variety of opinions and large differences in 'publication cultures'. Some researchers maintained that it is necessary to publish in top journals; others said that conferences are their major outlet of research results and that the most important result of their work is that they deliver good engineers to the big multinational companies in The Netherlands.

Pavitt: The people who have played the greatest role in the development of statistical methods for evaluating science over the last 20–30 years have been practising scientists and scientific policy makers, at organizations such as the NSF, the OECD, the Institute for Scientific Information (ISI), CHI (Computer Horizons Inc) and the National Science Board. It has been practical people dealing with practical problems.

In that sense we are following a model developed by one of the subject's pioneers, Derek de Solla Price (1984). People develop instruments that improve the measurement of things, and this throws up all sorts of interesting puzzles and possibilities. What we have today, because of these pioneering efforts based on practical problems combined with information technology, is the greatly improved ability to collect and analyse all sorts of data on science and technology. One can look at specific institutions in a managerial sense— that's extremely important—but to me the greater challenge will be to improve the sort of understanding that Stuart Blume and Alvin Weinberg talked about. I think we can put our understanding of the nature, determinants and dynamics of science, and its interaction with technology, on a firmer basis. We can now go beyond anecdotes and collect systematic information to improve understanding. One shouldn't play down the grubby practical purposes for which these issues were originally addressed and why the data were collected—it's a very honourable tradition. We shouldn't expect quick results, but to those working, like Stuart, to understand the nature, dynamics and consequences of science and technology, these databases and what one can do with them form an extremely important and exciting part of intellectual development.

Irvine: It is true that instrumentational developments are crucial. For this reason, credit needs to be given to Eugene Garfield for having developed the *Science Citation Index*, since this is the research tool on which Derek Price based much of his work. Indeed, Eugene laid the foundations for what we now know as scientometrics.

One of the reasons for using bibliometric and patent data in evaluation is to reduce uncertainty by employing additional independent information to back up expert judgements. As Keith Pavitt pointed out (this volume), it is advisable to use as many sources of data as are available—we need to use multiple indicators and to question the differences between indicators. It would seem self-evident that scientific assessments based solely on peer review are likely to be more subject to uncertainty than when complemented by bibliometric and other management information data.

Hill: There is an irreducible uncertainty in the *ex ante* evaluation of scientific proposals that no amount of intelligence and no amount of data about the current world can answer. It's profoundly in the nature of science to generate new knowledge and nothing will get you past that.

Irvine: I completely agree, but within those limits one can still reduce the uncertainty. This, and not how to achieve the impossible, is the concrete issue we are discussing. Taking the question of identifying promising new areas, let us focus on the example of superconductivity used by Dr Weinberg. In Japan, the general area of superconductivity had actually been identified as a priority topic two or three years before 1986 and many companies were actively developing a capacity in the field; they evidently expected a surprise. In Tokyo University, they also had a big programme under way and as a result were able to capitalize rapidly upon the IBM discovery. This included reproducing the findings, which was quite important for their acceptance. In the 1987 Science and Technology Agency (STA) 30-year outlook, which identified 1070 important technical targets for the future and polled scientists on when they expected them to be achieved, no less than 20 of the targets concerned superconductivity, including one explicitly dealing with the commercialization of high-temperature materials.

The scientists' poll got it wrong; they forecast that high-temperature superconductors would be achieved by the year 2011. This was highly embarrassing for the STA and they rapidly had to undertake a further survey to obtain forecasts on two revised targets. However, I would argue that the details of timing are unimportant: high-temperature superconductivity had been identified as a key target, and future surprises in the area were thus seen as likely. This shows that foresight techniques can be used to identify, in a general way, areas of science that are regarded as specially promising for the future.

Small: We are looking at peer review, on the one hand, which is a qualitative activity, and bibliometrics, on the other hand, which is primarily quantitative. I would like there to be more of a convergence of the qualitative with the quantitative. I'm not sure I endorse John's expectation of surprises as a method of doing this, however. We had occasion to develop some data on the field of chaos—a new burgeoning field of physics. You could ask physicists or lay people whether this is likely to bring about great practical applications in the next 5–10 years. Would people be willing to make a prediction about research into chaos? The large volume of publications in the field of chaotic phenomena would lead one, bibliometrically, to expect that something useful must come out of so much activity. There's at least as much activity in high-energy physics. Is that going to lead to practical applications? These are very 'iffy' types of predictions. The combination of the qualitative knowledge that we have about the subjects and the quantitative data that we can obtain from bibliometrics gives us the power we are seeking—it's certainly better than just one person's opinion on a purely qualitative basis, or just a big number that is not disaggregated.

Collins: There was a long exchange of papers in *Social Studies of Science* in 1985 about the Martin & Irvine approach to bibliometrics. One paper was memorable for its title, 'The case of the disappearing caveat' (Bud 1985). I am always conscious that when we discuss techniques we start every report by saying publications don't mean very much and citations mean rather less, and we then go on about the third decimal place! It's important to be aware of the extent to which the variables we discuss actually relate to the enterprises that we evaluate.

The organizers of this meeting were very keen to engage the users of evaluations in the debate about them and, equally, in their production. This leads us back to the earlier discussion about protecting oneself from being pressurized by the person commissioning the work. You stand a better chance of making sense and being taken seriously if you can put together a steering group which includes the consumer for your work and people who are independent of both the consumer and, equally importantly, yourself. The independent members should not have been brought up on bibliometrics or any other technique and should be able to give you a broader view.

Dixon: We ought to address the need for an acknowledged and respected forum, perhaps a journal, to authenticate, criticize and discuss these sorts of assessments in the normal manner of the scholarly community. You don't have to go far nowadays around Britain to find disgruntled academics. One source of discontent is the University Grants Committee's assessment of departments, the methodology of which has never been completely disclosed to the people most affected by the process. Contrast what the UGC did in Britain—looking at university departments and taking certain measures into account without publicly declaring them—with normal behaviour in the natural sciences, where papers begin with an introduction, describe the methods, and then go on to results and discussion. Why are we generally not doing that in the evaluation process? The discussion that has taken place amongst UK academics has been very spotty—a little bit in the *Times Higher Education Supplement* (THES), the odd disgruntled letter in a university newsletter, and one disgruntled and misguided piece in the *New Scientist* a while ago by an academic complaining about the way his department had been treated. We lack an acknowledged, respected forum where this sort of thing can be thrashed out in terms that make sense to the people who are most affected. Existing journals, such as *Scientometrics*, carry material of that sort, but they are not read by working scientists.

Collins: In defence of the UGC, the leaders of the British scientific community have come a long way in the last five years in opening up the processes of negotiation to public inspection—witness the publication of the Advisory Board for the Research Councils' advice to the Secretary of State at the Department of Education and Science, and the UGC's willingness to open up the second selectivity exercise and give everyone the opportunity to comment on the methodology and the principles for it.

Dixon: I accept that they have changed. My assertion, having talked with academics around the country, is that the methodologies are still not known. There have been quite a number of letters in the THES which have gone unanswered by the people who might have replied to those criticisms.

References

Bud R 1985 The case of the disappearing caveat: a critique of Irvine and Martin's methodology. Social Studies of Science 15:548–553

Chabbal R 1987 Reorganization of research evaluation in the Commission of the European Communities, CEC, Brussels

Kruytbosch CE 1989 The role and effectiveness of peer review. In: The evaluation of scientific research. Wiley, Chichester (Ciba Foundation Conference) p 69–85

Pavitt K 1989 Technology and its links with science: measurement and policy implications. In: The evaluation of scientific research. Wiley, Chichester (Ciba Foundation Conference) p 50–68

Price D de S 1984 The science/technology relationship, the craft of experimental science, and policy for the improvement of high technology innovation. Research Policy 13:3–20

Science and Technology Policy Bureau, Science and Technology Agency 1987 Report on the survey of the direction of science and technology developments in this country—report and forecast. STA, Tokyo

Tversky A, Kahneman D 1974 Judgement under uncertainty: heuristics and biases. Science (Wash DC) 185:1124–1131

Weinberg AM 1989 Criteria for evaluation, a generation later. In: The evaluation of scientific research. Wiley, Chichester (Ciba Foundation Conference) p 3–15

The evaluation of research training

Joe Anderson

The Ciba Foundation, 41 Portland Place, London W1N 4BN, UK

Abstract. The success of training award schemes for scientists can be assessed partly
by analysing course completion rates and career profiles, and partly by measuring
research performance following training. Quantitative measures of scientific
performance are now routinely used as 'partial' indicators in comparative
assessments of nations, institutes and research groups, but it is frequently impossible
to evaluate training award schemes on the same basis. As their careers develop,
trainees often become less identifiable as a cohort which makes it difficult to identify
a control group for comparison. In these circumstances, it is suggested that the
citation characteristics of journals in which trainees subsequently publish could
be used as a standard for comparison. This approach is tested using data from
a study of undergraduate research training in biomedical science. Subsequent
research performance is, however, only a remote indicator of the effectiveness
of training, and 'product' evaluations provide only one insight into the success
of an award scheme. It is also necessary to examine the *process* of training, and
as a model for this approach to evaluation, an assessment of the UK PhD system
is considered.

*1989 The evaluation of scientific research. Wiley, Chichester (Ciba Foundation
Conference) p 93–119*

The major industrialized nations spend very large sums of money each year on
training future scientists. It is surprising, therefore, that this activity has largely
escaped the kind of systematic, quantitative analysis now being applied to other
components of national science systems.

Scientists may receive formal research training at various stages
in their careers: as undergraduates in short-term projects; as postgraduates
through doctoral studentships; as postdoctoral scientists through training
fellowships and, later, through special laboratory courses and travelling
fellowships.

In the UK most of the support for training in basic science is provided
by the research councils and, to a lesser extent, the scientific charities
and industry. There are no reliable estimates for the *total* national annual
expenditure on research training, but figures for the research councils are
published in their annual reports. For the academic year 1985/86, these
were as shown in Table 1. Thus over £64 million, or about 10% of the

TABLE 1   Annual expenditure (1985/86) on research training by the UK research councils

Research council	Direct expenditure on training (studentships etc.) (£ million)	% of total annual expenditure in 1985/86
Agriculture and food (AFRC)	0.829	0.74
Medical (MRC)	7.028	5.40
Natural environment (NERC)	6.021	5.99
Science and engineering (SERC)	50.166	15.80

combined expenditure of the scientific research councils in 1985/86, was devoted to research training, predominantly in the form of doctoral studentships.

It is impossible to assess accurately the world-wide expenditure on research training because of the multiplicity of institutional courses, funding agencies and the extent of informal training which is not directly funded. One thing, however, is clear; with the advent of a condition of level funding for science in many countries (Ziman 1987) there is now pressure on laboratories, funding agencies and international organizations to examine their provision for research training against the competing claims of other scientific activities. In particular, it is necessary for these agencies to evaluate the efficiency, effectiveness and impact of their support for training and to demonstrate that this money is well spent.

In the UK, such pressures are being applied by the House of Commons Public Accounts Committee and the National Audit Office which have referred to the inadequate submission rates of doctoral theses as an indicator of the poor provision for the selection and training of students. As many as 42% of students supported by the SERC on three-year studentships fail to submit a thesis within four years (SERC 1987). Moreover, for the Economic and Social Research Council the situation is even worse: over half of their studentships are *never* completed. This has led to a series of sanctions on university and polytechnic departments, whereby departments with poor submission rates are denied further training awards. In addition, a series of committees and working parties have reported on aspects of postgraduate research training (ABRC 1982, CVCP 1986, ESRC 1987) and recommendations for reform have been made, mainly in connection with the management and supervision of training.

Given these pressures, there is an increasing need to develop further the methods for evaluating research training programmes. The purpose of this paper is to consider the range of possible approaches and to focus on some potential measures of impact. Two basic approaches to evaluation can be proposed — assessment of the product or of the process of training. Product evaluations treat the training programme as a black box and are concerned with measuring its output and impact. Evaluations of the training process, in contrast, look inside the black box to see how well a programme is able to provide the skills required of research scientists.

Product evaluation

Output measures

This is the most common approach to evaluation and it is used widely by funding agencies for basic accounting. The approach considers questions such as: 'are we selecting the best individuals for training?', 'how many trainees complete the course?', 'do they stay in research?', 'if so, have they changed field of research or emigrated?', 'what career positions have they achieved, and how quickly?' and 'does the number trained match the demands of a given research sector?'.

Postdoctoral research training in biomedical science.   An example of this approach is a study at the Ciba Foundation which is focusing on the Medical Research Council's scheme for training qualified doctors and non-medical scientists in techniques of medical research. About 35 postdoctoral training fellowships are awarded each year on a competitive basis to doctors, dentists and postdoctoral scientists. The awards are intended to provide individuals with specialized training in research techniques, but to date there appears to have been no systematic evaluation of how well the scheme meets its aim. A related scheme provides travelling fellowships to encourage researchers to broaden their training by working overseas for short periods.

Our study is at an early stage, but the following preliminary results illustrate the kind of issues which can be considered using data on the output of training schemes. The study sample consists of 347 training fellows and 187 travelling fellows who held awards between 1969 and 1979. Using publicly available reference sources, we were able to trace over 94% of the fellows and we are now compiling career profiles from their responses to our enquiries.

We have thus been able to analyse the net output of the fellowship schemes and identify some sources of loss to the UK research system. It is already clear, for example, that about 15% of the fellows are now overseas, particularly in the USA, Canada and Australia, and that there is a greater tendency for travelling fellows to accept appointments overseas than training fellows — whereas 13% of the training fellows were overseas in 1987, the corresponding figure for travelling fellows is 20%.

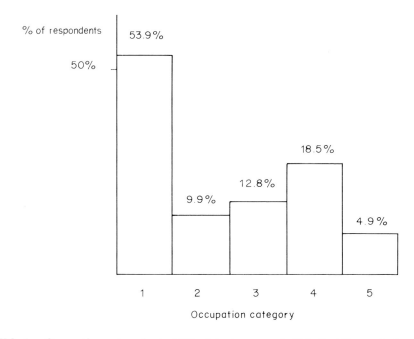

FIG. 1.   Occupation categories in 1987 of doctors awarded Medical Research Council Training Fellowships between 1969 and 1979. 1, academic, honorary clinician; 2, academic, no clinical duties; 3, clinician, honorary academic; 4, clinician, no academic post; 5, other (includes industrial research).

About 75% of the training fellows who responded were medically qualified and of those who chose to stay in the UK, a large proportion have developed careers that are either entirely devoted to research, or which involve a substantial element of research (Fig. 1). Only those individuals classified as 'clinicians' have no obvious commitment to research and these only represent 18.5% of the medical respondents. There is also some evidence that more of the earlier graduates in the study sample have focused on purely clinical careers in comparison with recently graduated fellows.

Other observations show that the training scheme has produced relatively few female researchers (11% of respondents) and that over half of the medical graduates used their awards to obtain a higher degree (PhD 53%, MD 38%, MSc 8%, MS 2%).*

---

*In the UK the MD and MS (Master of Surgery) are research degrees. The UK MD is therefore not equivalent to the MD award in the USA.

We are now extending the analysis, but the results so far serve to illustrate that this type of survey can provide useful statistics for making policy decisions on the future directions of training schemes. For example, it may or may not be acceptable to a funding agency to discover that about 30% of its awardees subsequently emigrate or pursue non-research careers, or that the scheme attracts and produces so few women scientists. It is a simple approach to evaluation and requires only limited expertise with survey procedures.

Undergraduate research training of medical students. An alternative, and more sophisticated, survey approach was used in our earlier evaluation of under-graduate research training in medical schools (Evered et al 1987). We started from a different reference point; not from lists of awardees, but from an audit of all the senior medical academics in the UK. These 940 readers and professors were matched with a control group on the basis of sex and date of graduation. This control group represented 'typical' medical graduates against which we were able to compare the undergraduate backgrounds of the academics, as shown in Fig. 2.

We discovered that the research medics were twice as likely to have attended Oxford or Cambridge Universities as a 'typical' doctor in the Medical Directory and over four times as likely to have taken an intercalated BSc.*

The significance of this is that the intercalated BSc scheme and the Oxford and Cambridge medical curricula have for a long time been the only means by which medical students can gain experience of research as undergraduates. At the time we published our results, the future of the intercalated BSc award scheme was threatened because it was seen by the UK National Audit Office as a form of *educational*, not research, support and therefore outside the remit of a research council.

Our data clearly demonstrated that the BSc scheme contributes substantially to the provision of medically qualified scientists in the UK, and effectively reduced the force of the argument that undergraduate research training is of no measurable value to the national research enterprise. We also found that, of the 16 UK medical schools, only two or three were 'net exporters' of senior academic clinicians (unpublished data). This observation has clear policy implications given the trend towards selectivity in institutional support.

The type of data discussed so far cannot provide an insight into the basis of the link between undergraduate research training and subsequent career attainment. In a previous study (Wakeford et al 1985), it was shown that early exposure to research has a positive influence on choosing a career in research, and so it may be that the intercalated BSc scheme does no more than select the

---

*This is an award, largely funded by the MRC, which enables a medical student to 'intercalate' a research-based science degree during their medical training at UK universities.

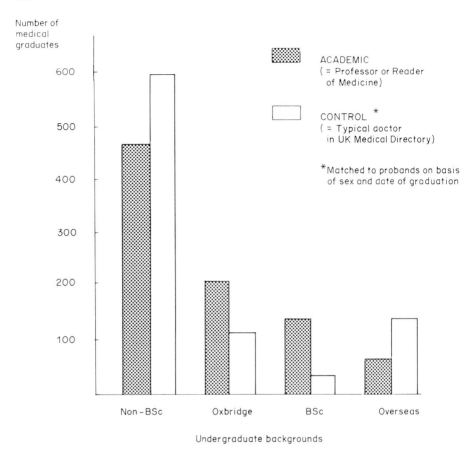

FIG. 2. Undergraduate backgrounds of all medically qualified professors and readers in UK medical faculties in 1985. Non-BSc, no undergraduate research training; Oxbridge, undergraduate research training at Oxford or Cambridge University; BSc, undergraduate research training during intercalated BSc; overseas, overseas graduates. The academic: control odds ratios (with 95% confidence limits) are: Non-BSc, 0.55 (0.47 to 0.63); Oxbridge, 2.11 (1.86 to 2.35); BSc, 4.58 (4.15 to 5.00); overseas, 0.43 (0.34 to 0.54).

most academically able medical students and encourage them to embark on a career in research. It may also be that the possession of a BSc enhances career prospects in a way that is unrelated to research ability. It is unlikely that such selection factors entirely explain the predominance of BSc graduates in senior academic positions, but one way of examining this hypothesis is to determine if there is any correlation between exposure to research as an undergraduate and subsequent 'research performance'. This approach is a departure from the 'output' method of evaluation discussed so far and brings us to a consideration of impact measures.

Impact measures

These measures attempt to answer questions such as: 'how good are the trained scientists?', 'what contributions have they made to science, technology or clinical practice?' and 'does the training scheme make a substantive contribution to science?'.

The concept of using quantitative measures to supplement value judgements, for example peer review, of quality in research has been the subject of extensive discourse, research and validation over the past ten years. It is now widely accepted that the most reliable quantitative measures are those based on publication and citation analyses, or 'bibliometrics'. The validity of bibliometrics in science policy analyses has been discussed in detail elsewhere (Martin & Irvine 1983, Moed et al 1984, ABRC 1986, Luukkonen-Gronow 1987, OECD 1987a, Chubin 1988) and it is sufficient here to quote Francis Narin: 'the results of bibliometric studies are seldom counter-intuitive: they usually agree with expert expectation' (Narin 1987).

Comparison of impact between groups with and without undergraduate research experience. In our evaluation of the intercalated BSc degree (Evered et al 1987), we used bibliometric analysis to generate comparative impact measures for the three groups studied (BSc awardees, Oxbridge graduates and non-BSc graduates). Care was taken to match the three groups being compared on the basis of date of graduation and sex as these are potentially confounding variables. Publications (original research articles only, not notes, meetings, reviews, letters etc.) were counted for each professor and reader in the specialty of medicine, the largest discipline in our study (a quarter of the population). Citation analysis was then conducted on a subset drawn from this discipline using the *Science Citation Index*. In addition, we supplemented these bibliometric measures with an analysis of the number of research grants obtained, taking this to be a proxy measure of assessments by peers. Full details of the methodology and analyses are given in Evered et al (1987) and the results are summarized in Tables 2 and 3.

The results showed clearly that the BSc group raised more grants, published more papers and were cited more often than their peers who had either received some undergraduate research training at Oxbridge or none at all. Thus, our various impact indicators were shown to converge. This is in accord with the widely used evaluation methodology proposed by Martin & Irvine (1983).

It should be remembered that we were comparing the performance of three closely matched peer groups in equivalent positions of academic seniority. The influence of the BSc award cannot therefore be entirely explained by the processes of self-selection by students motivated towards academic careers or accelerated career preferment arising from possession of a prestigious degree.

TABLE 2A   Numbers of original research papers published by professors and readers in the specialty of medicine between 1975 and 1985

Graduate group	Publication counts			No. (%) of subjects in each category[a]		
	Mean	Median	Range	High	Medium	Low
BSc	93.1	75	10–311	24(55.8)	10(23.3)	9(20.9)
Oxbridge	63.4	51	0–620	24(31.6)	26(34.2)	26(34.2)
No BSc	54.9	41	0–214	26(26.3)	34(34.3)	39(39.4)
All groups	62.8	48	0–620	74(33.9)	70(32.1)	74(33.9)

[a]Publishing category defined by 33.3 and 66.7 percentile points on publication frequency distribution for entire data set. Thus: High, >72 publications; Medium, 33–72 publications; Low, <33 publications. $\chi^2 = 12.22$, $P < 0.02$.

TABLE 2B   Citation figures 1983–85 for publications in 1981–83. Professors and readers in the specialty of medicine matched by date of graduation and publishing category

Graduate group	Total papers	Total citations	Citations/ paper	No. (%) of subjects in each category[b]	
				High	Low
BSc	346	2781	8.04	12(66.7)	6(33.3)
Oxbridge	347	2649	7.63	10(55.6)	8(44.4)
No BSc	293	1218	4.16	5(27.8)	13(72.2)
All groups	986	6648	6.74	27(50)	27(50)

[b]Citation category defined by median (50 percentile) on citation frequency distribution for entire data set. Thus: High, subject scores above 5.15 citations/paper; Low, subject scores below 5.15 citation/paper. Difference between BSc and non-BSc is significant. $\chi^2 = 4.00$, $P < 0.01$.

We would argue that the correlation between taking an intercalated BSc or attending Oxbridge and our performance indicators indicates that undergraduate training has a significant influence on subsequent research success.

The study also demonstrated the viability of applying bibliometric analysis to relatively small data sets. However, it is clear that great care is needed in such small-scale comparative work.

In earlier validation exercises, we found that substantial errors can occur when using bibliographic databases to count publications and citations for individual scientists. This was clear from checks we made on publications lists obtained directly from the scientists, and the most usual source of error was that authors with common names were attributed papers they had not written. There are other

TABLE 3   Project and programme grants awarded to medically qualified professors and readers by the Medical Research Council over the period 1974/75 to 1985/86 by graduate category and main specialty group

Graduate group	Number in group	Number (%) of subjects with grants	Programmes	Projects	Projects/ grantholder
Clinical specialties					
BSc	81	39(48)	10	120	3.08
Oxbridge	141	70(50)	15	170	2.43
No BSc	320	135(42)	22	285	2.11
Overseas	51	26(51)	12	52	2.00
Total	593	270(46)	59	627	2.32
Non-clinical specialties					
BSc	64	29(45)	3	78	2.69
Oxbridge	82	59(72)	15	155	2.63
No BSc	155	80(52)	16	191	2.39
Overseas	35	23(66)	4	75	3.26
Total	336	191(57)	38	499	2.61

errors in generating bibliometric data, but we found no systematic differences in error rates between our study groups. Nevertheless, very large single error rates could conceivably distort the overall bibliometric count for a group and this is why we avoided parametric analyses in our study. By converting our raw publication and citation counts into categorical data (high, medium, low), and testing differences between groups with non-parametric analysis, we reduced the influence of any large random errors. We believe that such categorical analysis is a more robust approach in small-scale comparisons of research performance than the direct comparison of citation counts.

Impact measures are thus valuable adjuncts to output measures in evaluations of research training programmes. However, it is not always possible to identify suitable groups for comparison as we were able to in our study of the BSc programme. For example, in our study of the MRC training fellowships, it is not possible to compare the relative performance of senior medical faculty with and without fellowships, because the number of ex-fellows is relatively small in this population (the ratio of MRC training fellowships:BSc awards made annually is about 1:9). Nevertheless, impact assessments are meaningless unless they are conducted with reference to some standard. The ideal control group is one in which the individuals are identically matched to the probands (ex-trainees) in every respect of ability and experience, the only difference being that the controls never received the training award under study. This is in most cases unattainable.

An alternative is to measure the research performance of ex-trainees against a reference standard which is set by their respective research communities. The average citation rate of the journals in which the ex-trainees publish might be identified as such a standard.

In this approach, the other authors publishing in the same journal set are considered to be competing for citations: they are, effectively, the research peers of the scientists under study. The reference standard which the scientists must exceed to be considered of high impact is then the average citation to publication ratio for their journal set. This approach has been applied by Moed et al (1985) in their 'level analyses' of research groups in the University of Leiden, and is equivalent to the 'relative citation rate' methodology used by Schubert & Braun (1986) and described by Braun et al (this volume). There are, however, several assumptions in this approach, one of which is that authors consistently publish in journals of a standard appropriate to their work. Before applying this methodology to our current evaluations of training programmes, we therefore wished to test its validity using data from our previous study of the BSc programme.

Impact studies of single cohorts using journal citation to publication ratios as internal standards.   We chose as our study group the 54 professors and readers of medicine whom we had previously evaluated using direct comparison of citation rates between the BSc (B), Oxbridge (O) and Non-BSc (N) groups. The pattern of performance for these three groups on the basis of grants raised, number of publications and number of citations was $B > O > N$. We wished to see if this pattern held when the groups were each compared against their own internal citation standards.

For each journal in which our study group published, the citation to publication ratio was calculated as the reference standard:

$$JCS = \frac{\text{number of citations in year x}}{\text{number of citable publications in year } (x-2)}$$

where JCS = Journal Citation Score* and 'citable publications' = articles, notes and reviews.

---

*Citations are counted two years after the publication date of a paper (i.e. in its third year) because papers in the field of biomedical science typically attract their greatest number of annual citations at this time. Thus, the 1985 JCS value for journal y is the total number of 1985 citations given by SCI source journals divided by the number of articles, notes and reviews published by journal y in 1983. There are other ways to calculate citation to publication ratios (e.g. the SCI Journal Impact Factor), but JCS, as first proposed by Moed et al (1984), has the advantage that it is more applicable to small samples of publications.

The figures for calculating JCS were obtained from the *Journal Citation Reports* (JCR) volume of the *Science Citation Index*. JCS values were calculated for 1984 and 1985 for the 242 journals in which our subjects published. These values then represented the 'expected' number of citations to articles, notes and reviews published by our study group in 1982 and 1983 respectively.

A total of 549 relevant papers was published by the group in 1982 and 1983. The number of citations received in 1984 by papers published in 1982 was then compared with the 1984 JCS value for the appropriate journal. If the observed citation score was above the JCS, the paper was scored as a 'high' (H) performer and if below, as a 'low' (L) performer. The same procedure was followed for papers published in 1983, citations to these in 1985 being compared with the 1985 JCS values. The results of this scoring exercise are summarized in Table 4.

As in our previous study (Evered et al 1987), these data demonstrate an association between graduate group and citation performance: 45.9% of all the articles published by the BSc group received more citations than the average for the journals in which they were published. This is higher than the equivalent figure for the Oxbridge group (39.4%), which in turn is higher than for the non-BSc group (21.9%). Hence, the pattern $B > O > N$ holds. This finding offers support for the use of internal citation standards to evaluate the performance of individual research groups or cohorts of scientists when comparative groups are not available.

However, there is a serious limitation to this approach. It is possible, for example, that the BSc group consistently published in lower impact journals than the other groups, so improving their apparent performance without actually having a higher absolute citation rate than their peers. In comparative evaluations this is a well-known problem. Is it 'better', for example, to be publishing papers

TABLE 4   Citations in 1984 and 1985 for publications in 1982 and 1983 respectively compared with journal citation scores 1984–85

	No. (%) of papers in each citation category[a]	
Graduate group	High ($>JCS$)	Low ($<JCS$)
BSc	90(45.9)	106(54.1)
Oxbridge	85(39.4)	131(60.6)
No BSc	30(21.9)	107(78.1)
All groups	205(37.3)	344(62.7)

$\chi^2 = 20.50,\ P < 0.001$

[a] Citation category is defined *for each paper* by the average citation score (JCS) of the journal in which it was published. Thus each paper is being judged by a standard set by its own specific scientific community. This is a different basis for comparison than for the data in Table 3 in which the citation standard was set by the combined (median) performance of the three groups.

which achieve above average citation rates in low-impact journals or below the average in high-impact journals? In some respects this question is a little artificial because the impact level of a journal set can depend on the field of science. Citation practices in fields such as mathematics mean that journals in this field have low citation to publication ratios when compared with fields such as biochemistry (Moed et al 1984). This is unlikely to have been a problem in the present exercise as the three groups of scientists were all drawn from the same specialty of medical research. Nevertheless, an alternative analysis can be used to reveal possible distortions in the publishing patterns of different groups.

This involves plotting the actual number of citations received as a function of JCS. When the axes of the graph are equally scaled, the orthogonal line represents the control above which papers are scored 'high' and below which they are scored 'low'. This is the general model proposed by Schubert & Braun (1986) who plot the position of a nation on such a 'relational chart' as a single coordinate according to their aggregated citations (see Braun et al, this volume). However, in some analyses, it could be more informative to disaggregate the data contained in a single coordinate by regressing observed on expected citations over the entire range of journals in which a group (or nation) publishes. Fig. 3 shows the regression lines for such an analysis of our data on the BSc, Oxbridge and non-BSc groups.

These lines clearly demonstrate the same relative performance pattern as obtained in our previous study (Evered et al 1987). Furthermore, it is clear that for each group the observed citations are positive linear functions of expected citations. Hence, as the groups published in higher impact journals, so they received more citations. In this kind of analysis, regression statistics such as the gradient and intercept could be of interest as new indicators of scientific performance. For example, the regression coefficient for the non-BSc group is very close to 1.00 (an orthogonal gradient), but the intercept is negative. In other words, the non-BSc line is below and parallel to the control line showing that this group consistently performed below the average with respect to their peers, regardless of the journal standard.

A different picture emerged for the BSc and Oxbridge groups. Both of these groups were high performers in low impact journals, but found it increasingly difficult to score above the average as they published in higher impact journals. In other words, their intercepts were positive, but their regression coefficients were less than 1.00.* Thus if the regression lines for the B and O groups are

---

*Positive regression coefficients above 1.00 would, of course, indicate an improvement in relative citation performance as a group publishes in higher standard journals.

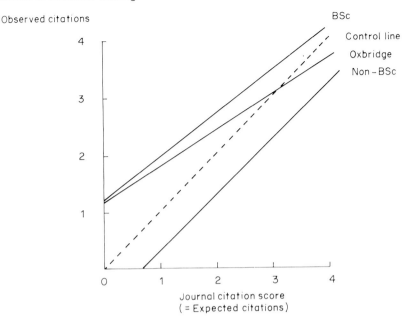

FIG. 3.   Regressions of observed on expected citations to publications by UK professors and readers of medicine. The data are for publications in the bottom 80% journals as defined by their Journal Citation Score. BSc, $y = 0.75x + 1.21$, $n = 149$ publications, $r = 0.41$, $P < 0.001$; Oxbridge, $y = 0.60x + 1.19$, $n = 164$, $r = 0.42$, $P < 0.001$; Non-BSc, $y = 0.97x - 0.66$, $n = 118$, $r = 0.48$, $P < 0.001$.

extended to the highest impact journals the relative performance of these groups falls substantially below the average for their peers in these journals (Fig. 4). The obvious explanation for this pattern is that the BSc and Oxbridge groups are only able to achieve above average citation rates for papers published in lower impact journals. A less obvious, but more reasonable, explanation is that the observed pattern is an artefact of the analysis.

The most obvious source of error in the methodology is that JCS values are computed as *mean* citation rates. As a measure of central tendency, the mean is only a reliable statistic when the distribution of the variable approximates to a normal curve. However, it is well known that citations are not distributed normally within journals: such distributions are heavily skewed in a positive direction. This can be illustrated for five leading biomedical journals (Fig. 5).

Some of these curves resemble the classic shape of a negative binomial distribution and, indeed, this is precisely the distribution predicted in a mathematical analysis by Schubert & Glänzel (1983). A more robust measure of central

Observed citations

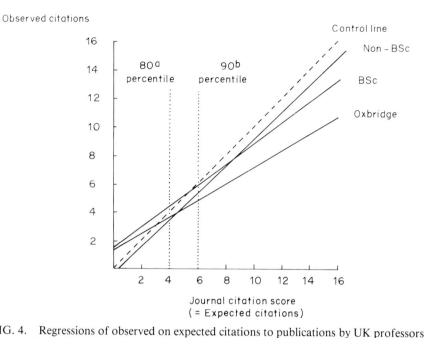

FIG. 4. Regressions of observed on expected citations to publications by UK professors and readers of medicine, using the complete data set, 547 publications. BSc, $y = 0.75x + 1.21$, $n = 195$, $r = 0.41$, $P < 0.001$; Oxbridge, $y = 0.60x + 1.19$, $n = 215$, $r = 0.42$, $P < 0.001$; Non-BSc, $y = 0.97x - 0.66$, $n = 137$, $r = 0.48$, $P < 0.001$.
[a] This point represents 80% of all publications in the data set.
[b] This point represents 90% of all publications in the data set.
All data are plotted but only 12 publications out of a total of 547 appeared in journals with a Journal Citation Score > 10.

tendency for this type of distribution is, arguably, the median (or 50 percentile).*

As illustrated in Fig. 5, median values are always lower than means for positively skewed distributions. Thus if JCS values are computed on the basis of median citations for each journal, the threshold for grading papers as 'high' performers is lowered. This may help to explain why all three groups produced more papers that were 'below average' than 'above average' despite the fact that these groups contain a large proportion of the most senior medical scientists in the UK (Table 4).

---

*Other authors have proposed using the top decile (Narin 1983), or decile contours ('decilotopes'; van Raan & Hartmann 1987) as reference points within citation frequency distributions, but these can only be computed if you have access to the complete citation data for journals. However, even when such data are available, certain evaluations remain more meaningful if group performance is compared against the average (median) citation rate than against, say, the top ten percent of papers.

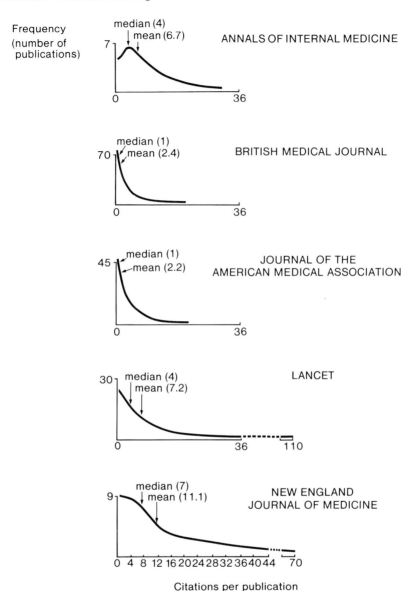

FIG. 5.   Frequency distribution for citations to articles, notes and reviews in five leading biomedical journals. Data for these curves were kindly provided by the Institute for Scientific Information (ISI) and are for citations in 1979 to publications in the first quarter of 1977.

The effect of using the mean instead of the median is more noticeable with high impact journals because the absolute difference between the two statistics is greater than for low impact journals. This may explain why all three groups appeared to be performing below the average in high impact journals (Fig. 4).

Another possible deficiency in the methodology is that the threshold for identifying 'high' and 'low' papers is set as the JCS value of a journal. This threshold may be too sharp, because it takes no account of the relatively high degree of random variation around the computed regression lines (see low r values in Fig. 3). Thus papers which fall close to the control line may have citation rates that are not significantly different from the JCS value, but these will still receive a high or low classification. In future analyses, it may be better to compute error rates for the regression lines and use these to identify 'outlier' thresholds (typically 1.96 standard errors either side of the regression line). This would introduce a category of 'equivalent' to the expected versus observed analysis and would improve the sensitivity of discrimination between above and below average papers.

Whatever the reason for the observed results, it would seem that JCS is, at present, an inadequate index of 'expected' citation rate, particularly for high impact journals. These arguments apply equally to the ISI Journal Impact Factor (JIF), or any other citation to publication ratio which is based on the mean of the citation distribution. In future applications of this technique, it will be important to consider the comparability of the frequency distributions for the expected *and* the observed citations. When there are substantial differences in the shape of these curves, it is clearly meaningless to compare them on the basis of their means. This is a potential source of error in the statistics on national performance as reported by Schubert & Braun (1986) and by Braun et al (this volume). For example, if the citation data for a nation are highly skewed and the (artificially high) mean of this curve is compared with the mean of a more normally distributed 'expected' citation curve, then the 'relative citation rate' value will give a false impression of that nation's performance.

Nevertheless, with further refinement and careful application, it is clear that journal citation to publication ratios could have significant potential as research standards when evaluating the performance of cohorts of scientists for which there is no obvious control group. As the technique stands, however, it is probably only reliable for journals with JCS values below 4.00 (the majority of journals indexed by ISI). Before the technique can be extended to higher impact journals, further analysis of citation frequency distributions will be needed.

In summary, with further development and careful application, impact measures should prove to be useful extensions to the traditional measures of output commonly used to evaluate training programmes. However, output and impact measures are both elements of a product-based approach to evaluation. A central problem with this approach is that it does not demonstrate how (or, indeed, *if*) the product is related to the process of training. If an evaluation of a training award scheme demonstrates that it is producing large numbers of successful scientists, it may be that the funding agency is merely operating as an efficient talent spotter for individuals who could have become good scientists without the training award. Good research performance may be the effect, but is training the cause?

This issue of causation is important and can only adequately be addressed by examining the elements of a training programme which make it effective or otherwise. In other words, when evaluating a training programme, it is important to supplement output and impact measures with a detailed inspection of the *process* of research training.

Process evaluation

This approach considers questions such as: 'how well does the training prepare scientists for research in their chosen fields?' or 'what are the needs of the labour market and does the training provide for these needs?'.

For short-term advanced courses, such as those offered by large national and international institutions (e.g. the Woods Hole Marine Biological and Cold Spring Harbor laboratories in the USA, the European Molecular Biology Laboratory in Heidelberg, and the NATO awards), it is relatively easy to identify whether the training programme is matched to the needs of the trainees. Such courses are, indeed, usually developed in response to a demand from the scientific community to introduce experienced scientists to new practical research skills (techniques in molecular biology, microscopy, etc.). Thus it is usually adequate for research administrators only to assess the output and impact (i.e. the 'product') of their courses.

For more widespread and basic programmes of research training, such as the PhD system, product-based evaluations alone are inadequate because it is more difficult to infer a causation between training and subsequent performance. Here, the priority must be on evaluations of the training process. As an example of the type of approach that may be desirable in process evaluation, we can consider our current study of the UK PhD system.

A series of reports has discussed various aspects of the PhD system in response to growing dissatisfaction with the way postgraduate training is managed in the UK (ABRC 1982, CVCP 1986, TCC 1986, ESRC 1987). These reports have considered how to improve thesis completion rates, whether or not the preparation of a thesis is relevant to training in the natural sciences, whether training should include a greater element of formal instruction (the so-called

'Americanization' of the PhD), the role of supervisors and how they can themselves be supervised, and various aspects of the labour market for PhD graduates. This labour market is particularly interesting because there have been significant shifts in the employment sectors favoured by newly qualified PhD graduates. The boom period for academic jobs was around 1965 when 53% of all PhD graduates found employment in universities, but since then there has been a substantial decline in numbers of PhD graduates starting academic careers (Hirsh 1982). Our data for the biomedical sciences (derived from the Universities Statistical Record) show that in 1986 only 31.1% of all newly qualified PhD graduates took university employment.

The assertion that the PhD is a 'training for independent scholars and research workers at the highest level' (CVCP 1975) must therefore be a little outdated. Indeed, in the latest report on this subject by the CVCP (1988) it is no longer claimed that the primary purpose of a PhD is for training. Instead, the Committee of Vice-Chancellors and Principals now sees two interrelated purposes of the award:

> (1) . . . to enable young people of high intellectual ability . . . to contribute new and significant ideas, and to make a positive contribution to knowledge . . .

> (2) . . . to provide a training in research methods which makes them capable subsequently of assuming the role of independent scholars and research workers at the highest level . . .

This represents a significant shift in emphasis and suggests that PhD students are now to be regarded an an important manpower resource in UK science. It reinforces the view, articulated in an earlier paper (Anderson & Evered 1986), that the 'training' element of a PhD is increasingly becoming simply a by-product of the process of getting research results. There is also concern over the '. . . perceived variable standard of the person who is awarded a PhD, the variable standard of the research problem set, the variable standard of the supervision and the variable standard of the PhD examination' (TCC 1986). This complaint, significantly, is heard not only from the universities, but also from those sectors of high-technology industry which employ PhD graduates.

It is timely, therefore, to evaluate the process of PhD training in the context of the needs of the labour market. If it can be accepted that at least one of the aims of a PhD degree in science is to train graduates to become competent researchers (wherever they subsequently gain employment) then a key issue for process evaluation is what this training should involve. It is no longer sufficient to assert that a PhD training engenders a high level of intellectual development and a rational approach to problem solving. Such general attributes could be developed in other ways and research councils may find it increasingly difficult to justify their support of PhD training on this basis.

Clearly, the training profile will depend very much on the scientific field and 'research environment' the student is being trained for, but within these boundaries it should be possible to identify the core skills required of a competent researcher. Once these skills have been identified, it is then reasonable to assess whether or not the PhD system adequately provides training in such skills.

To investigate the potential of this approach to process evaluation, the Ciba Foundation is studying the labour market for PhD graduates in experimental biomedical science and attempting to establish a consensus (within the different employment sectors) on the range of skills required of researchers in this field. Examples of skills being considered so far are: competence in experimental design and statistical analysis; a broad knowledge of analytical techniques and instrumentation; expertise in information retrieval; writing and oral skills in scientific presentations; and basic computing skills. These general categories will be added to as the audit progresses, but they are typical of our scale of analysis.

We also aim to describe the range of institutional approaches to PhD supervision and formal instruction and to examine how well the PhD process is able to equip scientists with the full range of skills identified in the national survey.

We consider this kind of process evaluation to be of primary importance, whereas the issues of managing the PhD system (improving completion rates, reforming supervisory practice, introducing taught courses) are of secondary importance. It is only when the skills needed by the academic and industrial research labour markets are fully understood that we can begin to shape the process of training to meet these needs.

The pressures on the postgraduate research training system are by no means confined to the UK. In The Netherlands and France there have been radical reforms of the systems for doctoral training (van Hout 1986, OECD 1987b) and it is not inconceivable that the UK PhD system will be similarly affected in the near future. The CVCP (1988) recommended that universities should introduce taught courses during PhD training. What these courses should teach, however, has not yet been publicly discussed. It is only through systematic evaluations of the needs, and the process, of training that we can provide a sound basis for change.

Conclusion

Research training programmes, whether advanced laboratory courses or national programmes, can be evaluated in terms of their product and process. Product evaluations measure the success of training award schemes through analyses of completion rates, career profiles and studies of manpower output. This kind of output analysis can be extended to examine the subsequent research impact of trainees, using a variety of quantitative measures such as counts of publications, citations and grants raised. It is always desirable to measure performance with respect to some standard. The conventional method is to identify control, or at least comparable, groups of scientists for simultaneous evaluation. This is not always possible with ex-trainees because as their careers develop they become less identifiable as a cohort. In these circumstances, it is suggested that a reference standard can be provided by the citation characteristics of journals in which trainees subsequently publish. However, caution should be exercised when using this approach, as there are considerable technical difficulties.

Finally, output and impact measures are, at best, only distant indicators of the effectiveness of prior training. It is difficult to demonstrate a causal link between training and subsequent research performance. As this is a key issue in evaluation, it is recommended that product-based studies should always be complemented by analyses of the process of training.

Acknowledgements

I would like to express my gratitude to colleagues at the Ciba Foundation for their help with preparing this paper. Special thanks are due to Frances Smyth and Stephanie Greshon for their valuable contributions to the analyses and to David Evered for reviewing the manuscript.

References

ABRC 1982 Report of the working party on postgraduate education (the Swinnerton-Dyer report) Advisory Board for the Research Councils, HMSO, London
ABRC 1986 Evaluation of national performance in basic research. A review of techniques for evaluating performance in basic research with case studies in genetics and solid-state physics. Advisory Board for the Research Councils, London
Anderson J, Evered DC 1986 Why do research on research? Lancet 2:799–802
Braun T, Glänzel W, Schubert A 1989 An alternative quantitative approach to the assessment of national performance in basic research. In: The evaluation of scientific research. Wiley, Chichester (Ciba Found Conference) p 32–49
CVCP 1975 Report of the study group on postgraduate education. Committee of Vice-Chancellors and Principals of the UK, London
CVCP 1986 Academic standards in universities. Committee of Vice-Chancellors and Principals of the UK, London
CVCP 1988 The British PhD. Committee of Vice-Chancellors and Principals of the UK, London
Chubin 1988 Research evaluation and the generation of big science policy. Knowledge: creation, diffusion, utilization 9:254–277
ESRC 1987 The social science PhD. The Economic and Social Research Council inquiry on submission rates (the Winfield report). Economic and Social Research Council, London

Evered DC, Anderson J, Griggs P, Wakeford R 1987 The correlates of research success. British Medical Journal 295:241–246

Hirsh W 1982 The postgraduate training of researchers. In: Oldham G (ed) The future of research. Society for Research into Higher Education/Leverhulme Foundation Monograph No 4

Luukkonen-Gronow T 1987 Scientific research evaluation: a review of methods and various contexts of their application. R&D Management 17:207–221

Martin BR, Irvine J 1983 Assessing basic research: some partial indicators of scientific progress in radio astronomy. Research Policy 12:61–90

Moed HF, Burger WJM, Frankfort JG, Van Raan AFJ 1984 On the measurement of research performance: the use of bibliometric indicators (3rd edition). LISBON Institute, University of Leiden, The Netherlands, p 199

Moed HF, Burger WJM, Frankfort JG, Van Raan AFJ 1985 The use of bibliometric data for the measurement of university research performance. Research Policy 14:131–149

Narin F 1983 Subjective versus bibliometric assessment of biomedial research publications. NIH Program Evaluation Report, US Dept Health & Human Services, National Institutes of Health, Bethesda, Maryland, USA

Narin F 1987 Bibliometric techniques in the evaluation of research programs. Science and Public Policy 14:99–106

OECD 1987a Evaluation of research: a selection of current practices. Organization for Economic Co-operation and Development, Paris

OECD 1987b The role and function of universities: postgraduate education in the 1980s. Organization for Economic Co-operation and Development, Paris

Schubert A, Glänzel W 1983 Statistical reliability of comparisons based on the citation impact of scientific publications. Scientometrics 5:59–74

Schubert A, Braun T 1986 Relative indicators and relational charts for the comparative assessment of publication output and citation impact. Scientometrics 9:281–291

SERC 1987 PhD submission rates. SERC Bulletin 3(9):26

TCC 1986 The careers of scientists and engineers (Report of a study commissioned by the SERC). The Technical Change Centre, c/o Policy Studies Institute, London

van Hout J 1986 Towards a new structure for postgraduate research training in The Netherlands. European Journal of Education 21:275–286

van Raan AFJ, Hartmann D 1987 The comparative impact of scientific publications and journals: methods of measurement and graphical display. Scientometrics 11:326–331

Wakeford R, Lyon J, Evered DC, Saunders N 1985 Where do medically qualified researchers come from? Lancet 2:262–265

Ziman J 1987 Science in a 'steady state', the research system in transition. Science Policy Support Group, London

Anderson: We searched by hand. We didn't bother taking out self-citations because we had previously done some calibration studies and found that the self-citation rate is remarkably constant in biomedical science at about 9% of all citations. Whether or not we excluded self-citations made no difference to our results, so it was easier to leave them in.

Braun: You said that mean values can be misleading and you prefer to use the median. We think that the mean value is a correct and relevant reference standard when one compares expected and observed citation rates, provided the sample examined is large enough. Because of the central limit theorem, the expected value of any distribution with finite variance has a normal distribution. Therefore the mean values of two sufficiently large samples can be compared by using *t*-statistics even if the underlying distributions are, say, negative binomials. This enabled us to use significance levels which help to discriminate between above and below average papers (see Braun et al 1985).

However, there is a simple method, which we call the procedure of shifted averages, for grouping populations of papers into different citation categories. The first average is the average number of citations per paper over the total population of papers in the group of journals considered. All the papers which are more highly cited than this first average are considered as a new population, and a second average is obtained. Repeating this method with the papers cited more highly than this second average gives a third average, and so on. Then one can work with any of these categories of papers, which can be said to reflect increasing quality or impact. You can do this with any population of papers and it avoids the problem of the median or the average.

Anderson: It makes no difference whether you shift the average or not. The point is that when you compare an observed citation rate with an expected citation rate the two mean values are based on different populations. For a country which has relatively few highly cited scientists, the mean observed citation rate will be artificially high because the distribution curve of citations is highly skewed. However, the mean citation rate of a large international population of scientists would probably have a less skewed distribution of citations. Any attempt to compare these two means will artificially improve the apparent performance of the evaluated nation. This is true whether or not you shift the average by selecting subpopulations of citations from an already skewed distribution.

However, there are some sophisticated techniques that you can use if you have the full citation data for journals instead of just totals or means as published in the *Science Citation Index*. Tony van Raan, for example, obtained complete citation data from *Science* and computed an elegant set of decile contours as citation reference points for this journal (van Raan & Hartmann 1987). The limitation of this technique is that data of this quality are not made widely available by the Institute for Scientific Information. Administrators wishing to conduct a quick in-house evaluation usually have to work with data that are already available; it is too expensive to buy in extra data.

Our evaluations were, in part, experiments with publicly available information to see what could be achieved without recourse to expensive databases or sophisticated procedures. It is important to show that evaluations can be straightforward, because policy makers can be suspicious of complex statistics. Data should always be simple and intuitive if they are to be widely accepted.

Braun: Do you have some data on the statistical reliability?

Anderson: We are hoping to extend our analysis to change the control line that I showed (Fig. 3) into a control bar which would include error rates.

Braun: If you give me the data, we can do the computation using the methodology I described in my paper (Braun et al, this volume).

Anderson: That's very kind of you.

Narin: Because we have the full database we use some of the sophisticated techniques. Our methods are analogous to those of Tony van Raan and Tibor Braun. We generally use as our reference set all the papers in a subfield, as Tibor does. We found, when dealing with the skewed distribution, that if you take the log of the distribution you can get a distribution which is at least approximately normal, and you can do relatively standard statistics in the logarithm of the citation distribution and do reliability tests. The other way is essentially analogous to Tony van Raan's method in that we take the most highly cited 10% of any distribution and see how many papers are in it. That has some nice advantages and it's essentially independent of both subfield and year. Therefore you have a measure that you can add together for many different years and for many different subfields.

Braun: The ten percentile method you are using is a 'fixed limit' method; you choose the ten percentile in an arbitrary way. Our shifted averages generate citation values which automatically belong to the field or to the topics we are investigating and we are not obliged to set an arbitrary threshold.

Narin: Except that the number corresponding to the 10% is determined entirely by the threshold and it might be five citations in acoustics or 40 citations in biochemistry.

Braun: Yes, but it depends on the time period; therefore if you have a low population of papers the method becomes unreliable.

Narin: We do it separately for each year and just add them together. Every year is done separately because we have all those distributions.

Small: The problem Joe Anderson is facing is not resolved by using a median or any other measure of central tendency. No matter where you put that line you are going to have more people and more papers on the low-cited side of it than on the high side, because the distribution continuously decreases with increasing citation rate. High citation is a very rare phenomenon; even in very elite groups, there will be papers published by Nobel Prize winners or other important people that are very lowly cited. Most papers in anyone's bibliography will be fairly infrequently cited.

Anderson: The very definition of median is that half of the papers are above this point and half below.

Hills: While I accept the value of the statistical analysis and admire the way it has been developed, I am concerned that we are trying to be very sophisticated about fairly soft data. A remark was made about the suspicion that policy makers have for statistics. In my policy making role I don't have a suspicion of statistics—I believe that I have a reasonable understanding of them—but I also recognize that statistics are only as good as the data on which they are based. Joe, you made a reference to the question of association versus causality. How have you satisfied yourself that there is causality and not just association? You dealt with the possibility that these groups were initially more intelligent but, for example, the people who did the intercalated BSc degree may have had a greater inclination towards research; I would think that was extremely likely.

Anderson: The difficulty of proving causation is an issue that goes right through the whole history of science and social science. But the lack of such proof hasn't stopped policy decisions being made in the past, particularly with respect to issues like cigarette smoking and cancer. Our study of the BSc scheme has not shown that undergraduate research training was the cause of superior research performance later in life. The study has simply revealed a link between training and performance that was not known before. This link is all the more interesting because we know that doctors generally do not make the decision to go into research until after they complete the BSc (Wakeford et al 1985). The argument that the people who did an intercalated BSc had a greater inclination for research does not hold. It is obviously desirable to look more closely at the relationship between training and performance. This can only be achieved through what I referred to as process evaluation. We need a better theoretical basis to describe many of the empirical results now available from quantitative science policy studies. But the field is still quite young and, because many of us are working inductively, we need data first before we can build theoretical models. This is not unusual in science. For example, taxonomy and palaeontology were around a long time before Darwin!

Hills: I accept what you say. I am not decrying the statistics. I am merely saying that we have to guard against the risk of becoming hypnotized by our sophistication in statistics.

Dixon: It would lend itself to the justification of the causal linkage if, for example, the people who had taken the intercalated BSc felt that had contributed to their research success and correspondingly if those who hadn't perhaps regretted it. Did you interview any of these people?

Anderson: No, we didn't. It's something we would like to do in our study of postdoctoral fellowships. I think it is an important point.

Blume: Evaluation of a scheme of education shouldn't necessarily focus on or limit itself to the technicalities of scientometrics. There's a long tradition of economic analysis of education. Do these sorts of data have any relationship to human capital arguments or rates of return arguments? In Amsterdam we have done some work, not on medical training, but on the performance of clinical research in the medical faculty of a university. It must not be forgotten that medical professors also have patients, and the nature of clinical, patient-related research is not easily captured in these bibliometric statistics. Medical people who do not publish much are not necessarily idle. You can't write off either the economics or the unique nature of medicine so easily.

van Raan: The results of our studies on the medical faculty in Leiden over 15 years of research performance (1970–1986) suggest a positive correlation between research performance and clinical performance.

Anderson: The medical profession already has well prescribed methods for evaluating clinical performance. What it does not have is a method for evaluating research performance. This is what we have been trying to develop in our studies. The urgent need for such methods can be illustrated by the hidden agenda for our study of the intercalated BSc scheme. About two years ago, the National Audit Office suggested that the Medical Research Council (MRC) should reconsider their position on funding the BSc scheme because it was primarily educational and had nothing to do with research. The MRC had no data with which to counter this. We therefore wanted to see if data could be found to show whether the BSc scheme had any impact on medical research. As I described, we found some very strong correlations. The results were published in the *British Medical Journal* (Evered et al 1987) and considered by the House of Lords Select Committee on priorities in medical research. Thus the study was useful in that debate. This proved to us that it is important to develop these methods further, but we fully accept that you can't just look at performance in terms of publications and citations; medicine is about much more than that.

Moravcsik: Postgraduate research training generally doesn't teach students, at least not in the United States, how to choose a research problem; the topic of a PhD is usually decided on by the supervisor. I wonder whether one can make a break-down in success rate according to whether the student chose his own thesis topic or not.

Anderson: Very few students choose their project in the UK. Generally a supervisor will make an application to a research council and get funding for a project and then find a student. The data would be limited for that kind of study.

Hill: I would like to comment on the aspects of the skills base of the PhD that you chose to mention: computer skills, knowledge of a variety of instruments, etc. They don't strike me as being central to what the doctoral degree is about, namely the ability to select important problems and to develop an appropriate strategy for gaining better understanding of those problems. If the skills you mentioned are indeed the central ones, they could be taught in a year of additional course work beyond the bachelors degree and wouldn't demand either the time or expense of extended PhD training.

Also, in my paper (this volume), I refer to the doctorate as poor training for certain other functions; it reinforces a tendency to stick with a problem long after the effort yields diminishing returns, for example. Could you elaborate on how you are looking at doctoral training and whether you think the skills you mentioned are the central ones?

Anderson: That's a very good point. People have for a long time seen the PhD as in some way engendering a high level of intellectual maturity; for example a rational approach to problem solving. We would take that as accepted. But, in addition, it is increasingly felt that the research councils must demonstrate that specific skills emerge from a PhD training because there are many other locations, such as in an industrial research post, where one can foster general intellectual development. The PhD system takes up about 10% of the combined budget of the UK research councils each year, and it seems reasonable for the labour market to ask what taxpayers are getting for this.

First, we have to ask by what criteria we are going to evaluate the PhD system. We felt the safest bet was to regard the PhD as a training for research (although this isn't universally accepted). We then have to ask the question 'what basic tasks should a scientist be able to do?'. Is it reasonable for a PhD graduate to know all about gas–liquid chromatography but very little about other related techniques, statistics, or computing? This is common at present. Increasingly, the feeling is that PhD graduates are getting their training largely as a by-product of the pressure to get results. Consequently, their training is polarized into one or two specialized methodologies in one or two narrow areas.

The Technical Change Centre (TCC) made a survey (1986) of industrial employers of PhDs on behalf of the Science and Engineering Research Council. Dissatisfaction with the research skills of new PhD graduates was prevalent throughout industry. It is thought that a PhD graduate is able to quickly learn new research techniques and to find his or her way round knowledge systems, but we are trying to demonstrate that there is also an inventory of skills that one can identify through a consensus survey of the UK's employers and PhD graduates.

Hill: I find that very disturbing and very compatible with what I consider to be the absurd notion that radio astronomy and high-energy physics are good training for industrial research because students learn how to run computers. If all that is involved in the doctorate is a series of functional skills that can be listed and which are probably better performed by high-school level technicians, who are better operators of many devices than doctoral people, then we have a real problem in our concept of what doctoral education is about.

Anderson: I think that we have got a problem and that is what we are studying. Doctoral graduates should, perhaps, be generalists, and this involves knowing what range of techniques are available in their research field.

Collins: The TCC study you mentioned might have covered this point. You wished to evaluate a training programme (the intercalated BSc) and what you have done is to look at people who developed careers in what they were trained for and who are now looking back at how they got there. Those are the people who, as it were, walk in a straight line. There are others who go through the training programme and then follow different careers. In the UK, we increasingly hear about bright scientists who subsequently work in the City. I would be interested to know whether that actually improves the City, and whether one could follow through how their scientific background has been of help.

Anderson: That sounds like a job for the Royal Society!

References

Braun T, Glänzel W, Schubert A 1985 Scientometric indicators. A 32 country comparative evaluation of publishing performance and citation impact. World Scientific, Singapore & Philadelphia

Braun T, Glänzel W, Schubert A 1989 An alternative quantitative approach to the assessment of national performance in basic research. In: The evaluation of scientific research. Wiley, Chichester (Ciba Foundation Conference) p 32–49

Evered DC, Anderson J, Griggs P, Wakeford R 1987 The correlates of research success. British Medical Journal 295:241–246

Hill CT 1989 How science policies are determined in the United States. In: The evaluation of scientific research. Wiley, Chichester (Ciba Foundation Conference) p 221–233

Technical Change Centre 1986 The careers of scientists and engineers (Report of a study commissioned by the Science and Engineering Research Council). The Technical Change Centre, c/o Policy Studies Institute, London

van Raan AFJ, Hartmann D 1987 The comparative impact of scientific publications and journals: methods of measurement and graphical display. Scientometrics 11:325–331

Wakeford R, Lyon J, Evered DC, Saunders N 1985 Where do medically qualified researchers come from? Lancet 2:262–265

The impact of different modes of research funding

Francis Narin

CHI Research/Computer Horizons Inc., 10 White Horse Pike, Haddon Heights, New Jersey 08035, USA

Abstract. The purpose of this study was to identify the principal contributors to selected Advances in cancer research, how they were supported, and where they performed their work, to determine if a significant relationship exists among the research event, the funding mechanism, and the location of the performer. Thirteen major Advances were selected to represent the broad spectrum of cancer research. Historiographic tracings ('Traces') of the 13 Advances were then prepared. Key events were represented by seminal research papers, and major research streams were identified. The key characteristics of these papers, including research support acknowledgements, author institution, co-authorship and citation frequency were tabulated and used to characterize the Advances covered by the tracings. Three comparison sets of related papers were also identified.

All the research settings, and all the support mechanisms (small and large grants, contracts, intramural NCI, etc.) contributed significantly to the Advances, with no single mechanism or setting disproportionately represented. More specifically, the National Cancer Institute (NCI) provided 37% of the acknowledged support for the Trace papers, there was a large amount of cooperative, multi-sponsor support for the Trace papers, and papers on the Traces, whatever the support mechanism, were extremely highly cited — eight times as frequently as expected.

1989 The evaluation of scientific research. Wiley, Chichester (Ciba Foundation Conference) p 120–140

The study underlying this paper entitled 'Assessment of the factors affecting critical cancer research findings' (Narin 1987a,b, Reisher 1987a,b,c, Reisher & Narin 1987) was the last of a series of studies aimed at understanding the research-to-innovation process. Figure 1 traces these precursor studies.

The first direct precursor to this assessment was the original TRACES study (**T**echnology in **R**etrospect **a**nd **C**ritical **E**vents in **S**cience; IIT Research Institute 1968) performed at the Illinois Institute of Technology (IIT) Research Institute in the late 1960s. The Traces developed in this study were modelled after the original TRACES methodology.

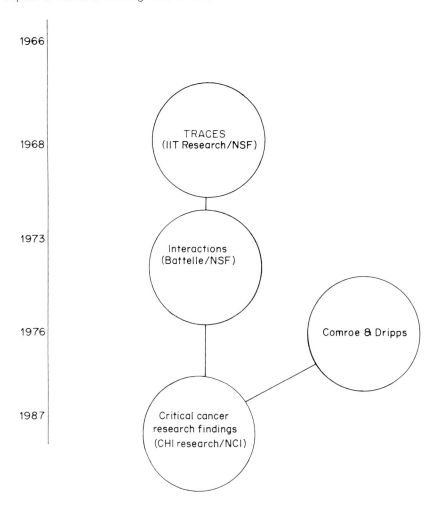

FIG. 1.   Tracing of precursor studies.

On the tracings that were developed in the original TRACES study each individual event was identified by the author, his location, the date and a small annotation. The events were classified by whether they were non-mission research, mission-oriented research, or development and application, and were grouped into streams of related research advance. This specific classification of events and the creation of the graphic tracing were the key methodological innovations in TRACES.

The importance of a specific, graphic tracing to an assessment of research activities should not be under-estimated. In contrast, the more classical scientific history tends to be descriptive, and thereby less objective. A good historian must have a thorough grasp of his material, but he is not forced—without the tracing—to make a specific decision as to the comparative importance of individual events. That forced specificity is a key part of the transition of the tracing methodology from the more subjective realm of the historian to the more quantitative realm of modern evaluative research.

The original TRACES study was extended five years later by the Interactions study at the Battelle Columbus Laboratories (1973) which added some tracings and surrounding data and some socioeconomic and managerial data. The assessment described here makes the first significant technical advances from the original TRACES study, by adding citation analysis to provide an independent measure of the impact of the Trace papers, and by adding control sets of related papers.

Another important study of the research-to-innovation process by Comroe & Dripps (1976) also used quantitative techniques to assess the origins of research advance by developing statistical evidence for the contribution that earlier basic research provided to ten important advances in cardiovascular and pulmonary diseases. They found that 41% of 4000 underlying articles were not clinically oriented, and concluded that clinical advances in cardiovascular and pulmonary diseases were strongly dependent on precursor, basic biomedical research.

Methodology

Statement of the problem

The National Cancer Institute (NCI) is responsible for the conduct and support of research related to the cause, prevention, diagnosis and treatment of cancer. In carrying out this mission, the NCI supports a significant share of the world's cancer-related research, using a variety of support mechanisms (contracts, grants, etc.) in a wide range of different institutional settings (intramural, extramural at various universities, medical schools, independent laboratories, etc.). The published output of this research includes approximately 7000 research papers per year in which one or more of the authors is supported wholly or partially by the NCI (Gee & Narin 1986).

An important issue is whether there are certain research settings, or certain research support mechanisms, which are more effective than others in bringing about important advances in cancer research. Our assessment addressed this issue by identifying key papers associated with 13 important Advances in cancer research, and analysing both the support source and the institutional setting of the papers.

Selection and tracing of Advances

The basic methodology used in this study involved the selection, by a senior advisory panel of experts, of a set of 13 important Advances in cancer research, and the identification of the major research events underlying each of the selected Advances. These research events were then arranged chronologically and thematically to produce a historiographical tracing ('Trace') for each selected Advance. Figure 2 shows a small portion of the Trace entitled 'The study of DNA repair mechanisms'. Each of these 13 Traces generated a set of key papers that are representative of important advances in cancer research — papers that have had significant impact.

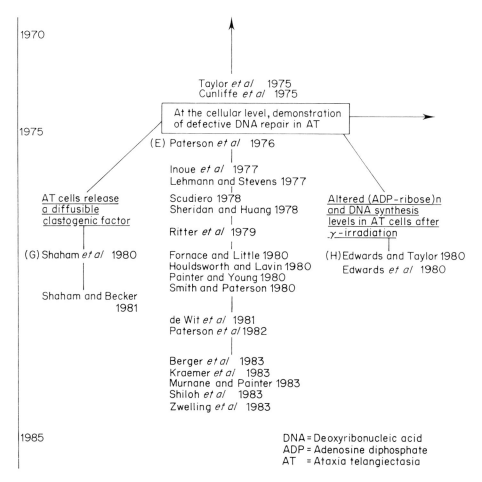

FIG. 2. Section of the Trace for the study of DNA repair mechanisms.

No attempt was made to compile a comprehensive list of all major advances in cancer research and treatment. Instead the senior advisory panelists developed a set of major advances that were representative of the broad spectrum of advance in biomedical research and clinical medicine related to cancer. The 13 selected Advances were:

1   Metabolic activation of carcinogens
2   Development of drug resistance in cancer cells
3   The study of DNA repair mechanisms
4   Elucidation of human lymphocyte surface antigens using monoclonal antibodies
5   Reverse transcriptase — techniques and biological mechanisms
6   Association of Hepatitis B virus and hepato-cellular tumours
7   The relationship of cellular transforming genes to viral oncogenes
8   Malignant transformation of mammalian cells in culture by chemicals
9   Bone marrow transplantation in humans
10   Radiotherapy of prostatic cancer
11   Combination chemotherapy of childhood acute lymphocytic leukemia (ALL)
12   Multimodal therapy in Wilms' tumour
13   Mammography as a screening tool.

Development of four data sets

When the Traces had been completed, a bibliography was prepared for each. Most of the references (90%) on the Traces were to scientific papers appearing in refereed journals, and easily found. The remaining references were to chapters in books, monographs, special reports and other materials. The analysis, however, was restricted to those papers in refereed scientific journals and dated between 1965 and 1982. The number of papers identified for each of the 13 tracings ranges from 84 (for multimodal therapy) to 273 (for reverse transcriptase). For the 13 tracings, 2016 papers were used in the analysis.

In addition to the Trace papers, there are three other sets of papers which serve as comparison sets whose properties are contrasted with the Trace papers. All four sets and their key characteristics are listed in Table 1. The cited and co-cited* papers were identified using various *Science Citation Index* (SCI) citation tapes. The Augmentation set are the contemporaneous papers nearest the Trace papers. The Science base contains the direct precursors of the Trace papers, and the Trace-related papers are a set of surrounding contemporaneous papers.

---

*If paper 'a' cites both paper 'b' and paper 'c', this constitutes a co-citation for papers b and c (Small 1973).

TABLE 1   Definition of sets of papers

I Trace papers

Papers on the Traces, directly associated with each selected major Advance.

Purpose: identify and characterize the direct contributors to each selected major Advance.

II Augmentation papers

Closely related contemporaneous papers cited with the Trace papers (identified through co-citation techniques). Each of these papers was co-cited 30 to 98 times with the Trace papers.

Purpose: control for bias in selection of Trace papers.

III Science base

These are papers cited by the Trace papers, representing the precursor knowledge upon which the selected major Advance was dependent.

Purpose: identify and characterize knowledge base which enabled the selected major Advance to occur.

IV Trace-related comparison set

Papers representative of an appropriate subset of biomedical research related to each selected Advance.

Purpose: background against which to compare prevalence of selected factors, such as NCI support.

Table 2 summarizes the sets of papers that were used in the analysis. The average number of Trace papers was 155 per trace. The number of Science base papers (11 730) is approximately five times as large, and is limited to Trace papers published in every third year. (Only every third year of the citation tapes was used in the project.) The number of different papers that were co-cited with the Trace papers was very large — tens of thousands — of which the most highly co-cited one percent were designated as the Augmentation set. The less highly co-cited papers were designated as the Trace-related comparison set. All citation data are based on every third citing year from 1970 through 1982.

Characterization of the four sets of papers

From each of the Trace papers that could be found the following information was obtained: the research support acknowledgement or acknowledgements, and the institution or institutions with which the authors were affiliated. The number of times each of these papers was cited was obtained from the computerized SCI tapes.

In addition to the Trace papers, random samples of approximately 1260 papers from the Augmentation set, 1600 papers from the Science base, and 2600 Trace-related comparison papers were selected. The sources of support and institutional

TABLE 2   Number of papers used for analysis

| Advance | Trace papers[a] (1965–1982) | | Augmentation papers[b] (1965–1982) | Science base papers[c] (1960–1982) | Trace-related papers[d] (1965–1982) |
	No.	% NCI supported[e]			
Metabolic activation	215	39.4	371	1046	8770
Development of drug resistance	85	46.1	143	582	3203
DNA repair mechanisms	148	20.0	305	829	6481
Monoclonal anti- bodies	115	26.7	729	622	14 474
Reverse transcriptase	273	48.4	739	2548	15 805
Hepatitis B	127	13.8	118	615	2968
Oncogenes	232	49.2	808	2188	16 597
Malignant trans- formation	210	46.9	479	1389	10 699
Bone marrow transplantation	166	35.2	273	696	6350
Radiotherapy/ prostatic cancer	146	20.2	78	341	933
Combination chemotherapy	124	40.6	443	479	5620
Multimodal therapy	84	49.4	100	224	1306
Mammography	91	32.0	23	171	542
	2016		4609	11 730	93 748

[a]Unique papers.
[b]Top 1% most highly co-cited; Trace papers excluded.
[c]Unique papers.
[d]Moderately highly co-cited (top 5–25%); Trace papers excluded.
[e]Fractional counts.

affiliations of these papers were also determined, and the number of their citations was also taken from the SCI.

Findings

Support sources for the Advances

The NCI played a central role, and participated in supporting 55% of the Trace papers. On a fractional basis, where a paper supported by NCI and by another organization is considered half of an NCI-supported paper, the NCI supported 37% of the research on the Traces. Column 3 of Table 2 shows, for each of the Advances, the fractional support by the NCI.

The impact of NCI research support was also apparent in the surrounding sets of papers. Twenty-eight percent of the Augmentation set papers were NCI-supported, as were 33% of the Science base papers, and 22% of the Trace-related papers. Thus, NCI support was also an important factor in the research surrounding the Traces.

Other components of the National Institutes of Health (NIH), most notably the National Institutes of Allergy and Infectious Diseases (NIAID), General Medical Sciences (NIGMS), and Diabetes and Digestive and Kidney Diseases (NIADDK) also contributed significantly. Collectively they accounted for 12% of the Trace papers on a fractional basis, and 13 to 17% of the papers in the other three sets. Non-US sources were approximately equal to the other NIH components, accounting for about 13% of the Trace papers, and 13 to 17% of the other three sets.

NCI support mechanisms

When the relative contributions of the various mechanisms that the NCI uses to support research were examined it was found that, in the aggregate, each of the major support mechanisms contributed significantly. Figure 3 shows the percentage of Trace papers with NCI support, by type of Advance and by funding mechanism.

The key funding mechanisms are: R01, the traditional research project grant; P01, the programme project grants; P30, the cancer centre support grants; N01, research contracts; the R10 (now U10) clinical cooperative research grants; and the NCI intramural programme.

The R01 traditional research project grant and the NCI intramural programme play parallel and prominent roles—each accounting for 10 to 25% of the Trace papers supported by the NCI. However, the importance of the other research support mechanisms is also evident with contract funds supporting almost a fifth of the NCI papers in the basic Advances and 40% in the epidemiological Advances. The one mechanism that appears only for the clinical Advances, the R10 clinical cooperative research grants, was designed specifically for clinical investigation.

Citation analysis

Citation analysis played two roles in the assessment. First, it provided an independent test of whether the papers chosen to represent the Advances were high impact papers, because highly cited papers are widely recognized as papers

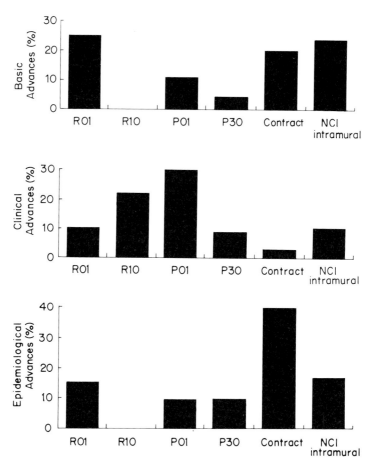

FIG. 3. Percentage of NCI-supported Trace papers by type of Advance and funding
mechanism. Basic Advances: metabolic activation, drug resistance, DNA repair,
monoclonal antibodies, reverse transcriptase, oncogenes and malignant transformation.
Clinical Advances: Bone marrow transplantation, radiotherapy/prostatic cancer,
combination chemotherapy and multimodal therapy. Epidemiological Advances:
Hepatitis B and mammography.

that have had important scientific impact. Second, the citation analysis allowed
for a comparative assessment of the various subsets of papers. Papers supported
by one support source versus another or papers supported by different
mechanisms can be compared on the basis of citation frequency.

The chief finding from the citation analysis is that the papers on the Traces,
and the papers in the surrounding sets, are extraordinarily highly cited — *eight*

times as frequently as typical papers in the same subfields in the same years. The average paper on the Traces is cited approximately 100 times in the first ten years after it is published. The papers in the Science base and Trace-related sets are cited almost as frequently, and the papers in the Augmentation set, which were chosen because they were highly co-cited with the Trace papers, are cited even more highly than the Trace papers. Thus, the milieu of research papers most closely related to these critical cancer findings is composed of papers of unusually high citation impact.

The citation performance data shown in Figs 4 and 5 are presented in terms of the percentage of papers in the 'top decile' of cited papers—that is, the

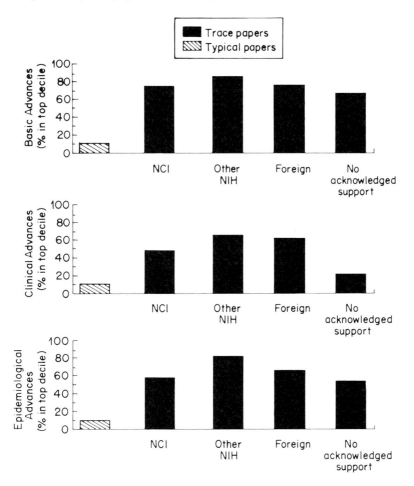

FIG. 4.   Top decile citation performance for Trace papers by source of support. The top decile citation performance is the percentage of papers in the most highly cited 10% of cited papers. Cited papers 1973–1978. Basic, clinical and epidemiological advances as defined in Fig. 3.

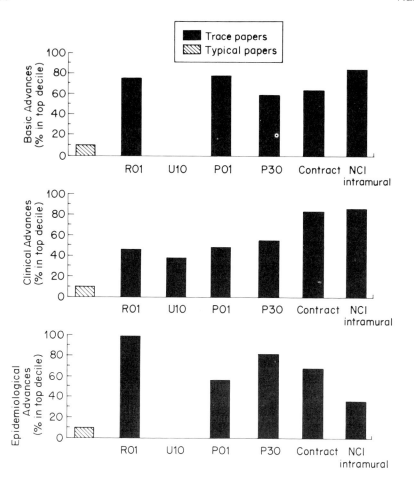

FIG. 5. Top decile citation performance (as defined in Fig. 4) for NCI-supported Trace papers by type of award mechanism. Basic, clinical and epidemiological advances as defined in Fig. 3.

percentage of papers in a given set that are among the most highly cited ten percent of papers in the subfields related to cancer research in the central years of the Traces, 1973 to 1978.

We use the 'top decile' because it allows us to combine papers from different years and subfields into one measure. Citation frequency varies substantially from subfield to subfield and from year to year. Top decile performance controls for this, because every subfield has a top ten percent in each year. As a result, the expected value of top decile performance in any set of papers is ten percent, and values substantially higher than ten percent indicate high citation, fully adjusted for subfield and citation year differences.

Figure 4 shows the top decile citation performance for Trace papers by source of support. The cross-hatched box, at ten percent, shows the expectation for typical papers. The figure shows that all the Trace papers—those supported by the NCI as well as those supported by the other components of the NIH, foreign-supported and the papers without support acknowledgement—are extremely highly cited.

The same type of analysis was applied to each of the mechanisms used by the NCI. The results of this analysis are illustrated in Fig. 5, which shows the top decile performance for the NCI-supported Trace papers, by type of award mechanism. The first and most important observation is that each of the mechanisms produces very highly cited papers. Among the basic Advances, the most highly cited papers are produced by the NCI intramural programme, closely followed by the P01 and R01 mechanisms. For the clinical Advances the most highly cited papers are again from the NCI intramural programme, but in this case followed very closely by papers supported by contracts. For the epidemiological Advances, for which the number of papers in each category is relatively small, each of the mechanisms also supported very highly cited papers.

Research setting

Although hundreds of institutions were represented by the cancer research papers examined during this study, certain institutions appear more often, regardless of the type of research papers examined. Table 3 shows the 12 research institutions whose papers place them among the top ten producers of Trace papers for at least three of the selected Advances. These institutions meet standards of both productivity and breadth. The twelve include not only US universities and the National Cancer Institute, but also two hospitals and a British research centre. Of the ten US universities, hospitals and medical schools, nine had NCI-supported cancer centres in recent years.

It should be mentioned here that when the citation performance (% of papers in top citation decile) of the 18 institutions that produced ten or more Trace papers between 1973 and 1978 is compared to the number of their papers on the Traces, only a low ($r = 0.24$) correlation emerges. This, plus the fact that the institutions shown in Table 3 are quite diverse in terms of size and location, indicates that institutional type and location are not significant factors. Important research Advances occur at both large and small research institutions, US and foreign institutions, universities and medical schools, as well as at the NCI itself.

TABLE 3   Institutions which ranked among the top ten for Trace papers in at least three Advances

Institution	Number of Advances			
	Total	Basic[a]	Clinical[b]	Epidemiological[c]
National Cancer Institute[d]	10	7	2	1
Harvard University/Medical School[e]	8	6	1	1
Sloan Kettering Institute/ Memorial Sloan Kettering Hospital[e]	6	2	4	—
University of California, San Francisco/Medical School	5	3	1	1
Johns Hopkins University/ Medical School[e]	4	1	2	1
Stanford University/ Medical School[e]	4	2	1	1
University of Wisconsin/ Medical School[e]	4	4	—	—
Imperial Cancer Research Foundation, London, UK	3	2	1	—
Massachusetts Institute of Technology[e]	3	3	—	—
M.D. Anderson Hospital[e]	3	—	3	—
University of California, Los Angeles/Medical School[e]	3	1	1	1
University of Washington/ Medical School[e]	3	1	1	1

[a]Metabolic activation, drug resistance, DNA repair, monoclonal antibodies, reverse transcriptase, oncogenes, and malignant transformation.
[b]Bone marrow transplantation, radiotherapy/prostatic cancer, combination chemotherapy, and multimodal therapy.
[c]Hepatitis B and mammography.
[d]Intramural NCI research only.
[e]Institution with NCI-supported cancer centre.

It may be concluded that support mechanisms and institutional settings are not key factors affecting research advance. By implication, the procedures used to screen research proposals at the NCI are, in fact, choosing high impact research regardless of the support mechanisms and institutional settings.

Acknowledgements

This paper is drawn from a study performed for the US National Cancer Institute by CHI Research/Computer Horizons, Inc., under contract N01-CO-33933, entitled 'An assessment of the factors affecting critical cancer research findings'. The Traces were developed under a subcontract by a team of biomedical scientists at the Dynamac Corporation, Rockwell, Maryland, under the direction of Dr Peter Woodman.

References

Battelle Columbus Laboratories 1973 Interactions of science and technology in the innovative process: some case studies. Final report prepared for the National Science Foundation under Contract NSF C-667

Comroe JH, Dripps RD 1976 Scientific basis for support of biomedical science. Science (Wash DC) 192:105–111

Gee HH, Narin F 1986 An analysis of research publications supported by NIH, 1973–1980. NIH Program Evaluation Report, US Department of Health and Human Services, Public Health Service, National Institutes of Health

IIT Research Institute 1968 Technology in retrospect and critical events in science. Report prepared for the National Science Foundation under Contract NSF-C535

Institute for Scientific Information 1970 through 1987 Science Citation Index (SCI). Philadelphia

Narin F 1987a An assessment of the factors affecting critical cancer research findings. Final report prepared for the National Cancer Institute under Contract N01-CO-33933, 100 pp

Narin F 1987b An assessment of the factors affecting critical cancer research findings. Executive summary prepared for the National Cancer Institute under Contract N01-CO-33933, 27 pp

Reisher SR (ed) 1987a An assessment of the factors affecting critical cancer research findings, volume III: Part A — advances # 1 to # 4 narratives, traces and bibliographies. Report prepared for the National Cancer Institute under Contract N01-CO-33933, 115 pp

Reisher SR (ed) 1987b An assessment of the factors affecting critical cancer research findings, volume III: Part B — advances # 5 to # 8 narratives, traces and bibliographies. Report prepared for the National Cancer Institute under Contract N01-CO-33933, 174 pp

Reisher SR (ed) 1987c An assessment of the factors affecting critical cancer research findings, volume III: Part C — advances # 9 to # 13 narratives, traces and bibliographies. Report prepared for the National Cancer Institute under Contract N01-CO-33933, 178 pp

Reisher SR, Narin F 1987 An assessment of the factors affecting critical cancer research findings, volume II: methodology. Report prepared for the National Cancer Institute under Contract N01-CO-33933, 208 pp

Small, H 1973 Co-citation in the scientific literature: a new measure of the relationship between two documents. Journal of the American Society for Information Science 24:265–269

DISCUSSION

Luukkonen-Gronow: You found that the different forms of funding (small and large grants, contracts, intramural National Cancer Institute etc.) all contributed significantly to the Advances in cancer research. What about the rest of the research that was funded by these different mechanisms? Did different forms of funding produce different proportions of less frequently cited papers?

Narin: We don't have data about individual funding mechanisms. We do have data on 90% of the papers that were supported by the National Institutes of Health (NIH). About 15% of the extramural papers supported by the NIH are in the most highly cited 10%. Of the 2000 papers produced each year by the intramural NIH programme, about 23% are in the most highly cited 10%. There are about 30000 NIH-supported papers a year, and although we have identified all the papers supported by the NIH over the last ten years, we have not matched them to the grant files to find out by which mechanism each was funded. We may do that in the future, but it requires a vast computation.

Weinberg: Having worked in a very large institution for most of my life, I was pleased by your finding that the large institutions are as good as the small science institutions. But from your statistics it seems to me that the NCI, which is by far the largest supporter of cancer research in the world (about $1 billion a year), only supports about one third of the important findings. When you consider the other NIH support as well, which adds up to $5 billion, that accounts for only about 45% of the total. Does that mean that the other agencies that support relevant work are on the whole much more effective?

Narin: No, that is wrong. This study only catches a small part of the output of the rest of the NIH—the cancer-related papers. If you did the same study on immunology you would see a much larger role for the NIH institutes.

Weinberg: Let's look at the NCI's $1 billion then. How much other money is being spent?

Narin: Probably at least that much or twice that much around the world. I doubt if the NCI is any more efficient than the Karolinska Institute (Sweden), the Imperial Cancer Research Fund or anywhere else. It's certainly very active at the top, but I don't know.

Kodama: In Japan we are discussing methods of research funding. Our discussion always focuses on whether we should use institutional funding or project funding; that is, funding without evaluation or funding with evaluation. Many Japanese scientists say that block funding, or institutional funding, is better for basic research than project funding, because it allows researchers to have a longer perspective. Three years ago, at a conference at the National Science Foundation, it was suggested, to my surprise, that block funding might be better.

Narin: Some of the mechanisms used by the NCI, such as the P01 programme project grants, are, in effect, block funding.

Kodama: Without evaluation?

Narin: No, not without evaluation; even the block funding through universities is on a competitive basis, but it may be five-year funding. The R01 individual investigator project grant is typically a three-year award. Some of the clinical grants offer five or ten years of funding. We have a pluralistic system; the Sloan-Kettering Cancer Centre may get a block of funds, but they're also expected to get other funds for the individual investigators from other sources. There are some programme funds in that and some project funds, and we don't see any real difference. All the grants are subject to the same review procedure at the NCI; none of them are automatic and none of them are automatically renewed. It's a very competitive system in the United States.

Kodama: In Japan, we have funding without any evaluation. I don't know whether it is more effective or not.

Hill: The intramural funding at the NIH is the most like long-term block funding. I am sure there is internal competition, and it's highly productive.

Anderson: How did you select the panel of experts who chose the key papers?

Narin: That was done by a subcontractor, the Dynamac Corporation in Bethesda. They considered factors such as prestigious awards, and drew up a list of 25 to 30 people whom they felt to be important in the field. Then we screened it down to people who would be available. The National Cancer Institute eliminated a few people whom they felt would be hostile to this study.

Anderson: Were the panel members all North Americans?

Narin: Yes; there is clearly a US bias here. There were not even any Canadians on the panel. From the NCI's point of view, that was not important because they were mainly interested in the research under US sponsorship.

Anderson: Would the results be different if you had a panel made up of experts from other countries?

Narin: No, I don't think the results would have changed significantly, but there would have been a higher representation of non-US advances. French cancer scientists would have chosen some other representative advances, ones that they had participated in. The results are so strong that I don't think anything would have changed what we found, but the US versus, say, European shares would have changed. If you go further into the data you do begin very rapidly to see the Karolinska Institute and other non-US institutions. A number of UK institutions appear in the top 30 or 40 institutions.

Pavitt: You were mainly concerned in your analysis with a sponsor, the National Cancer Institute. No doubt the sponsoring body wanted to see how it was doing in important areas of cancer research, and you focused on its particular problems.

Narin: The NCI did not choose either the tracings or the panels.

Pavitt: No, but they were interested in how well they were doing.

Narin: Yes, obviously.

Pavitt: From the point of view of national and international policy, some very interesting conclusions emerge from your very rich data. First, although the NCI supported a lot of the advances, this amounted to only 30–40% of the total. This suggests that pluralism is a good thing; you can't depend on any one particular funding source. Second, in spite of a possible American bias, there's quite a high participation of foreign science and foreign references in the developments. This is an important point to make in the USA, which is going through a period of scientific nationalism; even in areas where it's supposed to be far ahead, it depends quite a lot on foreign science.

Narin: I think the people in the NIH will agree with that.

Georghiou: One of the criticisms of the original Hindsight (Sherwin & Isenson 1966) and TRACES (IIT Research Institute 1968) projects is that however you construct a sequence of events it's always possible to find some sort of link that goes through them, but that you would perhaps ignore potential dead ends at the time. Did you investigate whether you could trace other events around those ones?

Narin: In a sense we did that by means of the Augmentation set. These are the papers that are in the vicinity of the Trace papers. Originally we planned the augmentation papers to be an alternate set which we would use to enrich the tracing. However, when we finished the tracings, the panel and others felt that there was no reason to enrich them; the papers on the tracing were sufficient to cover the Advance. As a result, we just used the Augmentation set as a control set; because it was computer generated, there is no direct selection bias. We have looked at it only for one of the tracings. About a quarter of the papers in the Augmentation set were actually on the tracing itself. Three quarters of the papers were not on the tracing, so people in the field had not picked them, even though they were as or more highly cited than the Trace papers.

What are these papers? A large fraction has to do with methodologies and instrumentation. They're contemporaneous papers on new methods. We screened the papers so everything's in the same time period, but we had given instructions to trace the intellectual development of the field, and not the relevant techniques. When we looked at the surrounding papers we found that they report instrumentation and methodological advances, because that is what is driving a lot of the sciences—the ability to see, do and measure. If we had tried an automatic creation of the tracing, many of the Augmentation papers would have been included.

Other papers that were prominent were alternate papers by the same investigators. We had specified that if there was a group of papers the most seminal, earliest paper should be picked. That's often not the most highly cited paper in the cluster; the second or third paper in the series is often the most highly cited. That comes up in the co-citation analysis, whereas we chose the paper that had the germ of the idea.

van Raan: I would question the validity of omitting papers on instrumentation. For example, the introduction of the fluorescence activated cell-sorting machine is important in medical research.

Narin: It was left out of the tracing itself, by design, because the tracing was the development of that event, but it shows up in the Augmentation and it shows up in the statistics because the Augmentation set caught all those things.

van Raan: More emphasis on instrumentation may reveal the interdisciplinary influence of other fields. In the example I gave, fluorescence-activated cell sorting will show the influence of physics.

Narin: We do have lists of some of the Augmentation papers.

van Raan: Perhaps medical research has claimed a discovery which was in fact given to them by physics or chemistry.

Narin: We were startled by the Augmentation set because as soon as you look around it, it's all, 'we can now do this and so we have found'.

Hill: Omitting instrumentation and methodology from the Trace might produce a bias against engineering development and the role of technology in facilitating science. We've been struggling for a long time to overcome that bias; Derek Price wrote his last paper on that (Price 1984). To say that something is merely methodology and technique, not the intellectual development of a field, also tends to mislead us about what's important in the development of new science. I wonder whether you would have obtained a different pattern of support of critical research if you had left the methodological papers in the Trace rather than eliminated them?

Narin: It would have been a little broader in that we would have caught what we caught in the Augmentation set and in the Science base. Those papers were caught in the surrounding sets which are broader; you see more of the other parts of NIH and a slightly decreased role for the NCI from 37% to about 32%. However, it would not have markedly changed what we found. In the final report, we said that one of the remarkable findings was the large role that instrumentation plays in supporting advances in cancer research. That was automatically apparent from the development of the control sets.

Blume: How should we interpret these interesting results? They obviously identify a sample of important cancer-related papers and tell us certain things about the work that gave rise to those papers. The history of previous exercises such as the TRACES (IIT Research Institute 1968) and the Comroe & Dripps (1976) studies, shows that there is a tendency in public discussion to go beyond the results and say 'this is how medical innovations take place', and to declare 'this kind of research is more crucial than that kind of research'. One difficulty is that there are important things that, as I understand it, we can't deal with or at least have not dealt with. For example, I would have thought that in making the kind of decisions that your work implies—where to fund, or how to fund—we need also to take account of *how* different kinds of research are important in the innovation. We would then look at delays in using research, at the organizational circumstances and motivations that brought the next steps about, at who did or did not take the next steps, and so on.

These are the kind of questions that people ask in innovation studies such as the ones that Keith Pavitt and others do. Is there any way you can investigate those issues? To say that a piece of research is important and then to add up all the important pieces does not provide a model of how breakthroughs are dependent on research. Neither does it tell us whether other work might have done the same job, nor explain the sort of delay that occurred before the work got used. This is not to denigrate the importance of what you have done, but rather to say 'how can we be careful about the interpretations of the work?'. I have learned from past experience that decision makers are loath to be careful in the interpretations they place on the studies we do in this area.

Narin: I agree with you. We have a classification of journals on a basic to applied scale. In the trace of monoclonal antibodies, the research went clearly from basic to applied; the original discoveries were in very basic literature and over the ten-year period the average went from 3.80, which is very basic, to 3.0, which is more clinical. For drug resistance, the papers originally scored 3.1, which is clinical, and over ten years the research became more basic because they kept finding more problems. So in other parts of the data you can see the feedback mechanism; sometimes it goes one way, sometimes it goes the other, and it is hard to generalize. This is a very rich data resource, but I don't know whether it will ever be used.

Small: How did you establish your links over time, your causality? Did the experts tell you what research came first and what it led to?

Narin: Yes, all the causality was the opinion of the people who compiled the tracings. First the skeletons were done by the senior advisory panel and then the people at Dynamac filled it in. They did not apply citation techniques.

Small: They didn't investigate whether the papers in the same Trace cited one another?

Narin: About a quarter of the co-citation augmentation papers, which are in fact papers that are co-cited by the Trace papers, in the one case we looked at, were already on the tracing. We excluded them in the statistics. Some of the Science base papers that were within the area of the Advance were also on the tracing. If you take the most recent papers, then the early papers that were cited were sometimes on the tracing, but often not.

Small: This is one of the problems; the arrow of causality.

Narin: That is a very difficult question. We did not look at whether the flow of citations matches the flow of knowledge.

Braun: Did the group of experts see the co-cited papers which they had not selected previously?

Narin: No, their role was to select the Advances and develop and supervise the Traces so that we would be confident that the traces did represent advances.

Braun: And you sorted out that all of them were highly cited papers?

Narin: Yes, we found that out afterwards. The average Trace paper was cited eight times as frequently as other papers in the same year and the same subfield.

Garfield: This issue is interesting in relation to a study that Irving Sher, Richard Torpie and I did 25 years ago. We tried to use citation data to trace the history of genetics from Mendel to Nirenberg (Garfield et al 1964). We investigated whether well-cited papers identify both the core events and lesser ones as well and whether experts remember these lesser events. The analysis highlighted several important connections that Isaac Azimov, the control, had forgotten.

This relates to how we select 'Citation Classics'. We have published in *Current Contents* almost 3500 original commentaries by authors of well-cited papers. Unfortunately, there are many important classic papers, especially of pre-war vintage, that have not achieved the appropriate threshold of citation until now because we only recently published the 1955–1964 *Science Citation Index*. However, 1945–1954 will be available at the end of 1988. In any case, we would leave out some very important papers by using absolute rankings or counts exclusively. I would be interested to determine which of the papers you identified would, in fact, satisfy our criteria for Citation Classics. However, as Table 1 illustrates, we could not deal with 10% of the literature—as a rough estimate, 1% of the 30 million papers published and cited to date gives us 300 000 candidates. The average well-cited author would have produced ten or more papers cited over 50 times, so this reduces the number of potential authors to 30 000 or fewer.

TABLE 1   (Garfield)   Citation frequency distribution data for 1955–1987 (SCI)

Number of citations	Number of items	% of file
Over 101	131 000	0.4
51–100	300 000	1.0
26–50	714 000	2.4
17–25	768 000	2.6
10–16	1 384 000	4.6
5–9	2 716 000	9.1
2–4	7 246 000	24.2
1	16 668 000	55.7
Totals	29 926 487	100.00

Narin: We can cut it at any level. For the papers that made it to the tracings, quite often there would be another paper by the same group in the Augmentation set that might be even more highly cited.

References

Comroe JH, Dripps RD 1976 Scientific basis for support of biomedical science. Science (Wash DC) 192:105–111

Garfield E, Sher IH, Torpie RJ 1964 The use of citation data in writing the history of science. Institute for Scientific Information, Philadelphia

IIT (Illinois Institute of Technology) Research Institute 1968 Technology in retrospect and critical events in science. Report prepared for the National Science Foundation under Contract NSF-C535

Price D de S 1984 The science/technology relationship, the craft of experimental science, and policy for the improvement of high technology innovation. Research Policy 13:3–20

Sherwin CW, Isenson RJ 1966 First interim report on project Hindsight. Office on the Director of Defense Research and Engineering, Washington DC

Evaluation of scientific institutions: lessons from a bibliometric study of UK technical universities

John Irvine*

Science Policy Research Unit, University of Sussex, Brighton BN1 9RF, UK

Abstract. After reviewing British attempts to evaluate scientific institutions, this paper outlines the main features of an exploratory study for the Advisory Board for the Research Councils which aimed to construct 'bibliometric profiles' of the research output of UK universities and other public sector organizations. The methodology employed is described briefly and a set of illustrative data presented to show the types of results obtained. By comparing the bibliometric profiles of a number of similar technology-oriented universities, it is shown that research excellence (or weakness) appears to be concentrated in certain institutions across a broad range of fields. In between, there are universities with uneven levels of research strength in different areas. This finding has possible implications for the restructuring under way in the UK academic system, although further work is necessary before conclusions sufficiently reliable for policy purposes can be drawn.

1989 The evaluation of scientific research. Wiley, Chichester (Ciba Foundation Conference) p 141–168

British science has recently been characterized as having entered a 'steady state' in which limits to growth are creating severe strains on the organization and management of research (Ziman 1987). On the one hand, pressures exist for an expansion of spending on basic science: the increasing cost and sophistication of equipment; continuing growth of 'big science' fields; recognition of the need for new centres to handle the multidisciplinary character of many emerging specialties; and the strategic importance of certain research areas. On the other hand, government is insisting that the maintenance of a dynamic research system will have to take place within the confines of level, or at best slowly increasing, funding from the public purse. As a result, a structural transition is taking place to a new form of scientific regime where selectivity, concentration, accountability, efficiency and strategic management have become the bywords.

---

*The views expressed in this paper are those of the author alone and do not imply endorsement by the Advisory Board for the Research Councils or any other organization.

Evaluation of research performance is coming to be seen as an integral part of this new state of affairs, with formal techniques of output measurement being considered as one element in a management information system to augment traditional peer review mechanisms (Irvine 1988). This should enable decision making not only to become more effective, but, most importantly, to become more open and transparent when the essential but difficult choices have to be made about curtailing existing research activities in order to expand others. Developing appropriate methods for evaluating research institutions is thus a central policy priority for the effective management of science in a 'steady state'. This paper addresses one dimension of the task — the development of output indicators for assessing the relative research performance of universities.

Institutional evaluation

Assessment of the scientific performance of institutions is in itself not a new development in the UK. The research councils, for example, have a long tradition of employing 'visiting committees' of distinguished scientists to evaluate periodically their intramural laboratories. The Medical Research Council, in particular, uses such evaluations as an integral part of the decision making process over possible closure of an institute on the retirement of its director.

There is little doubt that expert committees can function effectively in institutional assessment, especially where the research under review is in a single field (or in several related fields) and a disinterested group of relevant experts can be drawn upon as evaluators. However, problems arise when institutions undertake a wide range of research activities (making it difficult to constitute a suitable committee), or in fields characterized by institutional oligopoly (e.g. high-energy physics) with a limited number of centres and a distinct lack of neutral peers (Irvine et al 1984). The absence of suitable peers is also a major problem in national evaluations of the relative performance of all institutions (or university departments) in a particular field because it is far from easy to establish a disinterested committee unless all the members are drawn from abroad.* Consequently, when a domestic committee does carry out a comprehensive review of university research strengths which has implications for future resource distribution, strong criticisms are generally voiced as to its intrinsic 'lack of neutrality' and 'bias' towards established institutions from which the members are often drawn. This was certainly the case in the 1985/86 ranking exercise of academic departments and 'cost centres' carried out by the University Grants Committee (UGC) (see Healey et al 1988, Carpenter et al 1988, Phillimore 1988).

---

*This is a major reason underlying the Swedish policy of using committees of foreign scientists to review individual basic research fields (see NFR 1981).

The pressure to develop more formal methods of research evaluation has come from the desire to improve the quality of decision making in science, and to limit the possibility of mistakes being made (e.g. by overlooking the contributions of a small department in a narrow specialty, or through the quite understandable and often unconscious desire of committee members to protect their own field of work or institutional interests). It has also stemmed from the opportunities opened up by the availability of the *Science Citation Index*, coupled with developments in information science techniques and computing capacity necessary for data handling and analysis. As a result, it is now becoming accepted practice (as is demonstrated in several papers in this volume) to employ numbers of publications in leading refereed journals as an *indicator* of the scientific production of an institution, while citation counts are used to gauge the overall impact of its research output on the scientific community. Average citations per paper, in contrast, give an indication of the aggregate level of influence, while highly-cited papers reflect the more important contributions to the field. For example, the most cited experimental high-energy physics papers in each of the last three decades have been the only ones whose authors have been awarded the Nobel Prize (Irvine et al 1986).

The fact that Britain was among the first of the industrial countries where science entered a 'steady state' in the mid-1970s led to relatively early attempts to explore the use of bibliometric and other formal assessment techniques for policy purposes.* This began with a study by the Science Policy Research Unit (SPRU) in the late 1970s which aimed to develop methods for evaluating the research performance of big science centres in the fields of radio astronomy, optical astronomy and high-energy physics (see US House of Representatives 1985). The study resulted in the method of 'converging partial indicators' in which the research output and impact of a centre or experimental facility were compared with those of matched equivalents in other countries, with input figures (funding and staffing) being used to construct productivity and performance measures. Use of structured peer-rankings was an integral part of the method and showed that in many cases a strong association exists between bibliometric data and expert judgement. (The interviews with scientists also played a key role in interpreting the publication and citation analyses of institutional research output.)

Although this initially caused a stir within the scientific community — because of scepticism among researchers that their output could be measured, as well as worries that such external evaluations posed a threat to the peer review system — there has been a growing acceptance of such techniques. In particular, a number of senior scientists have seen that bibliometric analysis provides a

---

*Don Fuqua, Chairman of the US House of Representatives Task Force on Science Policy, remarked recently that Britain appeared to be 'well in the lead' in the evaluation field (US House of Representatives 1985, p 1).

mechanism for helping distinguish the institutions performing well in a field from those making little contribution, and therefore may assist in opening up the necessary but politically contentious debate on selectivity and concentration.

The first major step in the acceptance by the scientific community of such evaluations came in 1983 when the Advisory Board for the Research Councils (ABRC) commissioned studies exploring the utility for policy purposes of three different bibliometric approaches (co-word analysis, co-citation analysis, and simple publication and citation analysis; see Healey et al 1986, Phillips & Turney 1988). However, it was only when the Royal Society published the results of a follow-up study using bibliometric methods to assess the health of British basic science (employing the manual scanning approach) that their legitimacy really began to be established (see Royal Society 1986).

The research councils have now begun to use bibliometric techniques in institutional evaluation. In particular, the Agricultural and Food Research Council has successfully tested their utility in a study of avian virology (King 1988), while the Natural Environment Research Council (NERC) employed publication and citation analysis in an assessment carried out in 1987 of their marine biology centres (McGinnety 1988). The aim was to compare the results obtained from bibliometric analysis with those from expert review, so the visiting committee carrying out the evaluation was only given the results after having arrived at its conclusions. The committee found a high degree of agreement between the bibliometric data and its own findings, and felt it would have been useful to have been given access to the results of the analysis prior to the site visits (thus enabling, for example, more detailed questioning of researchers to be undertaken). The NERC Council subsequently agreed that publication and citation data should be employed in future as an input to institutional evaluation. Bibliometric techniques have also been used in as yet unpublished assessments of the Natural History Museum (PREST 1988) and earth science departments in British universities (undertaken by the Royal Society for the University Grants Committee). However, despite these initiatives considerable scepticism still exists within the scientific community about the viability and legitimacy of publication and citation data for evaluation purposes.

Bibliometric profiles study

Policy background

The 'bibliometric profiles' project was carried out during 1986/87 by teams* from CHI Research (Computer Horizons Inc.), Strathclyde University and

---

*Full details of the project and the division of labour among the three teams are given in Carpenter et al (1988).

SPRU as part of the ABRC programme on science policy studies. The aim was to explore whether an aggregate analysis of bibliometric data for the UK, broken down by research field and institution, could provide a useful input to future decisions on academic science policy. As such, it probably constitutes the main British initiative so far to study the potential for employing quantitative techniques in institutional research evaluation.

The origins of the study stem partly from the debates within the academic community as to the validity of the 1985/86 UGC ranking exercise which was undertaken to assist with decisions on the provision of infrastructural research support to the universities. The existence of apparent anomalies in the rankings meant that there was interest in testing whether committee judgements of this sort were supported by the results of bibliometric analysis. If so, then publication and citation data might be of relevance to the research councils in determining their policy on the award to institutions of both project/programme grants and studentships. Several issues could therefore usefully be addressed in the bibliometric profiles study:

(i) Is it now technically possible to compile relevant bibliometric indicators for all British research institutions, and, if so, how timely are they, what would be the cost, and under what conditions might they provide a valid measure of scientific output?

(ii) How do the results of bibliometric analysis relate to the judgements made by expert committees, and how acceptable are quantitative assessments likely to prove within the scientific community?

(iii) What further development and testing of the approach is necessary before it might be adopted to provide inputs to policy making by the ABRC and other organizations?

(iv) Finally, what do bibliometric data reveal about the size and structure of research activities across the main institutional sectors of performance (universities, polytechnics, medical schools, research council establishments and government laboratories) and within each sector?

These questions are addressed in detail in both Harris et al (1988) and Carpenter et al (1988) and will therefore be considered only briefly here. Instead, an attempt will be made to shed light on the central philosophical debate currently under way on the future of the academic research system in the UK. This concerns the relative merits of the UGC policy of restructuring the universities on a field-by-field basis. As part of this task, the UGC is carrying out a series of disciplinary reviews with the aim of making recommendations for future infrastructural support to departments irrespective of the overall performance of the host institution (as in the case of earth sciences; see Oxburgh 1987). On the other side are those like the ABRC who argue that the productivity and creativity of academic research (as well as its autonomy) are best protected by removing core research funding entirely from those universities with poor overall performance, and concentrating it in leading institutions and to a lesser extent in those with a strong record in at least some fields (see ABRC 1987). The rationale underlying the latter policy is the synergy between different fields, as a result of which it may well be shortsighted to terminate research in a less successful department in an elite university while continuing to support activity in one of the better departments in an otherwise moribund institution. The weight of academic opinion seems at present to have come down against the ABRC proposals for three categories of higher education institution (research-based, mixed research and teaching, and teaching-based) as not reflecting the highly distributed nature of research excellence across the academic system. It is therefore of some policy interest to determine whether the ABRC model has any basis in reality, or is merely a figment of the imagination of elitist scientists. Can a group of leading universities be identified which make a significantly greater contribution to science across a broad range of fields than a bottom group whose research performance is uniformly poor?

Methodological approach

The approach employed in the study was first to match all the publications listed in the 1983 and 1984 'Corporate Index' sections of the *Science Citation Index** with the institutional affiliations of their authors. Credit for papers was then allocated fractionally to the 499 UK organizations identified on the basis of listed author addresses.

Publications were also categorized into eight main fields (mathematics, physical sciences, chemistry, earth and space sciences, engineering and technology, clinical medicine, biomedical research and biological sciences) and approximately 100 subfields (e.g. chemical engineering or optics) on the basis of a journal classification scheme developed by CHI Research. In this way, computer analysis of the resultant data could produce a field breakdown for the two-year research output of all 50 or so UK universities (with attached research council laboratories and teaching hospitals being treated separately).

The second step was to calculate measures of scientific 'influence' for the papers from each institution. This was done by means of an 'influence weight' methodology based on the relative citation impact of the journals in which papers appear (normalized by field). It was recognized from the outset that this was an approximate method likely to have technical limitations, but it was employed because it was significantly less costly than matching up citations to individual papers, and because insufficient time would have passed for 1983/84 papers to be referred to in subsequent publications.

---

*At the time the study was conceived, 1984 was the latest year for which bibliometric data were available. Coverage of publications was limited to articles, notes and reviews in the 3000 or so journals scanned by the *Science Citation Index*. For details of the procedure employed, see Harris et al (1988).

Full details of the methodological approach employed, as well as the inherent limitations, are given in Harris et al (1988) and Carpenter et al (1988). Among the main conclusions drawn from the study are that technical problems exist with both the journal classification system and the 'influence weight' procedure. In addition, the breakdown of institutional output by field and subfield is not fully synonomous with departments (e.g. mechanical engineers often publish in applied physics journals). Consequently, the approach was judged to be unsuitable for detailed appraisals of individual universities at the departmental level, or assessments at the level of most subfields, because the numbers of papers involved are generally too small for disturbing factors like highly-cited review articles to be averaged out. Nevertheless, the bibliometric profiles methodology was regarded as providing a potentially useful means of assessing the overall output of institutions at the level of fields, where the publication volume is large enough to result in a general concordance between aggregate influence and actual citation data.* In what follows, bibliometric profile data for only the eight main fields are therefore employed.

Institutional profiles of universities

Basis for comparison

One of the main problems with comparing the research performance of universities stems from the fact that their institutional nature and function within the R&D system vary widely. A large arts and social science based civic university may have little in common with a smaller technical university concentrating on engineering and pure and applied physical sciences. Thus some of the technical universities (e.g. Salford) felt they were discriminated against in the UGC ranking exercise because it failed to take fully into account factors such as their not insignificant work for industry. For this reason, it is important to compare 'like' with 'like' and also to take proper account of size-related factors (such as funding or staff numbers).

One way to overcome these problems is to compare matched sets of universities having similar functions and broadly equivalent research activity profiles across the main fields. In principle, it is possible to identify a number of sets of comparable institutions,** but we focus here on the thirteen technology-oriented universities which probably constitute the most homogeneous group of

---

*One task in the study was to check empirically the level at which influence scores for papers from an institution equate with impact figures based on actual citations. This was done for the fields of physics and biology (see Carpenter et al 1988).
**These might include, for example, the 'redbrick' universities (e.g. Sussex), large 'civic' universities (e.g. Manchester), smaller 'civic' universities (e.g. Hull) and autonomous specialized institutions within collegiate universities (e.g. Queen Mary College, University of London).

institutions. These comprise the ten existing ex-Colleges of Advanced Technology
(e.g. Loughborough University of Technology) and their Scottish equivalents,
together with Imperial College of Science and Technology (University of
London), the University of Manchester Institute of Science and Technology
(UMIST), and the University of Wales Institute of Science and Technology
(UWIST). All have relatively similar profiles of activity, concentrating on
engineering together with the physical sciences, chemistry and mathematics. As
a group, they have a slightly more uneven effort in biological research, least
emphasis overall being placed on biomedical and clinical medicine specialties.
Although all have some activity in the social sciences and humanities, this is
not sufficient to introduce problems into the comparison.*

The broad similarity in the research activities of the thirteen institutions means
that the bibliometric profile data can be adjusted for size on the basis of general
university funds (GUF) provided by the UGC in the financial year 1983/84.
It might be argued that total institutional research funds (including grants and
contracts) should be used in weighting the output data, but these in themselves
provide an indicator of scientific success. The key policy question in the
restructuring debate is how to make more effective use of the research component
of GUF, irrespective of whether this is achieved by concentrating research in
designated departments within disciplines or through selective support of entire
institutions. Therefore, it is most appropriate to adjust for size using the
respective GUF figures for each university broken down by field.

There are consequently three main questions to be addressed in comparing
the research performance of the thirteen universities. How marked are the overall
differences by field among institutions? Is 'research excellence' distributed fairly
evenly across the set of universities, or concentrated in specific institutions?
And, similarly, is poor scientific performance institution specific, or evenly
distributed?

Results of comparison

Before considering the results of the analysis, let us first examine a set of
illustrative bibliometric profile data for Universities A and B shown in Table 1.
These are two large civic universities of comparable size and pattern of research
activities, both having strong traditions in earth and space sciences, physics,
chemistry and mathematics. This can be seen from the respective activity indices,
a figure of 1.0 representing an institutional research output in the field equivalent

*In terms of numbers of UGC-funded teaching staff, the technical universities on average devoted
only about 25% of their effort in 1983 to fields outside science and engineering. This was concentrated
in economics, applied social science, psychology, management studies and languages; see Association
of Commonwealth Universities (1984).

TABLE 1   Bibliometric profiles of two civic universities with comparable UGC funding, 1983/84[a]

Research field	University A			University B		
	No. of papers	Activity index[b]	Total influence $(\times 10^{-5})$[c]	No. of papers	Activity index[b]	Total influence $(\times 10^{-5})$[c]
Biological sciences	147.3	0.6	3.2	70.6	0.9	0.8
Biomedical research	282.6	0.8	17.3	72.7	0.6	2.5
Chemistry	325.8	1.5	8.3	105.3	1.5	2.3
Clinical medicine	103.4	0.1	1.0	68.1	0.3	0.7
Earth & space sciences	327.2	3.5	7.4	95.3	3.1	1.4
Engineering & technology	223.3	1.9	2.0	60.0	1.5	0.4
Mathematics	83.6	1.9	0.5	34.8	2.4	0.1
Physical sciences	469.2	2.5	10.3	144.7	2.4	2.7
Total	1962.4	1.0	50.0	651.5	1.0	10.8

[a]The total amount of UGC funds received by University B is about 17% higher than that by University A.
[b]Defined as percentage of each university's total papers accounted for by each field, divided by overall percentage of all universities' papers in that field.
[c]Defined as the product of 'numbers of papers' in the field, 'average influence' and 'percentage of papers with influence'.
Source: ABRC 'Bibliometric Profiles Data-Base' (held at SPRU).

to the percentage norm for all universities. Although University A receives a level of GUF 15% lower than University B, its overall publication output is significantly higher in all fields. This is also the case with 'total influence' which represents the product of 'number of papers', 'average influence per paper' (calculated, as noted earlier, on an aggregate journal basis) and 'percentage of papers with influence'. However, while a broad-based difference in performance seems evident between A and B, such a finding has no real policy significance unless representative of a wider pattern across all universities.

   The existence of such a pattern is made more plausible by the figures in Table 2 on the distribution of papers and influence across all UK universities with departments in the four fields of chemistry, engineering, physics and biological sciences. It can be seen that the top five universities (i.e. the upper decile) produced between 25.7% and 38.2% of all papers (respectively in biology and physics),

TABLE 2 Distribution of papers and influence across UK university sector 1983–84

Universities	Biological sciences (n = 50)		Chemistry (n = 54)		Engineering (n = 48)		Physical sciences (n = 54)	
	% of papers	% of influence	% of papers	% of influence	% of papers	% of influence	% of papers	% of influence
Top 10%	25.7	26.8	26.8	28.8	31.2	37.9	38.2	43.1
25%	48.8	49.0	48.4	51.5	53.8	59.4	57.8	62.6
50%	77.2	77.4	75.8	77.8	79.0	82.2	79.9	81.0
75%	95.4	96.4	91.7	92.8	93.0	94.4	93.4	94.2
90%	98.9	99.0	97.7	98.1	98.1	98.4	98.4	98.5
100%	100.0	100.0	100.0	100.0	100.0	100.0	100.0	100.0

Source: Carpenter et al (1988).

with the bottom quartile responsible for only between 4.6% (biology) and 8.3% (chemistry). The distribution of influence is even more concentrated. This raises the important questions of whether specific institutions are ranked in the top decile across all fields, and to what extent such a pattern is a function of concentration of research resources in larger universities. Answering such questions involves detailed analysis of expenditure and personnel data for each university, which is now being done at SPRU. Preliminary results show strong indications of overall concentration of research excellence, with three universities being in the top five for all four fields as well as in mathematics and earth and space sciences.

The bibliometric profile data for the thirteen technical universities in Table 3 provide the clearest evidence for the likely existence of an overall hierarchy of research institutions of the type posited by the ABRC. Comparison of performance is limited to the five fields in which the technical universities focus the greatest part of their research effort (the average activity indices for engineering, chemistry and physics are 3.4, 2.1 and 1.7 respectively). All figures have been adjusted to take into account institutional size* and have also been normalized to facilitate analysis. It can be seen that University 1 has significantly higher than average figures for both publications and influence across all fields, achieving levels respectively 2.1 and 2.5 times greater than the norm. This is followed by Universities 4, 8 and 10 which also show a consistently good performance, as well as being strong in their main discipline of engineering. In comparison, the records of Universities 5 and 7 are below average in every field, while the figures for Universities 6, 9 and 11 are not much better. In between, the performance of a group of four universities is somewhat uneven across the different fields. The universities have been listed in the table according to overall level of UGC funding (from highest down to lowest) and it is interesting to find that no apparent relationship exists between relative research performance and institutional size.

The absolute extent of the inequality in research performance is shown in Table 4, which classifies the thirteen universities into four categories ranging from 'leading research university' to 'poor overall performance'. The basis for classifying institutions is as follows: 'leading research university' ($n = 1$), overall figures greater than 2.0 times the norm for both publications and influence (see Table 3); 'other strong research universities' ($n = 3$), figures greater than 1.0 for

---

*Publication output and influence were both adjusted for institutional size using GUF data broken down by research field according to numbers of full-time staff financed by the UGC in 1983. This was estimated by classifying all science and engineering departments into the eight main field categories employed in the study (making pro-rata allocations in the case of cross-disciplinary departments). A ninth 'other' category was used to cover all other fields (primarily social sciences and humanities). Details of academic staff and departments were obtained from Association of Commonwealth Universities (1984). The method is approximate but adequate for the purposes of this paper.

TABLE 3 Research performance of UK technical universities: relative output and influence by main field, 1983/84[a]

University	Engineering and technology		Physical sciences		Mathematics		Chemistry		Biological sciences		Average	
	Publications	Influence	Publications	Influence	Publications	Influence	Publications	Influence	Publications	Influence	Publications	Influence
1	1.55	1.55	1.75	2.30	1.80	2.15	2.85	3.30	2.45	3.10	2.10	2.50
2	0.70	0.65	0.70	0.60	0.70	0.65	0.95	1.00	1.95	2.25	1.00	1.05
3	0.90	0.65	1.80	0.95	1.35	0.70	0.95	0.85	0.50	0.50	1.10	0.75
4	1.25	1.80	1.55	1.40	0.30	0.45	1.10	1.00	1.15	1.00	1.10	1.15
5	0.35	0.45	0.90	0.95	0.00	0.00	0.75	0.60	0.80	0.60	0.55	0.50
6	1.05	1.20	0.35	0.35	0.65	0.50	0.35	0.25	1.35	0.70	0.75	0.60
7	0.75	0.55	0.90	0.65	0.05	0.00	0.70	0.55	0.25	0.30	0.55	0.40
8	1.20	1.30	1.40	1.20	1.90	2.15	1.15	1.10	0.25	0.20	1.20	1.20
9	1.15	0.90	0.95	0.65	0.25	0.15	0.60	0.50	0.20	0.25	0.65	0.50
10	2.00	2.20	1.10	1.15	1.00	1.40	1.00	0.95	1.00	1.15	1.20	1.40
11	0.45	0.65	0.30	0.45	0.80	0.15	1.35	1.75	—	—	0.70	0.75
12	0.75	0.50	0.90	2.15	0.95	1.35	0.75	0.85	1.00	0.80	0.85	1.15
13	0.80	0.65	0.35	0.25	2.30	2.35	0.50	0.25	1.05	1.10	1.00	0.90
Average	1.00	1.00	1.00	1.00	1.00	1.00	1.00	1.00	1.00	1.00	1.00	1.00

[a] Publication output and influence have both been normalized within fields taking into account institutional size. Figures may not sum because of rounding.

Source: ABRC 'Bibliometric Profiles Data-Base' (held at SPRU) and USR (1985).

TABLE 4 Overall pattern of research performance in UK technical universities, 1983/84[a]

Classification of technical university	Aggregate research component GUF (£m)[b] (%)	Aggregate publications Field[c]						Aggregate influence ($\times 10^{-5}$) Field[c]						Research grants & contracts (£m)	
		1	2	3	4	5	Total	1	2	3	4	5	Total	Research councils	Industry
Leading research university (n = 1)	8.6 (15.6)	202 (23.2)	297 (36.0)	70 (35.7)	227 (23.1)	113 (36.5)	909 (28.5)	1.22 (23.0)	5.70 (42.8)	0.38 (40.4)	4.78 (27.6)	1.72 (41.6)	13.80 (33.6)	7.15 (34.0)	2.39 (27.5)
Other strong research universities (n = 3)	12.1 (22.0)	246 (28.3)	188 (22.8)	44 (22.4)	226 (23.0)	54 (17.4)	758 (23.8)	1.90 (35.8)	2.58 (19.4)	0.25 (26.6)	3.81 (22.0)	0.73 (17.7)	9.27 (22.6)	5.04 (23.9)	2.24 (25.8)
Mixed research performance (n = 4)	14.9 (27.1)	191 (22.0)	162 (19.6)	59 (30.1)	250 (25.4)	93 (30.0)	755 (23.7)	0.82 (15.5)	2.68 (20.1)	0.26 (27.7)	4.27 (24.7)	1.18 (28.6)	9.21 (22.5)	5.19 (24.6)	2.37 (27.3)
Poor research performance (n = 5)	19.4 (35.3)	231 (26.5)	179 (21.6)	23 (11.7)	280 (28.5)	50 (16.1)	763 (24.0)	1.36 (25.7)	2.36 (17.7)	0.05 (5.3)	4.46 (25.7)	0.50 (12.1)	8.73 (21.3)	3.68 (17.5)	1.69 (19.4)
Total (%)	55.0 (100)	870 (100)	826 (100)	196 (100)	983 (100)	310 (100)	3185 (100)	5.30 (100)	13.32 (100)	0.94 (100)	17.32 (100)	4.13 (100)	41.01 (100)	21.06 (100)	8.69 (100)

[a] All figures in brackets are percentages.
[b] This relates only to the fields covered. It has been assumed that the research component of general university funds is 40% of the overall total.
[c] The fields are: 1, engineering and technology; 2, physical sciences; 3, mathematics; 4, chemistry; and 5, biological sciences.
Source: ABRC 'Bibliometric Profiles Database' (held at SPRU) and USR (1985).

both publications and influence; 'poor overall research performance' ($n = 5$), figures less than 0.8 for both publications and influence; and 'mixed research performance' ($n = 4$), remaining universities. This enables the aggregate publications and influence by field of all the institutions in each category to be compared against the total infrastructural research funds (GUF) provided by the UGC.

It can be seen that the one 'leading university' has a research output and influence greater overall than the three 'strong research universities' combined (which together receive 41% more GUF), as well as the four 'mixed research performance universities' (receiving 73% more) and the five universities in the 'poor research performance' category (receiving 126% more). The difference between the top and bottom sets of institutions is particularly marked in the case of influence. It is perhaps not unexpected that the higher classified universities win a proportionately greater amount of research council grants (which are primarily awarded on criteria of scientific 'excellence'). However, it is interesting that they also receive a higher level of contracts and grants from companies — the leading research university received industrial funding equivalent to 27.8% of GUF, while the proportions for the other three institutional categories in declining order were 18.5%, 15.9% and 8.7%. There is apparently a strong linkage between output of high quality basic scientific and engineering research and its perceived utility to industry — a finding of some importance for academic policy, given the pressure today on the university system for shorter-term research with less potential for publishing novel results.

Finally, it should be emphasized that bibliometric data on research performance are intended to be no more than an input to the traditional committee and peer review based mechanisms for decision making. Even if developed further, bibliometric techniques will always be subject to a number of intrinsic technical and conceptual limitations. This does not, however, invalidate the role they might play in evaluation because peer review also seems to have its own problems (Roy 1984). Table 5 presents a comparison of the UGC rankings for physics (published in 1986) with the bibliometric profile results obtained in the ABRC study. While there is overall a strong association between the rankings and total influence (a correlation of 0.65), a number of apparent anomalies stand out — for example, Universities 6 and 12 seem to have been harshly judged in the rankings compared to Universities 21 and 23. Size-independent indicators such as influence per publication show rather less correlation. This is also the case in other fields like chemistry, with evidence pointing to the likelihood that the UGC rankings may have been overly determined by the size of departments (Carpenter et al 1988). It is for such reasons that bibliometric data would appear to provide a useful check on committee-based procedures for evaluation of institutional research performance.

TABLE 5 Comparison of research profile data with UGC rankings for physics

University	Number of papers	Total influence[a]	UGC ranking[b]
1	552.4	11 739	4
2	469.2	10 251	4
3	296.8	5697	4
4	144.7	2679	4
5	165.2	2499	3
6	121.3	2435	2
7	120.3	2254	3
8	105.3	2086	3
9	100.4	1993	3
10	99.2	1664	2
11	95.2	1637	2
12	65.0	1519	1
13	44.3	1508	2
14	94.8	1466	2
15	72.6	1426	2
16	98.2	1342	3
17	75.2	1278	N/A
18	62.4	1125	2
19	76.1	1088	2
20	81.1	1081	1
21	69.7	982	3
22	62.4	947	1
23	66.1	943	3
24	52.9	908	1
25	44.8	860	1

[a]Universities are ranked in terms of total influence. Only the top 25 institutions with physics departments have been included.
[b]UGC rankings: 4, outstanding; 3, above average; 2, average; 1, below average; N/A, not available.
Source: Carpenter et al (1988).

Conclusions

This paper began by reviewing British attempts to apply more formal techniques to the evaluation of institutional performance in basic research. As we have seen, the move towards 'steady-state' science has led to a situation where it is now recognized that bibliometric methods can play a potentially useful role as an adjunct to peer review. In simpler cases, where equivalent institutions working in the same research area (e.g. marine sciences) are being evaluated, publication and citation data are already routinely employed by a few agencies. However, for most policy applications the search is still under way for sufficiently reliable methods and techniques. This is especially the case with overall comparisons of performance in the higher education system by field and subfield. In future, assessment of scientific impact should probably be done where possible by actual citation counts rather than using the influence weight methodology. It is also necessary to develop improved methods for linking together the inputs and outputs of research at the level of the institution, department and field (Johnes 1988, Whiston 1988). This will inevitably take time, and important methodological contributions are likely to be made by a number of UGC reviews of individual fields (e.g. physics and chemistry) in which bibliometric analysis is playing a part.

This said, the aggregate set of bibliometric profile data does lend itself to making broad institutional comparisons and to testing general hypotheses about the correlates of research success. The data presented on UK technical universities suggest the existence of a strongly differentiated hierarchy of performance across institutions. Further work is certainly necessary before firm conclusions can be drawn about these universities. For example, it would be worthwhile examining in more detail the main components of performance within the larger engineering fields (in particular, chemical, electrical and mechanical engineering). Moreover, if such a hierarchy of performance were apparent in studies of other sets of matched universities, it would appear to provide support for the ABRC's currently unpopular view that the overall scientific strength of an institution should be an important part of the equation on future policies for selectivity, concentration and restructuring within higher education.

Acknowledgements

The work involved in preparing this paper was undertaken as part of the SPRU 'Programme on Science Policy and Research Evaluation', financed by the Economic and Social Research Council. Some of the empirical material presented is drawn from Carpenter et al (1988), which reports the main findings from the ABRC 'bibliometric profiles' study undertaken jointly by CHI Research, the Department of Information Science at Strathclyde University and the Science Policy Research Unit. Special thanks are due to Ben Martin for comments on an earlier draft of the paper and to Phoebe Isard for statistical assistance.

References

ABRC 1987 A strategy for the science base. HMSO, London.
Association of Commonwealth Universities 1984 Commonwealth universities yearbook, 1984. ACU, London
Carpenter MP, Gibb F, Harris M, Irvine J, Martin BR, Narin F 1988 Bibliometric profiles for British academic institutions: an experiment to develop research output indicators. Scientometrics 14:213–233

Harris MJ, Hipkins MF, Huntingdon AT 1988 Output measures of research: bibliometric profiles for UK research institutions. Advisory Board for the Research Councils, London
Healey P, Irvine J, Martin B 1988 Quantitative science-policy studies in the United Kingdom. Scientometrics 14:177–183
Healey P, Rothman H, Hoch P 1986 An experiment in science mapping for research planning. Research Policy 15:233–54
Irvine J 1988 Evaluating research performance: managing science in a steady state. Paper presented at British Association for the Advancement of Science conference on 'Managing science in a steady state', London, April 26th. Mimeo, Science Policy Research Unit, University of Sussex
Irvine J, Martin B, Oldham G 1984 Research evaluation in British science: a SPRU review. CPE Etude 35:142–184
Irvine J, Martin B, Skea J, Peacock T, Minchin N, Crouch D 1986 The shifting balance of power in experimental particle physics. Physics Today 39:26–36
Johnes G 1988 Determinants of research output in economics departments of British universities. Research Policy 17:171–178
King J 1988 The use of bibliometric techniques for institutional research evaluation: a study of avian virology. Scientometrics 14:295–314
McGinnety J 1988 The Natural Environment Research Council: recent experiences with quantitative science-policy studies. Scientometrics 14:283–294
NFR 1981 International evaluations of research projects supported by the Swedish Natural Science Research Council. Naturvetenskapliga Forskningsrådet (NFR), Stockholm
Oxburgh ER (Chairman) 1987 Strengthening university earth sciences. University Grants Committee, London
Phillimore AJ 1988 University research performance indicators: a critical review. Mimeo, Science Policy Research Unit, University of Sussex
Phillips D, Turney J 1988 Bibliometrics and UK science policy. Scientometrics 14:185–200
PREST 1988 Evaluation of the research activities of the British Museum (Natural History). Report prepared for the British Museum (Natural History), ABRC and the Department of Education and Science. Mimeo, PREST, University of Manchester
Roy R 1984 Alternatives to review by peers: a contribution to the theory of scientific choice. Minerva 22:316–28
Royal Society 1986 Evaluation of national performance in basic research. Science Policy Studies No 1, Advisory Board for the Research Councils, London
US House of Representatives, Task Force on Science Policy of the Committee on Science and Technology 1985 Science Policy Study—Hearings volume 13: British science evaluation methods. Report 59, Ninety-Ninth Congress, First Session, October 30th, US Government Printing Office, Washington DC
USR 1985 University statistics 1983–1984, volume 3—finance. Universities Statistical Record, Cheltenham
Whiston T 1988 Restructuring and selectivity in academic science. Concept Paper No 5, Science Policy Support Group, London
Ziman J 1987 Science in a 'steady state': the research system in transition. Concept Paper No 1, Science Policy Support Group, London

DISCUSSION

Moravcsik: How did the University Grants Committee (UGC) come to their judgement on the relative performance of university departments?

Irvine: Discipline-based committees ranked all relevant departments into five categories of research strength (subsequently reduced to four). This ranking was based on the expert knowledge of the committee members together with information obtained from departments. One of the main problems was that each department was asked to submit five publications regarded as representative of its work, irrespective of its size or whether its research covered a large number of specialties. Although it is not known for certain, it is believed that grants received from research councils were given stronger weighting than contracts received from industry, which may have disadvantaged the technological universities (a number of which were subsequently subject to harsh expenditure cuts). No use was made of output data, such as numbers of publications or citations. The UGC now recognizes that there were problems in this approach, and is trying to develop improved methods for the next round of assessments.

Luukkonen-Gronow: Your methodology assesses the performance of universities in given scientific fields compared to the average for that field in that country. This relative comparison is well founded because there are large differences in citing conventions among fields. As you said, it is not possible to apply this approach to smaller units, such as subfields or departments. However, in practice, at least in Finland, universities do need to compare the performances of departments. For example, one field you study is medicine, but medical faculties have a number of departments and they are looking for methods with which to compare the performances of these units. To make the task more difficult, medical faculties in different universities are not defined in the same way and have different types of departments. How would you deal with this need to assess institutional units?

Irvine: This limitation arises because we judged it too costly to allocate all the papers to individual departments and decided instead to rely upon a classification into fields and subfields. This led to the problem that these are not always synonymous with departments (for example, an electrical engineer might well produce a physics paper), although our approach is useful for assessing institutional research output across disciplines. We could easily have avoided this problem (at much greater cost) by sending lists of papers to universities and requesting that they classify them by department and field (which is difficult to do using the *Science Citation Index*) or, alternatively, supply classified lists of papers themselves. We could have avoided the other main technical problems by using matched citations rather than the influence methodology, although the improved accuracy would be counterbalanced by the introduction of a more historical focus (since it takes around two years for papers to be cited). So in principle it is not difficult to improve the approach we used to make it suitable for the task you have in mind in Finland, but the small numbers of papers for each department mean it would probably not be possible to use the journal influence methodology.

Garfield: By suggesting that departments should classify the fields for their papers do you mean that they would select journal categories from those listed in the SCI?

Irvine: No. They would allocate pre-defined field categories to each paper, rather than relying, as we did, on the CHI (Computer Horizons Inc) journal classification scheme. As you know, some journals cover a wide mix of disciplines and errors can be introduced by assuming papers match up with the field classification of journals. One would encounter similar sorts of problems in using the SCI journal categories.

Garfield: Would you use co-citation clustering?

Irvine: No, I don't mean clustering. That may be a good way of identifying the intellectual context of a paper, but it introduces all sorts of problems into classification.

Garfield: Classification is a very vague term and I don't think this is related to the problem of whether the categories used in the SCI are narrow or broad. The *Journal Citation Reports* and all other journal classifications are problematic unless you classify individual articles. How are you going to separate articles published in journals like *Nature* and *Science*? Co-citation clustering or classification can work if applied consistently to individual articles. Our clusters of research fronts are applied consistently. Small specialty journals can provide a rough classification system. We use them to identify Citation Classics. But if an author has published an equally important paper in another multidisciplinary journal, he can tell us that, or cite it in his commentary. Our co-citation clusters do work in this respect but are presently limited by their annual compilation. Five, ten or fifteen year cumulations would solve the problem.

Phillips: I think there is a fundamental problem here. Science can no longer be easily divided into discrete packages which everybody understands; for example, people designated as physicists now publish papers in chemistry and biology.

van Raan: One conclusion of John Irvine's study is that there are a few elite universities that are strong in all fields and then a second echelon where it's necessary to have some fine tuning to see what's going on. Here a focus on the departmental level by a method such as ours (van Raan, this volume) can be helpful.

You talked about some minor inconsistencies in the context of the subfields. But I don't think this is a minor problem. One of the most important subfields in physics, especially in German and British universities, is atomic and molecular physics. This subfield does not exist in the classification—it is 'general physics'. Modern optics, because of the development of lasers within atomic and molecular physics, is also part of 'general physics'. Thus you are not able to trace developments in modern optics. For a study at the departmental level, this can be a catastrophe. The only people who know which journals are important for their field are the scientists.

Irvine: These uncertainties are one reason the study of technological universities is limited to assessing performance at the level of broad fields. In the further development of this type of study, such as the work you intend to do in The Netherlands, one could explore alternative approaches to subfield classification. That will, as you say, inevitably involve the participation of scientists.

Narin: We didn't do this study at the departmental level simply because of the amount of work necessary to take the tens of thousands of UK papers and individually assign them to the departments. It could have been done, and in the future it might be done, by preparing a bibliography by field and university and then approaching the departments for help.

Irvine: In Britain we have a number of collegiate universities, such as Durham. Authors often list only their college addresses, which raises problems for departmental classification. This can only be overcome with access to the faculty listings of the universities concerned.

Braun: You are using 'fractional counting'. Does that mean that you give one point to a university which writes a paper alone and half a point when it is a collaborative paper?

Irvine: That is correct.

Braun: Do you not feel you punish collaboration?

Irvine: No, I do not. On the contrary, I think your method, in which you allocate one paper to each author, can introduce all sorts of biases into evaluation in cases of joint publishing. For example, it would be wrong to give 20 high-energy physicists from different departments who co-author a paper one publication each. And what if 19 physicists from one department write a paper with a single collaborator in another? Is it fair to credit one paper to each department? The question of fractional allocation is important here. On balance, the method has less technical problems than 'whole counting'.

Braun: This is an open question! Do you sometimes use the same journal allocated to different fields?

Irvine: Yes; journal allocation is also done on a fractional basis!

Braun: You implied that your top university is better because industry supports it. This could be interpreted as the reverse: it is good and therefore industry supports it.

Irvine: That is what I was saying; the university not only had a better record in terms of publications and influence, but it also seemed to be well regarded by companies because it received more industrial research funds.

Braun: Perhaps the reverse is true; industry began to support the university, and it improved because the funds were available.

Irvine: My paper was addressing the efficiency with which these UK universities use the infrastructural research funds provided by the UGC.

Hill: As you said, it's too early to use your work for policy making, but inevitably someone will leap to do so. If this were an American assessment, the obvious conclusion would appear to be that all the money and all the students should go to the Massachusetts Institute of Technology and Harvard! But there's another way to read the results: namely, the challenge to Britain in restructuring or reallocating resources is to find a way to strengthen the second and third tier universities, which are surely important for education, for regional economic development, and for many other national objectives. How do you see that playing out? Does an analyst have a responsibility to enter into the debate and outline the true range of reasonable policy alternatives?

Irvine: What you say is true. One of the key problems will be to strengthen the second and third rank universities, but if this analysis is confirmed by the wider study of all UK universities that we intend to do, one would certainly have to question whether the performance of the very lowest ranked universities merits their continuing receipt of institutional research support.

Another policy issue is whether the elite institutions should be subject to cuts of the sort that followed for some of them after the first UGC field review. The synergy across departments within an institution is important, and tampering with the better universities may have unforeseen negative consequences. Perhaps the health of British academic research is best protected by restructuring on an institutional basis, or at least taking the overall performance of a university into account. At present, restructuring is being undertaken solely on a field-by-field basis. One aim of my paper was to question the wisdom of that policy.

Lake: This study was the first of UK technical universities. How valid are the conclusions likely to be for the broader spectrum of universities? It is possible that the so-called technical institutions are likely to focus their research towards the strategic and applied end of the spectrum, as evidenced by the 28% of funding that comes from industry, and that if one studied all the UK universities, including those which covered a full spectrum of disciplines, one might get an emphasis more towards intellectual endeavour for its own sake and reach different conclusions.

Irvine: That seems unlikely. I have briefly compared the research output figures for the other universities with their overall UGC research support and I would guess that the conclusions are likely to hold, perhaps even more strikingly. The figure for industrial funding that you quote derives only from a comparison with the research component of UGC support and is not the proportion of the total support for university research.

Kruytbosch: There is a connection between the issue of the concentration of research excellence and the problems of technical manpower policy. Perhaps you are not focusing on manpower production, but it is an important issue in the USA.

Irvine: The issue of technical personnel is central in science policy, but in the UK we have a large number of polytechnics essentially funded simply to provide teaching. They do not receive infrastructural research support in the form of general university funds and yet industry is happy with the quality of their graduates. Moreover, overall comparison of the research activities of the two sets of institutions shows that the better polytechnics match the performance of the bottom universities. Why should such universities be treated differently from the polytechnics? Why should their staff be privileged in having a teaching load enabling them to allocate 40% of their time to research? Might it not be a better use of resources to restrict such universities to a teaching role, as suggested by the Advisory Board for the Research Councils (ABRC), and channel the research funds released to other institutions with a stronger track record?

Collins: How fields are defined is important. In practical terms, one has to remember why one undertakes these exercises at all, which has to do with resource allocation. You have to analyse performance at the level of the unit that is being financed—the department, for example. At SEPSU (Science and Engineering Policy Studies Unit) we studied bibliometric performance at departmental level in the earth sciences in the UK. The UGC, in the context of restructuring national provision for earth sciences, collected from each department a list of what its staff had written. Our analysis of this data supports your finding that there is a group of very good departments, a group of poor departments, and a group of departments in between. That conclusion is fairly consistent whatever indicator is used. If my guess as to the top university in your study is correct, and if earth science was not included under the five headings that you used, that university is good but not brilliant across all fields.

Irvine: My analysis is at the level of main fields and inclusion of the relevant 'earth and space sciences' category would make no difference to the results. It was excluded from the comparison because few of the technological universities are active in this field. The top ranked university is in fact relatively stronger in the field than in most others, partly because earth and space sciences are integrated as a main field in the CHI classification scheme.

Collins: So much the worse for that classification scheme! You have been collecting data from the *Science Citation Index* or derivatives of that database. We used comprehensive data from each department. Averaging all the departments over the period examined, we found that 20% of their journal publications were in journals not covered by the SCI. Thirty percent of all their publications were not journal articles at all. I don't know whether this figure for earth sciences is typical of other fields. But, given that contract work is also done in other disciplines, I should imagine that this figure is fairly typical. Thus 44% of all publications from UK earth science departments are not picked up by the SCI. The percentage is obviously much higher in some departments than in others, but it does raise a caveat about interpreting at departmental level data based on the *Science Citation Index*.

Garfield: Are you using only the SCI *Source Index* and not the *Citation Index* section? The publication can be cited in the journals we do cover.

Collins: I'm looking at the *Source Index*.

Irvine: What proportion of the 44% of earth science papers not scanned by the SCI are ever cited? You seem to be including in the overall publication figures final reports and other material like conference papers. Many of these papers might later be re-published as journal articles. This raises questions about your figures.

Collins: I haven't analysed the citation performance of SCI-covered publications against non-SCI-covered publications. That could be done with the data we have. I don't know how much duplication of content there is between the two sets of publications.

van Raan: We have studied chemical and electrical engineering in our technical universities in The Netherlands. We found that the better groups in both fields do publish in SCI journals. In the annual reports of the universities where all publications are listed, about half of the publications from technical departments are in conference proceedings. These are very important for engineering fields, and are not always published in journals. Books of proceedings are not source items in the *Science Citation Index*, but they can be cited by source journals and are often highly cited. PhD theses are also not a source in the SCI but can be cited. You have to take these factors into account in assessing performance, especially in engineering fields.

Garfield: Unfortunately, we didn't expect the SCI *Source Index* to be used so heavily. We publish a database called *Index of Scientific and Technical Proceedings*. It is not incorporated into the SCI database but it is available on-line. We have been contemplating a *Science Book Citation Index* which would cover all types of non-journal material, especially multi-authored book series. We already cover many serial publications that are considered books.

Collins: We defined an SCI journal as one that is included in the July 1984 list, *Journal Publications for the Science Citation Index*, published by ISI (Institute for Scientific Information).

Garfield: Many hundreds of journals are covered in *Current Contents* (that is, indexed by ISI) but don't go into the SCI. If you use the on-line *SCISEARCH*, via DIALOG or DATASTAR for example, the database includes what we call '*Current Contents* only journals'. I am not certain about the problems you have in the earth sciences. I corresponded with a UK professor of earth science who was unaware of the distinctions between the source journals and cited journals. It is widely and erroneously assumed that if a journal is not a 'source' for the SCI it will be excluded from the *Citation Index* (see Garfield 1988). We process every work that is cited. We don't process most books as sources but thousands are cited in the *Citation Index*.

Georghiou: I would like to raise a point that straddles the methodology and the policy implications of John Irvine's work. To make a comparison one needs a homogeneous population; in your study the universities are homogeneous in that they all want UGC funding and are competing for that resource. I am sure every study would show your top ranked university coming out first, second or third, but the policy debate is really about the top 12 or 15 universities. I wonder whether it's desirable for these institutions to be homogeneous, even in research terms, not just at the research/teaching divide. The ex-Colleges of Advanced Technology would probably argue that their objective is to further technological development, perhaps on a local and regional basis. Industrial funding is not the sole indicator of that. Perhaps more importantly, those departments that come under the label of, say, physics, are not all homogeneous; they do different things. A case study was made of a department that changed from specializing in acoustics to solid-state physics. Their citation performance soared, but that's probably because more people cite publications in that field and the department had a change of personnel. It's not necessarily that they were doing better work. That is a longitudinal comparison, but one has to get behind these data, and perhaps more in the way that the UGC is going about it, before drawing any policy implications.

Irvine: Bibliometric data of the sort I presented should never be used as the sole basis for judging the performance of universities. They are intended purely as an input to and a check on peer review decisions. You are right about the need to take into account the divergent roles in the R&D system of different types of universities. When we extend our study to all UK institutions, we shall analyse separately the performance of the large civic universities, smaller civic universities, 'red bricks', technological universities, and the more specialized institutions within collegiate universities like London. Academic research policy should certainly take into account the fact that universities are not homogeneous. It was intrinsically unfair for the UGC to compare the technological universities directly with the large civic universities because they have different functions. This is also why I compared a set of reasonably similar institutions in my paper.

Pavitt: I would like to make a plea for dynamic analysis as the next step in this study. Twenty years ago it was being debated whether big is beautiful (Galbraith) or small is beautiful (Schumacher) for productivity in making innovations. So one collected data and saw that in some sectors big was beautiful, and therefore one advocated mergers. But this got the dynamics wrong, because very often firms are big because they are good, rather than good because they are big. Understanding this dynamic process is important, but the discussion here is naive on this subject. That's why I dislike the word 'restructuring'; I don't know what it means. I want to understand how it's come about that we have some universities that are good in all fields, some that are good in some fields, and some that are not good in any fields. We need longitudinal data on this and we must model it. The structural evolution over time of academic institutions and research laboratories in universities has been sadly neglected by the policy community and by the sociologists of science, and it's an issue that needs to be developed.

Irvine: You are right, but this is the first time that comprehensive bibliometric data have been produced for the UK. They cover only the period 1983/84 and therefore do not allow time-series analysis. Although it would be interesting to undertake dynamic structural analyses of the academic system, we have to begin by answering the simpler questions. Certainly, there are many lessons we could draw from technology policy studies. However, I note that you have not yet made any systematic study of the validity and meaning of patent indicators!

Pavitt: Yes, I have!

Anderson: John, your conclusion was that the ABRC model was right and the UGC model was wrong.

Irvine: Yes, that seems likely.

Anderson: And then you also concluded that the research performance of the universities you looked at was due to synergy between their respective departments. I don't think you can say that from your data. To see whether the UGC model is right we need to extend your methodology and look at individual departments. What are the possibilities of going in that direction?

Irvine: As we have heard, several studies are under way or planned which focus on departmental performance. The UGC is engaged in exploratory studies in which all academic departments in certain fields are being asked to submit publication lists which will then be analysed in various ways. Citation studies may then be done; it will be interesting to compare the results to those of the evaluations by the UGC's committees. In The Netherlands, Tony van Raan is planning a comprehensive study of all academic departments which will begin with the SCI *Corporate Index* and then enlist the help of universities to classify publications by field and department and to identify missing papers. It would be worth doing a similar study in the UK, and the Science Policy Research Unit (SPRU) has submitted a proposal to do precisely this.

As for the bibliometric profiles study, a lot of work remains to be done to explain the factors underlying the pattern of institutional research performance and draw firm policy conclusions. Nevertheless, I would maintain that institutional comparisons at the level of main fields are adequate to explore the respective merits of the UGC and ABRC models, especially since the differences between universities are so great.

Georghiou: One of the main arguments in support of inter-departmental synergy comes from equipment sharing. At PREST (Programme of Policy Research in Engineering, Science and Technology) we are investigating this for

the ABRC by making a census of all scientific equipment and collecting
detailed information on those who use it. It will be fascinating to combine our
data with yours and to relate output to capital intensiveness in science. I can say
already that your top technical university has at least five times as many
instruments as the lowest five institutions.

Garfield: Certain university departments in the USA were closed down,
even though they were doing well in terms of research, because they were not
attracting enough students. The staff doing research went elsewhere.

The Roose–Andersen studies (1970) looked at 50 typical departments in 100
US universities. Each department was asked to rank every other department in
the same specialty. Subsequently, those studies were repeated by the National
Research Council (1982). They used SCI source data to identify each department's publications. Then they matched the peer judgements against rankings
based on publication productivity. It was Warren Hagstrom's study (1971) that
convinced us that citation data showed something significant and usually
seemed to correlate very well with peer review.

Narin: We did a bibliometric comparison with the Roose–Andersen and
National Research Council studies. It was done at a very aggregate level—
physics, chemistry and biochemistry—and not at a departmental level. The
correlations are quite good, varying from 0.6 or 0.7 to 0.9 or higher for a large
central field such as physics, where the literature is reasonably well defined.
What is evaluated when departments are given a ranking? We compared the
ranking of departments assigned by the Roose–Andersen study and that produced by bibliometrics, based again on the same general classification (Anderson et al 1978). Peer review gave a higher internal correlation between rankings: the peer review score for physics at the University of Chicago was much
closer to the peer review rankings for mathematics and chemistry at that
university than if mathematics, physics and chemistry were ranked bibliometrically. Thus there is a 'halo' effect in the peer review.

Irvine: That is an important point, because funding decisions in the UK have
been strongly influenced by the UGC rankings. Departments have been heavily cut as a result of committee judgements made in some cases on the basis of
rather limited information. The key question is: would such UGC decisions
have been improved by access to the sort of bibliometric data I have presented?
I would answer yes, even though the data are technically limited and the
method needs further development.

Moravcsik: For the peer review rankings of US university science departments in the last 20 years (e.g. Cartter 1965, Roose–Andersen 1970), my
recollection is that the uniformity—universities are good in all fields or poor in
all fields—that you found in the UK was not found in the US. Thus one
university science department could be, say, 20th out of 110 whereas another
science department in the same university was ranked 50th.

Narin: But overall those rankings across departments were closer when done by peers than when based on publications.

Moravcsik: Yes; the publication studies probably give even more disparate results. That's different from what John finds in the UK.

Irvine: My guess is that a limited number of US universities are strong across all fields. There are probably only four or five such institutions in Britain.

Pavitt: You don't have to worry about them. That's the problem.

Garfield: Why did you leave out the social sciences in your study of the technical universities?

Irvine: The technical universities are primarily oriented to research in the physical sciences and engineering. More importantly, basic questions remain about the validity of using bibliometric techniques in the social sciences. Problems are likely to exist with coverage, because much research in the field is published in book form whereas the *Social Sciences Citation Index* mainly covers journals. It is also much more Anglo-Saxon biased than the *Science Citation Index*, which raises problems for international comparison.

Blume: Whereas in some countries, including the UK, the USA and Japan, there's an *a priori* assumption of a rank order of universities; in many other European countries, including Germany, Scandinavia and The Netherlands, such an idea does not exist. These assumptions structure the policy questions. Thus the question of how to target resources more effectively towards places where good research is being done emerges in a different way when there is no assumption of hierarchy. For example, in The Netherlands there is a scheme called the 'conditional financing of research'. The same underlying policy objective—better deployment of resources—took the form of saying that universities had to enter into research agreements with the Minister. They had to put forward programmes of work of certain magnitudes within certain fields, and broadly define five-year programmes which involved large groups of people on a scale that could be discussed at a policy level (also in Parliament). On the basis of an external peer group assessment of these large programmes, a university could earn back part of its block grant. This scheme has now been operating for five years and we have been following it under contract to the Ministry (Blume & Spaapen 1988, see also Spaapen et al 1988). I do not wish to focus on what happened, but rather to make the point that there's nothing sacrosanct about the step that precedes John's analysis. In The Netherlands and in Germany, you would tend to carry out a different analysis because you would not be making the same original assumption. There is nevertheless the same underlying wish to improve the use of resources.

Montigny: I agree. In France, for example, there is officially no difference between the universities, even though newspapers (like *Le Monde*) try each year to classify them. In France young people have no choice: they have to go to the university in their region. That is why the questions you are addressing here in Britain are not the same as the ones we face in France. This helps to explain differences between the use of bibliometrics in the UK and in countries like France and Germany.

van Raan: It's true that in Germany and in The Netherlands there is no formal difference in status between the universities. But, for example, universities in Germany are now ranked on the basis of the number of special grants (Sonderforschungsbereiche) from the German Research Council. This gives another approach to the ranking of universities. So the discussion on differences between universities does take place. This is unavoidable because the number of universities in many countries, including Germany, has increased greatly in the last 20 years.

Weinberg: The issues we are discussing make sense in so far as decisions on the allocation of resources are based on criteria of scientific and technical excellence. But as far as public policy is concerned, especially in a large country like the USA, the issue of geographical distribution is at least as important. I used to maintain, coming from the interior and, some would say, rather backward part of the United States, that the idea had grown up that the only places where good thinking on any subject could be done were places within sight of salt water! Texas has rather solved the problem by using oil money to buy excellent people from the North-eastern United States.

References

Anderson RC, Narin F, McAllister PR 1978 Publication ratings versus peer ratings of universities. Journal of the American Society for Information Science 29:2

Blume SS, Spaapen JB 1988 External assessment and 'conditional financing' of research in Dutch universities. Minerva 26:1–30

Cartter AM 1966 An assessment of quality in graduate education. American Council on Education, Washington DC

Garfield E 1988 The impact of citation counts. Times Higher Education Supplement. July 15, p 12

Hagstrom WO 1971 Inputs, outputs and the prestige of university science departments. Sociology of Education 44:375–397

National Research Council 1982 An assessment of research-doctorate programs in the United States: a series. National Academy Press, Washington DC

Roose KD, Andersen CJ 1970 A rating of graduate programs. American Council on Education, Washington DC

Spaapen JB, Vansuyt CAM, Prins AAM, Blume SS 1988 Evaluatie van Vijf Jaar Voorwaardelijke Financiering. The Hague, Ministry of Education and Sciences

van Raan AFJ (1989) Evaluation of research groups. In: The evaluation of scientific research. Wiley, Chichester (Ciba Foundation Conference) p 169–187

Evaluation of research groups

A. F. J. van Raan

Science Studies Unit, LISBON-Institute, University of Leiden, Stationsplein 242, 2312 AR Leiden, The Netherlands

Abstract. Research groups are, in many fields of science, the most important 'unit of action'. Therefore, evaluation of such groups is a crucial part of monitoring progress of science. There is no clear definition of a research group; its size may vary between one person and, say, 10 researchers. Research activities are characterized by a high coherence of research subjects and of collaboration; thus a group often represents a particular specialty or niche in its field of science.

Evaluation of research groups is, implicitly or explicitly, a well-established part of the scientific enterprise. 'Peer review' in different forms and on different levels (ranging from refereeing an individual publication to visiting committees or institutional self-evaluation procedures) often eventually acts as (part of a composite) evaluation of a group of scientists.

This paper focuses on the use of several quantitative methods and techniques to monitor research performance as a 'support system' for peer review and for research management. Distinction is made between 'micro-scale monitoring' of individual groups, and 'macro-scale monitoring' to put individual groups in the broader context of their scientific fields and subfields. Together, both monitors can provide a powerful tool for corporate planning in research organizations.

1989 The evaluation of scientific research. Wiley, Chichester (Ciba Foundation Conference) p 169–187

To a large extent, science is a 'self-evaluating' system. Scientific publications and contributions to conferences are not only meant to present research findings, but also to evoke comments, improvements, comparison with other work, etc. One can maintain that the continuous generation and application of knowledge automatically demands a permanent evaluation of the intermediate knowledge steps. Science is evaluation, to put it boldly. Furthermore, the infrastructure of science is also based on a continuous evaluation. In this respect, scientific organizations and institutions do not differ from other organizations or institutions that strive for optimal performance. In universities, research councils, institutes and laboratories a considerable amount of time is devoted to the evaluation of the scientific work of groups or individuals for appointments, promotions, grants, (honorary) degrees, prizes and awards, acceptance of publications, etc.

I shall refer to the self-evaluating character of science as 'cognitive evaluation' to avoid confusion with institutional self-evaluation procedures. Cognitive and infrastructural evaluation are strongly interrelated and these concepts partly overlap. This is, for example, obvious in the review of research proposals and of articles submitted for publication. This paper primarily addresses infrastructural evaluation. Strictly speaking, evaluation means an analysis of the extent to which activities have reached earlier specified goals (Gibbons 1984). Often, however, 'evaluation' is used to indicate an analysis of past or ongoing performance, on various levels of aggregation, in different contexts and for different purposes, without a specific assessment of goal-attainment. In fact, the 'quality' of past or ongoing work as such is the object of analysis, and the process is more accurately described by 'monitoring'. However, often there is no clear division between evaluation in the strict sense and monitoring (Luukkonen-Gronow 1987) and therefore I shall use both terms interchangeably.

The evaluation of scientific activities lies, almost by definition, in the hands of the scientists themselves, the peers. This is a well-established system and it is crucial to all aspects of the scientific enterprise. Why then the rapid increase of interest in the evaluation of research? I shall not dwell on this important question here: much has been already said and discussions on this point are still going on. I therefore refer, for example, to the work of Luukkonen-Gronow (1987) and the references therein, and to other contributions to this conference. I shall just mention a few important reasons for the increasing demand for evaluation. First, there are problems with the peer review system, especially when budgets are hardly increasing or even decreasing, when an assessment of social or economic relevance is required, and in the judgement of inter-disciplinary research. A second reason is the necessity for 'accountability', often at the macro-level. For example, a Minister of Education and Science has to defend his budget for research against the many other needs in society.

I shall focus attention on the assessment of scientific performance of research groups at a level just above the researchers, e.g. by the board of a research institute, the board of a faculty, or the board of a disciplinary research council — briefly, research evaluation as part of the management of an institute or of a discipline within a research organization. I think this is the most important form of research evaluation because it is most close to the daily, current work of scientists. Here peer review is a central method of evaluation, but it can take different forms, for example 'institutional self-evaluation' by 'in-house' research committees, evaluation by external visiting committees or a combination of both.

What are the main issues of research performance assessment by peer review? In fact there is only one: the judgement of the competence of a group or of an individual scientist to perform high-quality research. This is a very general formulation. Therefore, I distinguish the following aspects. The prerequisite is a 'basic competence', i.e. soundness of craftsmanship and a reasonable productivity. The next aspect is the choice of scientific problems: are they original, innovative?; do they have 'synthetic' capacities (to mention the high-quality side of the spectrum)? Furthermore, the choice of scientific methods and techniques is important; are they well-chosen and promising? Finally, consider the efficiency of the work: is the work done in a reasonable time-scale?

What are the flaws of the peer review system directly concerning these aspects of performance assessment? Peers can be partial, favouring more 'visible' scientists, protecting old and possibly declining fields in order to defend their colleagues. They can differ in their assessments of new emerging fields of research. They might find it difficult to assess research in the context of social and economic needs (see, for example, King 1987). Various studies have found evidence for these flaws, but the interpretations of the results of these studies differ and the peer review system has not been proven obsolete in any way.

Accepting peer review as the core process of scientific research evaluation, but also admitting the flaws in the process and the external pressures of accountability, we must conclude that the peer review system requires support by more objective data. In my opinion, this support can be given by quantitative, bibliometric indicators that should both be sophisticated and contain a sufficient variety of information. In this paper I shall discuss the use of bibliometric (i.e. publication and citation-based) 'micro-scale' indicators to monitor the performance of research groups, and of 'macro-scale' indicators to position a group or institute in a 'map' of the scientific field(s) concerned.

Micro-scale monitoring by bibliometric indicators

Basic method and techniques

Here I shall review some of our earlier as well as more recent experiences with research performance indicators, based on bibliometric data applied to research groups within a university. The research performances of groups in two large faculties of the University of Leiden (Faculty of Mathematics and Natural Sciences, and the Faculty of Medicine) have been analysed for a long period of time (1970–1983, partly updated until 1987) using data on international publications (about 10 000) and citations to these publications (about 80 000). These two faculties cover many fields and subfields within the disciplines of mathematics, physics, astronomy, chemistry, biology, pharmacy, clinical and non-clinical medicine. As far as I know, such a detailed 'micro-scale' monitoring (about 100 research groups involved) is unique. An extensive and detailed presentation of this work (the Leiden Science Indicators Project) was given by Moed et al (1983, 1985) and, in a follow-up study, by Moed & van Raan (1988a).

The core of this work was an investigation of the possibilities for and the constraints on the development of research performance indicators based on quantitative data from scientific literature, in particular in the natural and life

sciences. An important presupposition here is that results of scientific work are
published in the serial literature (primarily journals). This can be an inaccurate
assumption for applied fields of science, and for the humanities and social
sciences. In these fields, books, reports, 'grey literature', or even 'products'
are commonly regarded as important carriers of research results. However, work
by our group shows that for the applied and engineering sciences, as well as
for the humanities and the social sciences, international journals and conference
proceedings (often published as a special journal issue) do play an important
role in the dissemination of knowledge (chemical engineering, see Peters et al
1988; electrical engineering and electronics, see van Vianen et al 1988; linguistics,
literature, social history, anthropology, public administration, and psychology,
see Nederhof et al 1988). From these studies we learned that the applicability
of bibliometric data has to be investigated carefully for each field of science.
Large differences in applicability emerge, even within disciplines. This is also
true for the (basic) natural and life sciences. In general, as a good first
approximation, one may say that the applicability of bibliometric indicators
for a specific field of science strongly depends upon the extent to which
publication databases and, more particularly, citation databases cover the
communication channels used by researchers in that field.

   We return to the Leiden Science Indicators. Two important concepts play
a central role: scientific production or output, measured by the number (and
type) of publications; and scientific impact (considered to be an important and
'measurable' aspect of 'scientific quality'; see Moed et al 1983), measured by
the number of citations received by publications within a certain period of time.
We make a distinction between short-term impact (citations counted in the first
three years after publication) and long-term impact. The necessary data were
obtained from the *Science Citation Index* (SCI) of the Institute for Scientific
Information (ISI), Philadelphia. Data-handling was mostly computerized using
specially developed software.

   Figure 1A shows the indicators used in this study. Curve (a) represents the
number of publications in international journals (as far as covered by the ISI);
curve (b) indicates the number of citations received by these publications in the
first three years after publication ('short-term citation window'). We excluded
'in-house citations', i.e. citations given by members of the same research group.
For example, the numerical value for curve (b) in the year 1978 is the number
of 'external' citations for all 1978 publications of the group received in the years
1978, 1979, and 1980. Thus, Fig. 1A presents a trend indicator of a group's
scientific production and its short-term impact. Beside trends, a reference with
respect to the impact level is necessary. We compared the actual citation per
publication ratio of a group with the 'expected' ratio, i.e. the average citation
score per publication for the journals in which the group publishes. We assume
that this comparison of actual and expected impact provides, at least as a first

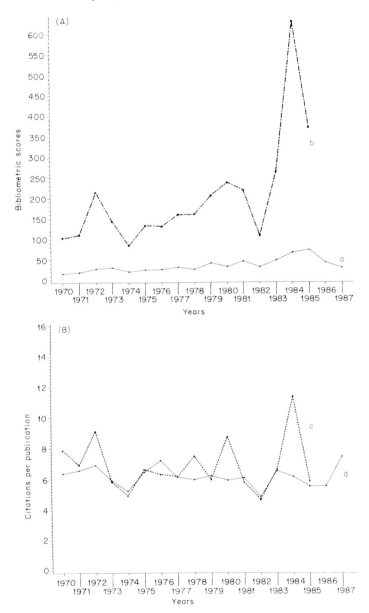

FIG. 1. Bibliometric indicators of a research group. A. Curve (a), number of publications (production); curve (b), number of short-term citations (short-term impact). B. Curve (c), actual (short-term) impact per publication; curve (d), expected (short-term) impact per publication.

approximation, a reasonable indicator of the international impact of a research group. Fig. 1B shows this type of analysis, for the same group as in Fig. 1A and for the same period of time (for details see Moed et al 1983, 1985).

Possible use of micro-scale indicators

What can we learn from these indicators, in particular to support peer review? First, there is no doubt that the indicators (assuming adequate coverage of communication channels) give a good impression of 'basic competence'. Together with their own knowledge of the general publication practices in a field and acquaintance with the infrastructural characteristics (like size) of the group(s) concerned, peers now have comprehensive information on a group's productivity and impact as a function of time and compared with a reasonable international impact reference; they can judge whether there is at least a 'sufficient' form of activity in these terms.

If the observed value of impact per publication is higher than the expected value (as is the case in Fig. 1B), the peers must diagnose the reasons for this: is it because the group continues to work on new, innovative research topics; or do they produce, in a well-established field, important data with specific methods and techniques? Furthermore, if the short-term impact (absolute numbers) rapidly increases in a recent period (as is the case in Fig. 1A), the peers are confronted with possibly very influential recent work consolidating the previous above-average international performance.

This is an example of the way peers involved in institutional research management can use our 'micro-scale' monitor in their assessment of research performance. The year-by-year displays make it possible to identify successful publication years and it is a challenge, from the viewpoint of research management, to relate these findings with excellent PhD work, appointments of new professors and senior researchers, or, indeed, the start of pioneering scientific work. For instance, the strong involvement of the Leiden Department of Astronomy in the international IRAS (Infra-Red Astronomical Satellite) programme and their successful elaboration and explanation of the enormous amount of observational data was visible in their indicators display ('Fig. 1A-type' display).

In the 'Fig. 1B-type' display, the year-by-year registration of the observed versus expected impact per publication enables us to investigate the influence of the chosen journals on the obtained impact. The often strikingly similar forms of the observed impact and expected impact curves reveal that this influence is indeed quite strong. Therefore, the choice of journals is crucial for the obtained impact value. This does not mean, however, that we can simply replace the obtained impact (the analysis of which is, no doubt, the most labour-intensive aspect of the work) by the expected values based on journal impact. Although the forms of the actual and expected impact curves might be similar, the important point is the difference in absolute values between the actual and the expected impact. This difference gives an indication of the impact level as compared to an international average.

Instead of a year-by-year display of the bibliometric data, we can use successive and partly overlapping four-year averages on the time axis, which gives a more smooth impression of the impact trends as a function of time. This makes it easier to study the influence of the chosen 'citation window'. As discussed, we use in our bibliometric analysis the short-term impact (citations are counted in the three-year period after publication, taking publication year as 0; we indicate this short-term citation window as [0,2]). It is, however, important to investigate what differences may occur when using other citation windows.

In Fig. 2A we compare, for the same research group as presented in Fig. 1, the impact trends for citation window [0,2] (the 'standard' short-term), and citation window [3,4] (i.e. counting citations on a longer term neglecting the short-term counts) (Moed & van Raan 1988b). There is a clear difference in absolute values. The simple explanation is that most publications in this field receive an increasing number of citations until the second or third year after publication, whereas in later years the number of citations decreases. The most striking observation is that there is no significant difference in the form of the impact trends given by the two different citation windows. We also observed this phenomenon for other groups. This means that we shall find the same impact trend for different citation windows and thus we can confine our attention to the short-term impact.

However, there can be exceptions, as shown in Fig. 2B. This is an interesting and important finding: as measured on the short-term, the group shows a continuously decreasing impact (after an important discovery at the end of the sixties). However, measuring the impact on the longer and somewhat 'delayed' term (citation window [3,4]), we see after an initial decrease a 'revival' in more recent years. It is clear that a simple citation analysis would never have revealed these subtleties. Such subtleties help us to understand important aspects of the research performance of this group, which are also not immediately obvious to peers or even to the researchers concerned. What are these aspects? We arrived at the following explanation after discussions with senior researchers in the group (within the field of experimental molecular physics). After the important discovery at the end of the sixties, the group continued their work with further refined and increasingly difficult experiments, and by doing so it established almost a world monopoly in this research. The interest of other experimental physicists flagged, resulting in a decrease in short-term impact. After some time, the experimental results became increasingly important for theoretical physicists. Their 'response time', however, is longer, in general, than for experimentalists

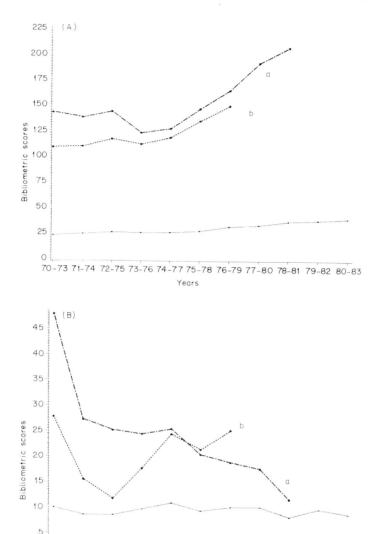

FIG. 2.   Short-term impact compared to longer-term impact. A. For the same research group as in Fig. 1: curve (a), short-term impact (citation window [0,2]); curve (b), longer-term impact (citation window [3,4]); solid line, number of publications. B. For another research group: curve (a), short-term impact (citation window [0,2]); curve (b), longer-term impact (citation window [3,4]); solid line, number of publications.

and this explains the recent increase in longer-term impact. We are verifying this *prima vista* explanation by carefully analysing the lists of citing papers for the whole period of time, and our preliminary findings confirm it.

The important methodological conclusion of this study is that there can be no question of a strict validation of quantitative (bibliometric) indicators over qualitative findings. In fact, the method has an interactive character. But this is precisely what can be expected from a monitoring system that is useful as a support for peer review. We have discussed the potential of our bibliometric 'micro-scale' monitoring system as a tool for institutional research management. In our opinion, it is a valuable tool. Much work was done to reach a level of sophisticated computerized data-handling. Therefore, further work can now be done at a reasonable cost. We are preparing to 'Netherlandize' the method, i.e. to extend our method from application to only one university (Leiden) to all universities in The Netherlands. Then, 'micro-scale monitoring on a macro scale' will have some interesting policy-relevant results. First, each university will be able to identify its strengths and weaknesses in a cross-disciplinary survey. Second, taking the results field-by-field, strengths and weaknesses within a field will become visible on a national level. Here the research councils for each discipline can use these results for their 'corporate planning'.

Macro-scale monitoring of research performance

Mapping of science: the state-of-the-art and problems

In this section I discuss the possibilities of monitoring the position of research groups in a broader context. With this I do not mean the 'micro-scale monitoring on a macro scale' (the 'Netherlandizing'), but methods and techniques to display the position of a research group on a 'map' of its field or discipline.

Several techniques have been developed to construct maps of scientific fields. Essentially, all these techniques are based on co-occurrences of particular items in specific sources, e.g. published material. Such items are, for example, references or words in publications (co-citation or co-word relations, respectively) but also field classification codes assigned to the publications (co-subfield relations), authors (co-author relations) or journals (journal-to-journal citation relations). Co-occurrences of items from a sufficiently large set of sources yield linkages between these items (e.g. arranged in a large matrix). With cluster analysis or other data-analytical techniques, these structural relations can be displayed in two-dimensional space. Not only are co-occurrences between similar items possible: 'hybrid' co-occurrences of different items like author-to-subfield or journal-to-subfield also yield artificial 'maps' (Peters et al 1988, van Raan & Peters 1988). The interesting question is what all these pictures mean, how they relate to each other, and how they can be applied. The two major (bibliometric) mapping techniques are co-citation and co-word analysis. Their applicability in science policy and research management are central themes in the development of these techniques.

Pioneering work in co-citation analysis was done by Small and co-workers. For discussions, primarily on methods and techniques, see Small & Sweeney (1985) and Small et al (1985). In co-word analysis the group of Callon, Turner & Courtial in Paris did the pioneering work (Callon et al 1986). For discussion of the applications of mapping techniques, see Healey et al (1986), Hicks (1987) (especially on co-citation analysis) and various contributions in van Raan (1988), in particular chapters by Rip (general problems of 'science mapping'), Franklin & Johnston, Weingart et al, and Oberski on co-citation analysis, and Turner et al on co-word analysis. The two major problems in the mapping of science are cognitive (interpretation, meaning) on the one hand, and methodological/ technical, on the other hand. They are strongly related: substantial improvement of methods and techniques might enhance the cognitive value of the maps. A striking example is the development of scientific fields as a function of time. As yet, mapping techniques do not allow for a reliable 'linkage' of maps from successive periods of time. In other words, the static pictures cannot be combined into an acceptable 'movie'. Even the single, static pictures (maps) still have large methodological problems: stability of the calculated clusters with respect to (small) variations of threshold values; significance versus 'noise'; and, not least, the degree to which the field(s) concerned are representative.

Improvements to put research groups on the map

In our group we are currently developing an extensive programme on the mapping of science, with a variety of methodological approaches as well as different data-analytical techniques. First, we succeeded in a substantial improvement of co-citation analysis by a combination of data from different databases. In this 'combi-approach' we collected from *Chemical Abstracts* all publications (about 3500 worldwide) of one year (1985) for the field of agricultural biochemistry. Then we collected the references (i.e. cited articles, about 55 000) cited in these 'source' publications. With these references we performed a co-citation analysis (Braam et al 1988a,b). The resulting co-citation 'clusters' consist of a 'core' which is a structure of linked co-cited pairs of papers (cited articles), surrounded by a 'cloud' of (source) publications citing (one of) these core papers. We found that only 14% of the original source publications appeared as (citing) publications in the co-citation clusters. In other words, 86% of the original source 'disappeared' in the analysis. This illustrates an application problem, in particular for small or medium-size countries (like The Netherlands) and, *a fortiori*, for institutes or groups. Their 'shares' in the different clusters are, generally, so low that it is not possible to find their participation in a field of science as represented by the co-citation map.

Because our source publications were collected from *Chemical Abstracts*, we were able to compare keywords of the 14% 'involved' publications with those of the remaining 86%. A word-similarity analysis allowed us to extend the co-citation clusters by approximately a factor of four. This substantial increase of 'cluster participation' considerably improves the ability to monitor the role of institutes or groups. Furthermore, the word-similarity analysis appears to be a powerful tool to test the significance of the co-citation cluster composition and stability (Braam et al 1988b). We are improving the 'combi-approach' and expect to have first results on the 'macro-scale mapping of groups' with this technique soon.

A second important part of our work on mapping of science concerns a project on chemical engineering. As well as explorations of mapping by journal-to-journal citation analysis, journal-to-subfield analysis, and co-subfield analysis (Peters et al 1988, van Raan & Peters 1988), we performed a co-word analysis on a database (CILO) of Dutch chemical engineering research projects. From the records in this database, we compiled all keywords, field classification codes, and institutional affiliations. A large data matrix represents all possible co-occurrences of these items. Then submatrices around specific items can be analysed by appropriate data-analytical techniques. As an example, the submatrix with 'water purification' as the central item is shown (Fig. 3). We see a co-word display picturing all keywords, classification codes, and institutes that are related to water purification. We see the position of several university departments (Delft, Health Technology, Chemical Technology; Enschede, Inorganic Chemistry) in relation to specific subfields like fluidized-bed combustion, environmental health, flocculation, and, more remote, refrigeration machines. Although these results are preliminary, we think this method is in principle a powerful tool to display specific parts of large databases or information systems, in particular the position of groups in their 'scientific' context. This is especially helpful for interdisciplinary fields.

Another possible way to monitor the position of research groups is author(group)-to-subfield analysis. As an example, we analysed the position of 14 outstanding chemical engineering research groups in different countries. We collected from *Chemical Abstracts* all publications of the 14 groups in the period 1977–1986 (about 700) and put the number of times publications were assigned to a specific *Chemical Abstract* section (subfield) in a group-by-subfield matrix. With correspondence analysis (Tijssen et al 1988) we displayed this matrix in two-dimensional space, as shown in Fig. 4. From this figure we see that the groups FR and SA are active in, for example, subfields 51 (fossil fuels, derivatives, and related products), 22 (physical organic chemistry), and 67 (catalysis, reaction kinetics, and inorganic reaction mechanisms). The core subfield of chemical engineering is 48 (unit operations and processes) and we see that most of the 14 groups are concentrated around this subfield. This

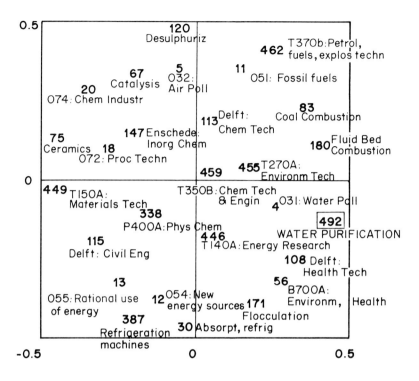

FIG. 3.   Co-word analysis on the Dutch CILO Database for Chemical Engineering, Subfield Water Purification. The map is constructed with the multi-dimensional scaling programme SMACOF. Boldface numbers are codes from our computer programme; they mark the position of the indicated items. These items are (see text): research subfields, according to the NABS classification (e.g. 074) or to the ISN classification (e.g. T350b); keywords (e.g. Coal Combustion); or affiliations (institutes, departments, e.g. Delft Chem Tech).

technique, however, clearly focuses on activities of research groups outside the core subfield of chemical engineering.

These techniques are useful to find the positions of groups in the context of their disciplines. They are, however, at an early stage of development; further work is in progress to improve the applicability of the techniques.

Conclusions

We have discussed the potential of quantitative (bibliometric) indicators as a support for the evaluation of research groups by peer review as part of institutional or organizational management. We distinguished methods and

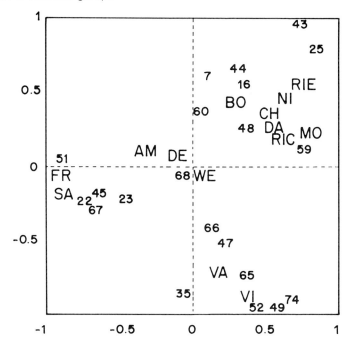

FIG. 4. Group-by-subfield analysis in chemical engineering (Map constructed with correspondence analysis, two-dimensional solution; 60.1% variance accounted for). Bold numbers, *Chemical Abstract* sections (subfields); letters, groups. See text for examples.

techniques to monitor the performance of individual research groups ('micro-scale monitoring') as well as methods and techniques to monitor the position of research groups in their disciplinary or, if necessary, their interdisciplinary context ('macro-scale monitoring'). Quantitative indicators can be used as tools for research evaluation by peers, provided that they are sufficiently sophisticated and that they can offer a variety of relevant data. We presented a number of applicable methods and techniques that form together an information system of composite indicators which might improve the assessment of research performance by peer review. Whilst micro-scale monitoring is fairly well-developed, macro-scale monitoring of research groups is still at an early stage of development.

It is important to stress that these quantitative indicators should not be used by non-peers, for example officers of university executive boards or of ministries. This is because interpretation of these indicators needs an 'interaction' between the data provided by these indicators and background knowledge. This situation can be compared, to a large extent, with the use of medical expert systems by physicians.

Acknowledgements

Special thanks are due to my colleagues Henk Moed, for discussions and carrying out the citation analysis with the different 'windows', and Robert Tijssen for analysing data with special data-analytical techniques.

References

Braam RR, Moed HF, van Raan AFJ 1988a Mapping of science: critical elaboration and new approaches. A case study in agricultural biochemistry. In: Egghe L, Rousseau R (eds) Informetrics 87/88. Elsevier Science Publishers, Amsterdam, p 15–28

Braam RR, Moed HF, van Raan AFJ 1988b Mapping research specialties and their interrelations: a combined co-citation and word analysis of chemoreception. ECRO (European Chemoreception Research Organization) Newsletter No. 30, p 360–363

Callon M, Law J, Rip A (eds) 1986 Mapping the dynamics of science and technology. MacMillan Press Ltd, London

Franklin JJ, Johnston R 1988 Co-citation bibliometric modeling as a tool for science & technology and research & development: issues, applications, and developments. In: van Raan AFJ (ed) Handbook of quantitative studies of science and technology. Elsevier Science Publishers, Amsterdam, p 325–389

Gibbons M 1984 Methods for the evaluation of research. OECD, IMHE Program, Paris

Healey P, Rothman H, Hoch PH 1986 An experiment in science mapping for research planning. Research Policy 15:233–251

Hicks D 1987 Limitations of co-citation analysis as a tool for science policy. Social Studies of Science 17:295–316

King J 1987 A review of bibliometric and other science indicators and their role in research evaluation. Journal of Information Science 13:261–276

Luukkonen-Gronow T 1987 Scientific research evaluation: a review of methods and various contexts of their application. R&D Management 17:207–221

Moed HF, van Raan AFJ 1988a Indicators of research performance: applications in university research policy. In: van Raan AFJ (ed) Handbook of quantitative studies of science and technology. Elsevier Science Publishers, Amsterdam, p 177–192

Moed HF, van Raan AFJ 1988b, to be published

Moed HF, Burger WJM, Frankfort JG, van Raan AFJ 1983 On the measurement of research performance: the use of bibliometric indicators. Science Studies Unit, University of Leiden

Moed HF, Burger WJM, Frankfort JG, van Raan AFJ 1985 The use of bibliometric data or the measurement of university research performance. Research Policy 14:131–149

Nederhof AJ, Zwaan RA, De Bruin RE, Dekker PJ 1988 Assessing the usefulness of bibliometric indicators in the humanities and the social sciences: a comparative study. Scientometrics, in press

Oberski J 1988 Some statistical aspects of co-citation cluster analysis and a judgment in physicists. In: van Raan AFJ (ed) Handbook of quantitative studies of science and technlogy. Elsevier Science Publishers, Amsterdam, p 431–462

Peters HPF, Hartmann D, van Raan AFJ 1988 Monitoring advances in chemical engineering. In: Egghe L, Rousseau R (eds) Informetrics 87/88. Elsevier Science Publishers, Amsterdam, p 175–195

Rip A 1988 Mapping of science: possibilities and limitations. In: van Raan AFJ (ed) Handbook of quantitative studies of social science and technology. Elsevier Science Publishers, Amsterdam, p 253–273

Small H, Sweeney E 1985 Clustering the science citation index using co-citations, I: a comparison of methods. Scientometrics 7:393–404

Small H, Sweeney E, Greenlee E 1985 Clustering the science citation index using co-citations, II: mapping science. Scientometrics 8:321–340

Tijssen RJW, De Leeuw J, van Raan AFJ 1988 A method for mapping bibliometric relations based on field-classifications and citations of articles. In: Egghe L, Rousseau R (eds) Informetrics 87/88. Elsevier Science Publishers, Amsterdam, p 279–292

Turner WA, Chartron G, Laville F, Michelet B 1988 Packaging information for peer review: new co-word analysis techniques. In: van Raan AFJ (ed) Handbook of quantitative studies of science and technology. Elsevier Science Publishers, Amsterdam, p 291–323

van Raan AFJ 1988 Handbook of quantitative studies of science and technology. Elsevier Science Publishers, Amsterdam.

van Raan AFJ, Peters HPF 1988 Dynamics of a scientific field analysed by co-subfield structures. Scientometrics, in press

van Vianen BG, Wachmann L, van Raan AFJ 1988 The role of quantitative indicators in the assessment of electrical engineering research. Research report to the Netherlands Advisory Council for Science Policy. Research Report SSU-88-07. Science Studies Unit, University of Leiden

Weingart P, Winterhager M, Sehringer R 1988 Bibliometric indicators for assessing strengths and weaknesses of West German science. In: van Raan AFJ (ed) Handbook of quantitative studies of science and technology. Elsevier Science Publishers, Amsterdam, p 391–430

DISCUSSION

Phillips: What is the meaning of the dimensions of the maps showing co-occurrence of items (eg. the co-word matrix, Fig. 3)?

van Raan: Sometimes dimensions are meaningless, as in a geographical map where the directions north–south and east–west have no specific meaning, other than their spatial meaning. But in other cases the dimensions indicate specific characteristics, as in factor analysis. An example is the two-dimemsional display of the citation relations of seven astronomy journals (see Tijssen et al 1987). We displayed this citation matrix with the quasi-correspondence technique. This is a special data-analytical technique in which the influence of the matrix diagonal is strongly reduced, and that's important in the journal-to-journal citation analysis because journal self-citation is the major citation traffic. In the resulting display, the horizontal dimension showed a division between European journals and American journals, and the vertical dimension a division between typical observational astronomy journals and the more physics-oriented astrophysical journals.

Thus, it is sometimes possible to explain the two dimensions, but there can also be a third or a fourth dimension. An example is the group-versus-subfield analysis (Fig. 4): 60% of the variance is accounted for in the first two dimensions, so 40% of the information is in the third and higher dimensions.

Anderson: Earlier, we heard about the possibility of measuring performance against the average citation score of scientific journals. Is there any theory about whether scientists publish in journals of the standard appropriate to their work? One could imagine a tactic of publishing in low grade journals so that even a few citations would pull the relative score above the average for the journal. This would obviously distort the data. Equally, one could, of course, improve one's absolute citation score by publishing in high impact journals. Have you looked at that?

van Raan: We have analysed about 150 research groups and the 'monitor pictures' were discussed with the project leaders of these groups. From the discussions a new field emerged—citation engineering! People observed that they could change their citation score by choosing better journals. In one of the examples I showed, the appointment of a new professor in one of the chemistry departments led to a great increase in the absolute number of citations. The reason for this was shown by the expected versus actual impact curves: the new professor changed the 'publication culture' of the research group by deciding to publish in journals with a higher average citation score. That worked almost immediately; you become more visible by choosing a journal with, generally speaking, a higher impact factor. But you always have to wait for the actual citation results and compare these with the expected values.

Anderson: There must be an optimization process. For groups with poor research performance, we found that no matter which journals they publish in they consistently attract a lower number of citations than the average for those journals. So were they optimizing their citation score or could they have done better if they had published in other journals? This must be studied if this bibliometric technique is to gain wider acceptance.

Luukkonen-Gronow: You have shown that if you use data based on longer time periods fluctuations in citation counts are not so evident. Nevertheless, citation data are always based on past performance and this may be a problem when they are used as a basis for the allocation of resources. Although there is a high correspondence between the past and future performances of research groups, there are some discrepancies. I am involved in a comparison of citation data and peer review on groups in the field of cardiovascular research in Norway and Finland (T. Luukkonen-Gronow, unpublished work 1988). The peer review assessments show that discrepancies, although rare, do exist. For example, one group that used to do excellent work has now gone in unwise directions, and a group that performed badly previously is now doing excellent work and has good plans for the future. If decisions are based on citation data alone, mistakes can be made. One should always combine peer assessment with the citation data, particularly when dealing with small units, such as research groups or individual scientists.

van Raan: That is why it's important to observe trends over a longer period. The minimum is, I would say, two 'generations' of PhD students, say eight years.

Luukkonen-Gronow: Is it possible to apply this to larger databases, such as that for all the universities in The Netherlands? Are you able to collect such detailed information for such a long period?

van Raan: Yes, that's part of our plan to 'Netherlandize' the Leiden Indicators Project. For the Leiden project we developed a large amount of software to handle many problems. One of the tools I described is 'co-author mapping', to give a first overview of the structure of a university. This technique allows us to assign about 50% of the papers to specific departments, but the remainder of the work must be done by the universities themselves and it takes time. For the study at the departmental level, you need help from the universities to check carefully the completeness of the publication lists, etc.

Irvine: The methodology that you have described stems from what might be termed your policy of 'scientometrics in one university'. You have been trying to develop an indirect technique to make imputed comparisons between the performance of groups in your university relative to a hypothetical norm based on journal publishing behaviour. However, if you compare the results of your analysis with studies of matched groups in other universities, you might discover some technical problems. For example, papers from some of the specialized Leiden groups may have a greater impact than the norm for the journals in which they are published because those specialties are characterized by high citation impact. Because this can only be established empirically, you may be introducing a statistical artefact into the comparison which could have major implications for university research policy. I would urge you, therefore, to identify some matched research groups against which you can make real comparisons, rather than using averages for journals.

Other criticisms I have heard Dutch scientists make of your methodology concern the definition of a 'group'. How does a group differ from a research collaboration, team, or laboratory, and are there any size constraints on the applicability of your methodology? Most importantly, how do you handle the difficult problem of groups working in two or more specialties?

Finally, I do not see why you need a complex co-word analysis to identify papers from a university. Why not just produce a listing of papers and ask the university to check completeness and to undertake the classification by department? This is much simpler, cheaper, and avoids the need for high technology.

van Raan: In answer to your point about specialized groups, the reverse is possible, and perhaps more likely. When you work in a rather exotic specialty, the number of people involved is small and the number of citations received will therefore be relatively low.

Irvine: That depends on the fundamentality of the area. Fundamental work may be cited by researchers in diverse fields and therefore the size of a specialty may not be important.

van Raan: But you cannot predict what will happen with a speciality and how fundamental it is or will become for other scientists. Finding matched groups is extremely difficult. When extending the method to other universities we can compare, for example, biochemistry groups in Leiden with biochemistry groups in Utrecht and study the characteristic differences or similarities. We plan to do such an investigation when we expand the method. I am sure new problems will arise.

The rationale behind 'co-author mapping' is that it enables us to study inter-group connections within a university. Researchers were interested in this map because it clearly showed the relationships with other groups; it provided a global view of the research structure of the university.

Anderson: In my paper (this volume), I showed that comparing three research groups which are matched with each other gives exactly the same pattern of performance as applying Tony's methodology. To some extent, this is a validation of Tony's approach.

However, getting publications lists from universities is not necessarily the best way of ensuring that you have the complete data. We checked this in our early work (unpublished) by comparing the *curricula vitae* and publications lists supplied by 600 scientists with lists generated from the hard copy *Science Citation Index* (SCI). We found that the SCI was more reliable than the authors' publication lists. Most of the scientists had an average of 80 to 90 publications over a 10 year period but they were often careless in compiling their bibliographies. Sometimes they even omitted important papers in journals like *Nature* and *Science*. When we asked some of the scientists why they had omitted these papers, they admitted that they had simply forgotten. On the other hand, the bibliographies may list papers in journals that the SCI does not cover. The discrepancy between the two sources is sometimes quite high.

Irvine: I was suggesting sending a provisional list to universities and asking them to do the departmental classification. This is rather different and seems unlikely to be open to major systematic error.

Anderson: Then you would get a heterogeneous classification; different groups might classify papers in different ways. You need a central system for classification and then you can do rational analysis on the data.

Hill: Scientists do not have complete control over where they publish. There is both a supply and a demand aspect, and the outcome depends on who will take your paper as well as on where you would like to put it.

All the discussion here has to do with averages of various measures, and yet scientists would claim that most of what is published isn't very valuable and that only a very few very important works really matter, at least in science, although perhaps not in engineering. Therefore, in looking at the quality of the department or the individual, what's important may not be the average citation performance but the citation performance of those few highly cited or very important papers. Has that been studied? Do the rankings differ when you focus on the citation performance of the very best work rather than the average work? Would that lead you to different conclusions about who really matters?

van Raan: That's why I present two monitor pictures. The upper graph in Fig. 1 is not an average at all. It's the absolute number of citations received by publications per year and has many peaks.

Hill: That's still integrated over all publications, yet it may be that one paper published in the ten-year period completely re-defined the field.

van Raan: It is not integrated over all publications; it is the citation score of the publications for that specific year. At the level of a research group, this number is relatively low. Thus, one very important publication receiving many citations (in the short-term period) will undoubtedly be clearly visible as a peak in our monitor picture. This phenomenon gives the very 'noisy' character of the upper half of the monitor pictures. The number of citations varies markedly per publication. Therefore it's dangerous to make 'snapshot' citation analysis in one year, or over just a few years, because you can have a year with a large peak followed by a year with a 'valley' in the citation performance.

References

Anderson J 1989 The evaluation of research training. In: The evaluation of scientific research. Wiley, Chichester (Ciba Foundation Conference) p 93–119

Tijssen RJW, De Leeuw J, Van Raan AFJ 1987 Quasi-correspondence analysis on scientiometric transaction matrices. Scientometrics 11:351–366

The contemporaneous assessment of a big science discipline

Michael J. Moravcsik

Institute of Theoretical Science, University of Oregon, Eugene, Oregon 97403, USA

Abstract. This paper discusses the contemporaneous assessment of a scientific discipline of the 'big science' type. Eleven indicators are proposed, of which some are methodological and some are based on the sociology of the scientific community. They pertain to the interaction of theory and experiment, to the cumulative nature of scientific research, to conceptual new ideas, to the non-mathematical initial motivation for new ideas, to unification of different subfields, to simplicity, to applicability, to tolerance within the scientific community, to a vigorous critique of the various current research directions, to aesthetic satisfaction, and to high morale. Ways of quantifying these criteria are discussed. It is suggested that the peer review system needs to include scientists from neighbouring disciplines. The pioneering work to experiment with such novel methods of assessment is best done by unofficial and flexible organizations.

1989 The evaluation of scientific research. Wiley, Chichester. (Ciba Foundation Conference) p 188–200

The evaluation of scientific research is called for and practised in many different situations. Often, units of scientific manpower are being assessed, such as individual scientists, research groups, research institutions, or whole countries. In such studies the disciplinary context is given and is kept fixed, and hence no deep epistemological problems arise. Furthermore, such assessments are usually only comparative ones.

The period of assessment may be in the past, in the present (contemporaneously), or in the future. The first type of assessment is the easiest, because in retrospect human factors play a less important role, and science can be effectively separated from the scientists involved in its development. Contemporaneous assessment is more difficult because the various human factors become intermixed with the elements of the scientific method itself. Nevertheless, contemporaneous assessment and assessment into the future form the backbone of science policy and management. For example, the awarding of research grants, the preparation of the budgets of large science support organizations, the assignment and promotion of scientists, and the selection of research directions to pursue in the near future all involve such contemporaneous assessment. The main problem with assessments in the present and in the future is that the scientific method, which in the long run promises to yield unambiguous results and works in a way that can be supported by consensus in the scientific community (i.e. is 'objective'), is seriously disturbed and interfered with in the short run.

Assessment of a 'big science' discipline

In this paper I wish to discuss an assessment that differs markedly from the customary types of assessment in that it deals not with individual scientists or groups of scientists, but with a whole research area, and this research area is of the 'big science' type. The task is made more difficult by the disciplinary context not being given or fixed. Indeed, that is what we evaluate. It is not sufficient to claim, for example, that applying bibliometrics provides quantitative indicators for such an assessment, because it is not only how much but also what we communicate that is under scrutiny. Thus substantive knowledge of the discipline to be assessed is needed to make the evaluation. Therefore, specialists in the discipline appear to be the only people capable of making the assessment but are also the people who are being assessed. Although the assessment is of a discipline, to the practitioners of that discipline it will appear that they themselves are the subject of the investigation.

Characteristics of big science

'Big science' refers to those areas of scientific investigation in which the research is very expensive, requires large and usually highly centralized installations, takes a long time to complete, and is carried out by large teams of people. I wish to show that these hallmarks of big science are interrelated and are merely symptoms of a unifying, underlying feature of big science.

At the beginning of modern science, some 400 years ago, the subjects of investigation were phenomena that could be observed directly with our human senses; little, if any, technology was needed for scientific research. At the same time, the technology of the period, also being made up of components easily perceivable by the human senses, could progress by the trial-and-error method and hence was not dependent on scientific knowledge.

In time, science turned increasingly to realms of nature remote from direct human experience. It dealt increasingly with very tiny or very large distances, with very short or very long times, or with very low or very high temperatures. It investigated phenomena that cannot be detected directly by human senses, such as most electromagnetic waves. Science has turned to atomic and then nuclear phenomena, and now to elementary particle physics. Science has turned to molecular biology, to very rapid chemical reactions, and to the cosmology of events that happened very quickly a very long time ago. To create these phenomena and to convert signals from these phenomena into something directly observable, we have to use elaborate technological devices; science has thus become increasingly dependent on technology. Equally, technology has also become dependent on science because technology no longer uses only experience from everyday life, but is based upon the laws of Nature scientifically discovered earlier. Thus the trial-and-error method no longer suffices: technology has become science-based.

These changes in the nature of scientific research have had important consequences for the very process of research. Because more elaborate technology is used, the specific cost of acquiring new scientific information is increasing faster than our resources, the size of a research team needed for a given scientific experiment grows by leaps and bounds, and the time needed to do such an experiment lengthens rapidly. There are corresponding problems on the theoretical side of science. It becomes increasingly difficult for the human mind to grasp the laws governing those distant realms of Nature, laws that are more and more drastically different from the laws governing the functioning of our brains.

These factors also alter (and in fact degrade) the sociology of scientific communities and the use of the scientific method. With respect to the latter, the great time delay in the interaction between theory and experiment allows theorists to dwell on incorrect theories too long, and means that too little guidance is provided for experimentalists. People whose enjoyment of science comes from creative individual efforts are discouraged from entering science, where they would be constrained to working in huge research teams for many years before gaining any opportunity for individual initiatives. In the absence of the regulative interchange of experiment and theory, persuasive and articulate scientists gain undue power in deciding the directions that research should take.

We can summarize the situation in these big science areas as a massive need for and accumulation of resources and manpower, combined with a distortion and temporary switching-off of those elements of the scientific method which in more 'normal' situations assure progress in science. Thus the various characteristics of big science are interrelated and they all follow from our attempt to probe Nature at increasing distances from the 'natural' range of human beings. We also see that this trend is inevitable. Clever ideas and developments can here and there delay science from getting 'bigger and bigger', but these temporary improvements are soon neutralized by our moving farther and farther away from the human scale.

If all this is correct, we are approaching the limits of perceptibility. That is, science is becoming more difficult and hence scientific progress becomes slower. We shall reach a limit beyond which practically no scientific progress will be possible, not because we shall have understood and explored everything, but because our capacity to generate progress will not match the difficulty of making further progress.

In many areas of science, these big science syndromes are not yet in evidence, but in areas such as high-energy physics, certain branches of astronomy, plasma physics and some areas of molecular biology the signs are beginning to be visible. These areas are manifestly already big science, and therefore present difficult challenges for someone wanting to evaluate science and, in particular, a scientific discipline.

All the evaluation and assessment methods we use in areas which are not big science are based, to various degrees, on the scientific method itself. For an annotated bibliography on measurement of research output, see Daniel & Fisch (1986). But the operation of the scientific method is distorted, impeded, delayed and degraded in the big science areas, making assessment more difficult. Yet the need for assessment has never been greater. Because big science strains our resource base, demands a growing share of our scientific manpower, and employs some of the best brains, it requires particularly thoughtful and thorough assessment. The practitioners of these big science disciplines, fully aware of the severe demands their activities place on society, adopt a siege mentality, trying to present a united front to the outside. Hence they cannot be relied on to suggest, or even less to conduct, such as an assessment by themselves. Thus the initiation of assessment must come from the outside; but can the evaluation be made entirely from the outside, or perhaps jointly with the insiders, and, if so, what criteria could be used?

Methodological criteria for the health of big science

Let us consider the formulation of a methodology and criteria for assessing a big science area. I have suggested that the scientific method becomes distorted and cumbersome in these areas. Yet progress in science comes from the successful operation of the scientific method. I propose, therefore, that criteria for assessing the health of a big science area must derive from an investigation of how well the various components of the scientific method function and how well the associated elements of the sociology of the scientific community operate. I suggest eleven criteria which may be suitable for the purpose. Seven of these are methodological criteria; four are sociological or psychological. The methodological criteria are:

(1) The interaction of speculation, explanation and theory, on the one hand, and observation, experimentation and measurement, on the other, is strong when a field progresses satisfactorily, but the reinforcing chain is broken when the field stagnates.

(2) In times of satisfactory progress, scientific knowledge and exploration are strongly cumulative: new activities are based on previous ones. In contrast, when stagnation sets in, many unrelated attempts and directions run in parallel, and the field appears fragmented and incoherent. Thus a kind of 'Brownian motion' takes place in the research community.

(3) In times of progress a new concept arises — a new type of insight, a novel way of looking at the problems — which appears as a qualitative, attractive and new idea and can be expressed in a simple, *anschaulich*, picture-like way. There follows a more detailed and mathematical formulation of the ideas, for the purpose of making quantitative predictions.

(4) The fourth criterion is related to the third. It states that the motivation and origin of these new ideas and breakthroughs lies in novel scientific concepts and not in new mathematical manipulations or equations. The new idea must precede its mathematical treatment. There are more pretty mathematical concepts than there are laws of Nature, and if the initial selection of a new direction is made on the grounds of mathematical elegance and clarity alone, it is almost certain that the approach will not be one that is found in Nature. It is important to stress this criterion nowadays when scientists frequently claim that a mathematical structure that they have devised or found in the literature is so beautiful that it must surely be used in Nature. This is a poor argument in favour of a new theory and promises almost certain failure. It is true that natural laws often have beautiful mathematical structures, but such beautiful mathematical structures are not necessarily natural laws.

(5) Great scientific breakthroughs often relate phenomena hitherto thought to be quite distinct and unconnected. In assessing such unification it is important to keep in mind that the unifying idea must work 'naturally', without requiring many additional assumptions or adjustable phenomenological free parameters which are included simply to fit the data.

(6) The sixth methodological criterion stresses economy and simplicity. A new idea may at first seem startling, 'unnatural', or strange, but these impressions are different from simplicity or economy. Once we have become used to the new ideas, they should be simple to articulate and understand, simple to implement, and economical, in that a large set of phenomena should be explained on the basis of only a few ideas.

(7) A successful stage of a big science field should be applicable. I do not necessarily mean technological applicability. That is also important, and inevitably follows good progress in science, but the time lag may be considerable. For a contemporaneous assessment, success in technology cannot therefore easily be used. I mean here that the new concepts can be applied to solving problems in science, perhaps in the same subdiscipline, perhaps elsewhere. This implies that the new insight is formulated not only 'in principle' but together with an algorithm that enables us to make quantitative prediction for new experiments.

The currently fashionable theory of the strong interactions of elementary particles illustrates the need for this last criterion. I am referring to quantumchromodynamics, which is now commonly claimed to represent *the* solution of the strong interaction problem. In this area, only the most rudimentary calculations can be made, covering only a fraction of the experimental observations. For most of the accumulated data relevant calculations cannot be done and hence predictions cannot be made. Thus, for the most part, such a theory cannot be evaluated and has no legitimate claim to be correct until an algorithm is devised which broadens the range of observed phenomena that the theory can predict.

Sociological criteria for the health of big science

Let me now suggest four sociological or psychological criteria for progress in big science disciplines.

(1) When real progress is being made in an area of science there is a relaxed attitude in the scientific community which enables people to pursue their own directions of investigation. This arises from the belief that the scientific method is working well and can, objectively, sort out who is right and who is wrong. In contrast, when a field is stagnant, scientists are more insecure; they argue and maintain their own point of view more intolerantly, knowing that their intellectual survival depends not on the workings of an objective scientific method but on rhetorical and 'political' factors.

(2) When progress is being made, scientists are involved in vigorous criticisms of each other's ideas and work, knowing that a critique on scientific grounds is based on the objective elements of the scientific method to which most scientists subscribe. If a field stagnates, exercising criticism may simply invoke counter-criticism and hence damage inflicted on oneself. As a result, scientific communication among different researchers becomes tenuous, and, as suggested in (1), interaction is dominated by non-scientific factors.

(3) In times of progress, researchers are dominated by the aesthetic satisfaction of gaining deeper insights into Nature. (This is perhaps the strongest motivation for scientists.) When a field stagnates, and the science produced does not have the hallmarks of beauty and power, people lack this aesthetic motivation and find solace in more external and formal gratifications, such as long publication lists and technological and methodological achievements.

(4) Finally, in a period of good scientific progress the morale of scientists is high and their confidence is evident. They are proud of publicizing their success to people outside the sciences, and are relaxed in the face of external criticism, knowing that they stand on solid ground. When stagnation sets in, scientists develop a siege mentality and become insecure and defensive when facing criticism and inquiry from the outside.

Are these criteria quantifiable?

The validity of the eleven proposed criteria must be established by demonstrating that they hold for examples from the past. To do this one needs measures for the various methodological and sociological components. We have quantitative indicators for some of these components. One can measure the interaction between theory and experiment through references in theoretical papers to experimental papers, and *vice versa*. One can explore the cognitive structure of a field of science to see if there were many parallel approaches or whether cumulation was pronounced, again using bibliometric methods. One can establish whether new trends arose as qualitative ideas or were derived from mathematics. The degree of unification brought about by periods of scientific research can be determined. Simplicity and economy can be characterized. Whether the results of a given field are taken over by other areas of science can be revealed by bibliometric and other methods. Thus, we have an impressive array of applicable and measurable indicators for the proposed methodological criteria.

Assessing the sociological components is more difficult. Whether a *laissez-faire* attitude prevails in the scientific community, and whether a vigorous scientific critique is exercised, may be detectable, but difficulty to quantify. Aesthetic satisfaction and morale are more difficult to assess, because these relate to the character and personality of individual scientists.

Compound indicators

Some of these criteria may appear to conflict with each other. For example, the absence of a *laissez-faire* attitude in a time of scientific crisis may seem to contradict the assertion that at such a time the field is disjointed, with many parallel approaches, resembling Brownian motion. A second look at these two criteria, however, suggests that they can co-exist, in the form of several parallel scientific trends, quite intolerant of one another.

Nevertheless, it is necessary, because of the speculative and partial nature of each of the indicators, to rely on the concept of a compound indicator — that is, a converging set of individual indicators. When several of these indicators are used, and they all point in the same direction, one can be more certain that the conclusion they lead to is correct. This idea of compound indicators has been used with considerable success in the past in other kinds of assessments.

For example, in assessing the performance of a research institution, one can use any or all of the following indicators: the number of publishing scientists; the total number of publications; the number of publications weighted with the impact factor of the journal where the publications appeared; the number of citations; the number of highly cited publications; the longevity of the citations; the publication output divided by the financial input into the institution. Each of these indicators pertains to a different aspect of 'performance'. A compound indicator would then contain all these indicators, possibly weighted by the personal preferences of the evaluator as to which of the above aspects are thought to be the most important.

Peer review

Besides 'impersonal' indicators measuring along the suggested criteria, the assessment of a big science discipline needs also to involve the other main evaluative tool, peer review. Here a major new obstacle arises. On the one hand, the big science field may be so technical and so unrelated to other areas of science that only specialists from within the field appear qualified to assess it. On the other hand, specialists in the field are sufficiently influenced by the prevailing siege mentality of the field to be unreliable. The use of the scientific method itself falters in these big science fields, and other, more subjective human qualities come to play a predominant role, resulting in deviations from the objectivity that is the foundation of reliable judgement.

There is a way to solve, at least partially, this dilemma. The peer review must include scientists from outside the big science specialty, but sufficiently close to it cognitively that they can make substantive contributions to the assessment. Even if they are not familiar with all the technical details they can judge the extent to which the criteria stemming from the scientific method are being used in the assessment. For example, they can assess the power of a theory to predict measured data, and can judge for themselves whether the theory was tempered or embellished with extraneous parameters to provide agreement with the data. The function of such an outsider may be akin to the football referee who may not be an expert player but can judge whether the game is played according to the rules.

What has been done in the past?

There has been no report of a contemporaneous assessment of a big science field as a whole. Pioneering assessment work has been done by Martin & Irvine (1984), but their aim was the *comparison* of various institutions. They did not claim that the composite set of indicators they used in the fields of high-energy physics and radio astronomy measured the overall rate of progress in these fields; they used them to rank the groups and institutions. Their work was nevertheless a major conceptual contribution, particularly because they stressed the necessity of using a set of converging partial indicators for a reliable and credible assessment.

Another assessment, also markedly different from what is suggested here, was made by the US Department of Energy in 1984 to review high-energy physics. This assessment had a largely political purpose, to bolster the image of high-energy physics. It was performed by peer review entirely from inside the field. The result was thus twofold: it presented a glowing picture of high-energy physics without, however, articulating the criteria used to reach this conclusion; and it strengthened conformity within the field by praising the

approaches that were then fashionable and disparaging approaches which lay
outside the momentary mainstream. That such an exercise could be undertaken
in this manner illustrates the need for a systematic methodology with which
to assess whole areas of big science.

Agenda for action

What then should be the future course of action? We first need to obtain
evidence for or against the validity of the eleven proposed criteria. This may
involve studying historical examples, or more recent episodes of science where
the outcome is already known. The only one of the eleven criteria that has been
tested in a specific situation is the first of the methodological criteria, the strength
of the interplay between experiment and theory. A study of the recent history
of interactions in high-energy physics, and of parity non-conservation and the
so-called V-A interaction in particular, showed the criterion to be valid for that
example.

A second area of investigation is more practical in nature. An assessment
must be made of several big science fields, using whatever criteria and tools
are already available. Such an assessment would fulfil at least three aims. First,
it would show us the extent to which such criteria and tools can be used in
practice. Second, it may lead to the development of further criteria and tools.
Third, it would provide information on the progress or lack of progress in those
areas of big science. This would be welcomed by science managers.

Such experimental assessments using new methodology pertaining specifically
to big science fields can be best taken up by independent and flexible
organizations interested in contributing to the strengthening of the sciences. For
pioneer projects the financial requirements are quite modest. Once the feasibility
and value of the new methods have been demonstrated, it is more reasonable
to expect that the large routine science support agencies will take over these
methods and use them in their daily operations.

Undoubtedly, these initial attempts would be imperfect and, because of the
sensitive climate in the big sciences, would also be controversial. I welcome this.
It is through such high visibility that one can focus attention on this interesting,
difficult and timely problem of assessing big science fields, with the further hope
that more powerful methods will be developed with which to approach these
problems.

References

Daniel H-D, Fisch R 1986 Messung von Forschungsleistungen, eine Annotierte
    Bibliographie (1910–1985) und Synopsis. Institut fur Gesellschaft und Wissenschaft,
    Erlangen

Martin BR, Irvine J 1984 CERN: past performance and future prospects. I CERN's position in world high energy physics. Research Policy 13:183–210
Martin BR, Irvine J 1984 CERN: past performance and future prospects. II The scientific performance of the CERN accelerators. Research Policy 13:247–284
Martin BR, Irvine J 1984 CERN: past performance and future prospects. III CERN and the future of world high-energy physics. Research Policy 13:311–342

DISCUSSION

van Raan: Science evolving beyond human perceptibility is a major concept in your description of big science, Dr Moravcsik. The 'old' quantum mechanics and the 'old' theory of relativity are also completely beyond human perceptibility, yet we are still playing around with them because we have brains and we can use mathematics. So I think that we are already far beyond 'direct' human perceptibility, and therefore this 'problem' (if it is a problem) is not specific for high-energy physics. It seems to me that the only problem here is money, because the experiments to test or to provoke theoretical work are extremely expensive.

Moravcsik: I use 'perceptibility', which may not be the best word, in two different ways; to mean understandability or to mean explorability. We can argue about the understandability, but I think quantum mechanics is well understood, because I am a physicist. The proof that we can understand quantum mechanics is that we can make good predictions. Ordinary quantum mechanical phenomena are also explorable; simple experiments can be done. I don't know whether we can understand particle physics because as yet we do not. But let's focus more on the explorability; exploration is certainly easier if you have money. The point I was making is that you might simply never have enough money because the amount generated by previous steps in science simply will not be sufficient to finance the next step.

Phillips: You said that no one had yet tried asking referees from neighbouring fields to look at a particular field. The Kendrew Committee, set up by the Advisory Board for the Research Councils and the Science and Engineering Research Council to review the UK role in high-energy particle physics (especially in relation to CERN) did not include any particle physicists.

Moravcsik: I should have mentioned that review. I was thinking more of the USA. The controversy about high-energy physics arose in Britain before it arose in America. The issue was Britain's participation in CERN (Centre Européen pour Recherche Nucleaire) which is an international consortium. Britain's contribution to CERN was fixed in Swiss francs and rose every year. Other scientists expressed the fear that too much money was being syphoned into this one field of science. So that approach has been used, but I think there is scope for more experiments, especially with the criteria that I proposed.

Hill: Your argument from scale is an interesting one. However, medieval scientists could navigate by the stars and when a cave man urinated in a fire the colour change he observed was caused by quantum mechanical phenomena, so we have been able to perceive and use very large and very small phenomena for a long time. What possible use could we imagine for the understanding that could flow from the particle physics at the instant of the big bang? If one had the money, it would be a nice indulgence, but one shouldn't expect to justify such research on practical grounds. Thus, I believe the argument from scale is only a partial argument.

Moravcsik: Some quantum mechanical phenomena are certainly observed in everyday life; an example can be seen in sodium street lights. But in general as you go farther and farther away in scale the phenomena which you want to understand become less and less accessible.

Weinberg: Freeman Dyson has said we have alternatives to the superconducting supercollider. Some people disagree with him but W.K. Panofsky, the former head of the Stanford Linear Accelerator Centre, has pointed out that, as far as the technologies are concerned, there are two fundamental limits. One is an energy limit, the other is the rare event limit; the first applies to heavy particles and the second to electrons. These limits make the business massive, difficult and very expensive. For the rare event limit at least, improvements in our ability to deal with huge quantities of data and tease out a single event from a vast amount of noise lead me to believe that if we were able to wait ten years then the work would be much less expensive.

On the subject of possible practical applications, I attended a meeting at which there was a vigorous discussion about the possibility of achieving so-called 'cold fusion' or 'muon-catalysed fusion', one of the totally unexpected spin-offs of high-energy physics. It doesn't work, but it comes within a factor of five of working, which I think is remarkable.

Narin: Are there any fields other than high-energy physics where this transition to big science is happening now?

Moravcsik: Yes; some areas of astronomy and maybe some areas of plasma physics, and it's beginning in some areas of molecular biology. The human genome sequencing project has some characteristics of a big science project. One of the objections to these projects is that, as Alvin said, if you wait you should be able to do it much better. To some extent that is true; if you're smart you can cut off a factor of five or ten, but very soon you will be caught up again in the same dilemma. The effect I am talking about is unavoidable.

Narin: But you are talking about a situation where the theoreticians are just way out-pacing the experimentalists. Computational capacity, for example, is still increasing by a factor of ten every four years—that offers enormous potential.

Moravcsik: A great deal of computation is already done in high-energy physics and it doesn't necessarily help.

Lake: You said that the technology created from a science may not create wealth at a rate sufficient to advance that science further. We might learn to apply this big science dictum rather more generally. We have focused on the benefits to science from the science that we are assessing but, in the UK at least, science must also show that its endeavours are leading to exploitable technology. One way of looking at this would be that a particular endeavour in science must be seen to have the eventual capacity to create enough wealth to support further work in that area. Have you addressed this problem at all? Dr Weinberg mentioned that physicists were within a factor of five of big wealth creation by cold fusion to create energy. So there is a probabilistic aspect, and if exploitation was successful the huge return would justify further research investment. The probability of wealth creation isn't explicit in your list of criteria.

Moravcsik: It is imposssible to predict what technology will come out of a field of science that we don't yet understand. We had an experimental observation supporting muon-catalysed fusion. Therefore researchers could make calculations, and we know that it almost works. But that's a relatively immediate application of something that we already know about. We already use other applications of high-energy physics—pions to irradiate cancer patients, for example. In my opinion, if we ever understand high-energy physics these will be considered trivial applications compared to those that we cannot yet anticipate.

Georghiou: My colleague, Michael Gibbons, has made an eponymous contribution to science policy studies; Gibbons' first law states that there is no indicator yet devised which the physics community cannot turn to its advantage within 12 months. Do you think giving them eleven simultaneously would clarify the situation?

Moravcsik: No comment!

Pavitt: I'm going to be ruder about physicists: they do have a tendency to equate gigantism with progress. This is not only true for basic science—it's also true about nuclear energy, which has been strongly advocated by physicists asking for bigger reactors, more fusion research, and fast breeder reactors. The outcome is similar to what Mike Moravcsik has described. Economists would call it decreasing capital productivity: increasing size doesn't lead to sufficient further output to compensate for the increasing cost. This is a classic example of diminishing returns, which is why there has been a slow-down in nuclear energy. On the other hand, other technologies are moving faster. Francis Narin said computing costs go down by a factor of ten every four years. This means that small can now be beautiful; I can have a computer in my office which you couldn't get into a building ten years ago. I am very suspicious about the way in which physicists use this argument of scale. I am impressed that in industry you can have cheap computing. I am impressed that biologists, with improvements in methods of measurement and detection, can do very creative experiments quite cheaply. We face the danger, as in giving too many resources for nuclear energy outside normal market processes, of supporting costly areas of basic physics outside the normal resource allocation system.

Moravcsik: I would agree with that. But I don't think that waiting so that you can do experiments in a more miniaturized and less expensive way will get you out of the long-term difficulties. The long-term trends are already there.

Pavitt: But that's high-energy physics; it's not true of biology today. You can compare nuclear energy and electronics.

Moravcsik: At the moment, it's not true for biology. My conjecture, which I won't be able to prove because the time-scale is probably such that nobody in the room will be here by the time it can be tested, is that eventually all areas of science will be in the same boat. That is, those areas of science which are not will have been essentially exhausted by then, and new areas of science will arise as big science fields. Therefore we'll have the difficulties I have described. Of course I might be wrong!

How research investment decisions are made in Japanese industry

F. Kodama

National Institute of Science and Technology Policy, Science and Technology Agency, 1-11-39, Nagata-cho, Chiyoda-ku, Tokyo, Japan

Abstract. With the emergence of 'high technology', various changes are occurring in the whole framework of research investment decision making in industry. In many Japanese manufacturing companies, research and development investment is much greater than capital investment. Thus the corporation is shifting from being a place for production to being a place for thinking. Investment decisions are no longer based on rates of return. It is more like the principle of surf-riding; the waves of innovations come one after another and you have to invest; if you miss you are killed. The pattern of competition is also changing; the competitor used to be another company within the same industrial sector, but in many cases nowadays the competitor is a company in a different industrial sector.

1989 The evaluation of scientific research. Wiley, Chichester (Ciba Foundation Conference) p 201–214

With the emergence of 'high technology' the whole framework of decision making on research investment in industry is changing. In Japan a fundamental redefinition of the company is occurring. The company is traditionally a place for production and the economist's formulation is a production function: capital plus labour make things. But in many Japanese companies capital investment is now much less than research and development (R&D) investment (Table 1). A survey of 68 major manufacturing companies in 1985, 1986, 1987 and 1988 also shows this trend (Fig. 1). In 1985, the total capital investment was much larger, but in 1987 and 1988 the R&D investment was larger than the capital investment. So the change to R&D investment surpassing capital investment is quite recent and is occurring rapidly. This signals a paradigm change; if R&D investment begins to surpass capital investment the corporation could be said to be shifting from being a place for production to being a place for thinking.

TABLE 1   R&D expenditure compared with capital investment in major Japanese companies (financial year 1986)

Company	R&D expenditure (hundred million yen)	Capital investment (hundred million yen)
Hitachi Ltd.	**2515**	1008
Toyota Motor Corporation	2500	2970
NEC Corporation	**2400**	1600
Nippon Telegraph and Telephone Corporation	1775	16 132
Toshiba Corporation	**1716**	1195
Fujitsu Ltd.	**1580**	846
Nissan Motor Co. Ltd.	**1550**	950
Mitsubishi Electric Corporation	**1120**	620
Matsushita Electric Industrial Co. Ltd.	**924***	120
Mitsubishi Heavy Industries Ltd.	**870**	707
Mazda Motor Corporation	800	1100
Nippon Denso Co. Ltd.	619	870
Canon Inc.	**609**	540
Sharp Corporation	**590**	516
Nippon Steel Corporation	550	1650
Sony Corporation	**507***	504
Sanyo Electric Co. Ltd.	506	655
The Tokyo Electric Power Co. Inc.	468	11 302
Fuji Photo Film Co. Ltd.	421	424
Kobe Steel Ltd.	362	835
Ricoh Co. Ltd.	**353**	182
Takeda Chemical Industries Ltd.	**349**	221
Asahi Chemical Industry Co. Ltd.	345	532
Mitsubishi Chemical Industries Ltd.	320	380
Komatsu Ltd.	**312**	128
Kawasaki Steel Corporation	307	1049
Ishikawajima-Harima Heavy Industries Co. Ltd.	**300**	137
Isuzu Motors Ltd.	**300**	296
Sumitomo Metal Industries Ltd.	288	823
Victor Company of Japan Ltd.	281	198

(*continued*)

TABLE 1   (*Continued*)

Company	R&D expenditure (hundred million yen)	Capital investment (hundred million yen)
Nippon Kokan K.K.	274	784
Oki Electric Industry Co. Ltd.	**249**	213
Matsushita Electric Works Ltd.	**247**	230
Sumitomo Chemical Co. Ltd.	243	323
Fuji Heavy Industries Ltd.	241	556
The Kansai Electric Power Co. Inc.	240	6561
Fuji Electric Co. Ltd.	**216**	152
Kawasaki Heavy Industries Ltd.	212	225
Sankyo Co. Ltd.	**204**	99
Asahi Glass Co. Ltd.	200	420
Sumitomo Electric Industries Ltd.	199	290
Shionogi & Co. Ltd.	**193**	101
Fujisawa Pharmaceutical Co. Ltd.	**190**	76
TDK Corporation	188	272
Eisai Co. Ltd.	**187**	47
Konishiroku Photo Industry Co. Ltd.	180	194
Kao Corporation	175	557
Chubu Electric Power Co. Inc.	156	5104
Kokusai Denshin Denwa Co. Ltd.	126	455
Matsushita Communication Industrial Co. Ltd	**120***	10

*Indicates companies whose settlement terms are different from the others. Financial year 1986 starts July 1985 and ends June 1986. Bold face numbers indicate companies whose R&D expenditures are greater than capital investment.
Source: Japan Companies Handbook (1987).

Secondly, there has also been a change in the dynamics of the research and development process. I would like to show that the R&D process in 'high-technology' industry is quite different from that in conventional industry, such as the steel industry, or in the so-called science-based industries, such as chemicals. High-technology R&D lies between these examples.

The pattern of innovation in 'high-tech' industry can be illustrated by the field of microelectronics. An old example in the field of transistors or integrated circuits is the replacement of the vacuum tube by transistors and then integrated circuits and VLSIs (very large scale integrations). The innovations occurred one

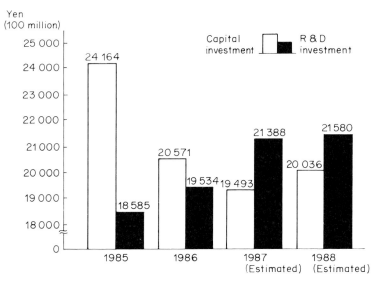

FIG. 1. R&D investment and capital investment of 68 major Japanese manufacturing companies. Source, NRI (Nomura Research Institute) Search 1987.

by one, like waves approaching the shore. When the semiconductor innovations arrived, in the USA the companies who produced the receiving tube lost their market share; their market share was only 26% in 1966 and new firms, like Texas Instruments, had 65% (Tilton 1971).

A more recent example is the development of the DRAM (Direct Random Access Memory) memory chip field, which illustrates how rapid, and in some senses, destructive, innovation can be (Fig. 2). The x-axis in Fig. 2 is the number of units of DRAM produced and the y-axis is the cost, in dollars per Kbit. The dotted line is the curve for 1 Kbit memory and starts with 1972, when it was introduced. The cost decreases as innovation or technological progress continues but in 1975 another product, 4 K memory, was introduced into the market. The amount of production of 1K memory was reduced drastically. The 4K product also benefited from technological progress but in 1978 another product was introduced in the market and, because of the scale of production, the cost per unit was greater than before. This is repeated. What is the decision making process in those companies? The investment decision, I presume, is not based on the rate of return. It's more like the principle of surf-riding. The wave comes and you have to invest; if you miss you are killed. Those are the kind of dynamics I have in mind.

As a policy scientist I want to prove that situation in an empirical way using R&D investment data. What kind of data is appropriate to describe the dynamics

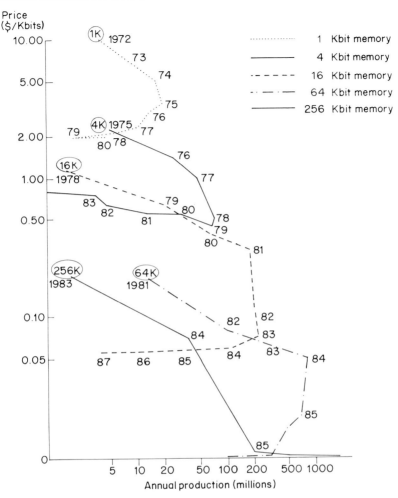

FIG. 2.   The relationship between price and production in MOS-type DRAM. Source,
Data Quest Co.

of the R&D process? Since 1970 the details of intramural expenditure on R&D
by industry and by product field have been available (Statistics Bureau of Japan
1970–1987). There are 21 industrial sectors, such as the food industry and
textiles, and 32 product fields. The matrix of these data indicates, for example,
how much money the electrical machinery industry invests in the field of oils
and paints. The data show that many Japanese companies have wide interests
and do not stick to their principal field. The minimum unit of the R&D process
is perhaps the cell of the matrix and this might reflect the dynamics of R&D.

If the electrical industry invests some amount in ceramics, it means they are interested in fine ceramics. Therefore, if the amount of investment grows, they are doing well; if it becomes zero, they have failed.

As there are 21 industrial sectors and 32 product fields, there are about 600 data points available for each year: over 10 years we have more than 6000 data points. They show an exponential distribution (Fig. 3); many programmes get a burst of small investments but many turn out to be failures. Only a few programmes survive to receive larger amounts of R&D investment. The area where the investment level is low is the exploratory phase of research and development; the area where investment is higher is the advanced phase of R&D. So the R&D process proceeds from left to right in Fig. 3. Thus we can formulate the R&D dynamic process as a model of survival (Kodama & Honda 1986).

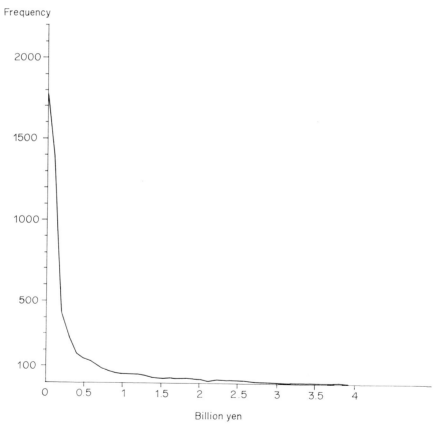

FIG. 3.   Frequency distribution of R&D expenses outside the principal product field of each industrial sector.

If the distribution of investment is strictly exponential, the model of survival implies that at each level of investment there is a death rate. In terms of R&D dynamics we can call this the 'cancelling rate'. If this is constant, it is independent of the state of the programme (Fig. 4). Usually, in the exploratory phase the cancelling rate is much higher than it is during development. In many cases the cancelling rate becomes zero. Thus I envisage two types of pattern; one where the cancelling rate is constant, and one where the rate becomes zero as the programme advances. The cancelling rate is another indicator of risk. A constant cancelling rate means you cannot reduce the risk by having R&D; this pattern is observed in the 'science-based' industries. In the conventional pattern, for the steel industry for example, the risk falls to zero. In between there are patterns where the cancelling rate can be reduced slightly but not totally; some risk remains after the programme has passed from research to development. We call that the 'high-tech' pattern.

Using a statistical test (Table 2) we can see which industry assumes this high-technology pattern. The criterion is whether the value of the t statistic is above 2 or not. Thus drugs and medicine, ordinary machinery, electrical machinery, communications and electronics, and precision equipment show the high-technology pattern. By applying this test we can identify the pattern for each industry (Table 3).

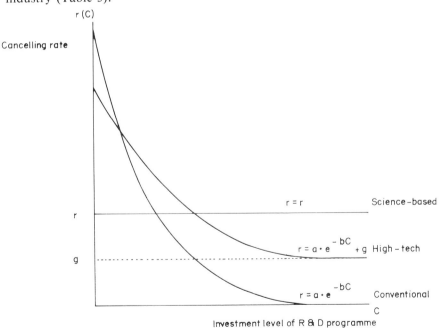

FIG. 4.   Three types of cancelling rate functions.

TABLE 2   Statistical test for high-tech pattern of R&D dynamics

Industrial sector	Estimated parameter value			Coefficient of determination
	a	b	g	
Food	0.4411 (29.94)	0.4016 (8.15)	0.0029 (0.52)	0.9145
Textile mill products	0.3292 (20.79)	0.1906 (5.30)	0.0015 (0.14)	0.9198
Pulp & paper products	0.5602 (50.68)	0.5963 (14.28)	0.0083 (1.13)	0.9968
Printing & publishing	0.5535 (7.40)	0.2971 (1.92)	− 0.0229 (0.36)	0.9212
Industrial chemicals	0.1112 (0.32)	0.0062 (0.11)	− 0.0274 (− 0.08)	0.8865
Oil & paints	0.4505 (24.42)	0.3233 (5.94)	0.0009 (0.11)	0.8967
Drugs & medicines	0.5303 (63.24)	0.7069 (17.88)	0.0077 (2.23)	0.9900
Other chemical products	0.3819 (37.51)	0.2664 (9.82)	0.0022 (0.40)	0.9683
Petroleum & coal products	0.4679 (31.06)	0.5484 (9.77)	0.0095 (1.43)	0.9735
Rubber products	0.4575 (9.91)	0.2597 (2.55)	− 0.0069 (− 0.19)	0.9154
Ceramics	0.2991 (21.43)	0.1482 (5.08)	0.0004 (0.04)	0.9111
Iron & steel	0.2908 (29.40)	0.2390 (9.25)	0.0065 (1.10)	0.9461
Non-ferrous metals & products	0.2776 (15.00)	0.1367 (4.15)	− 0.0005 (− 0.03)	0.9388
Fabricated metal products	0.2947 (21.73)	0.1950 (6.47)	0.0047 (0.48)	0.9573
Ordinary machinery	0.1463 (10.48)	0.2474 (4.28)	0.0356 (2.97)	0.8013
Electrical machinery	0.2764 (100.30)	0.8036 (35.98)	0.0294 (21.19)	0.9569
Communication & electronics	0.4454 (272.10)	0.5236 (79.87)	0.0008 (3.32)	0.9886
Motor vehicles	0.2762 (43.02)	0.1471 (10.71)	0.0016 (0.39)	0.9644
Other transport equipment	0.3996 (108.00)	0.2683 (25.57)	0.0002 (0.22)	0.9755
Precision equipment	0.4045 (47.31)	0.5027 (16.23)	0.0118 (2.75)	0.9841
Other manufacturing	—	—	—	—

a, b and g are parameters from the cancelling rate function where the cancelling rate $(r) = a.e^{-bC} + g$ (see Fig. 4).
Figures in parentheses are t statistics. Industries which show the high-technology pattern of R&D investment are indicated by t-values > 2.0.

TABLE 3 Identification of the pattern of R&D dynamics for each of 21 industrial sectors

Pattern	Industry
Science-based	Industrial chemicals
	Other manufacturing
High-tech	Drugs and medicine
	Ordinary machinery
	Electrical machinery
	Communication and electronics
	Precision machinery
Conventional	Remaining 14 industrial sectors

What are the implications of these patterns, especially in terms of evaluation? How should science-based industries manage their R&D investment? You cannot reduce the risk so you must support as many projects as you can. That is the extreme case. You need a strong financial basis in order to support many programmes.

How should industries showing the 'high-tech' pattern be treated? This is more manageable, but not totally so; some competitor may show up with a result based on a quite different scientific principle that performs much more effectively than your product. In the field of microelectronics, or DRAM, I showed waves every three years (Fig. 2), but the competitor was a company within the microelectronics industrial sector. In many cases the competitor is now a company belonging to a different industrial sector. For example, in the Japanese development of optical fibres, the first production was by a glass manufacturer. The original product had two problems — fragility and high transmission loss — which were not solved by the glass maker. To reduce transmission loss, a glass maker thinks in terms of purifying the glass, which obviously has a physical limit. This problem was solved by NTT (Nippon Telegraph and Telephone Company), a user of optical fibres, by discovering that using longer wavelengths drastically reduces the transmission loss. The fragility was resolved by a cable manufacturer who invented a coating technology that reduced fragility. Thus those two problems were solved by companies in other industrial sectors. The mass production method for optical fibres was developed by a consortium of the cable manufacturer and NTT, not by the glass maker.

References

Kodama F, Honda Y 1986 Research and development dynamics of high-tech industry. The Journal of Science Policy and Research Management 1:65–74
Statistics Bureau of Management and Cordination Agency of Japan 1970–1987 Report on the survey of research and development, intramural expenditure on R&D disbursement by industry and product field.
Tilton J 1971 International diffusion of technology. Brookings Institution, Washington DC

DISCUSSION

Georghiou: I am particularly struck by the ratio of R&D investments to capital investment in recent years. For chip manufacture the scale-up requirements in the past decade have risen from $10 million for a new plant to $100 million and the next generation, which is currently the subject of R&D, will cost one billion dollars.

Kodama: That is why I likened decision making to surf-riding.

Georghiou: Is the ratio likely to stay that way? Is knowledge becoming completely dominant over capital investment, or are companies going to have to use that knowledge and go back into an investment cycle?

Kodama: I don't know. There are two interpretations. R&D investment may surpass capital investment because the latter had been reduced so much. So, in good economic conditions, capital investment will increase and might surpass R&D investment again. While capital investment is decreasing R&D investment increases constantly. I think capital investment requirements are becoming less because the life-cycle of products is getting shorter and so companies are becoming more cautious about making large capital investments.

Georghiou: I don't know the answer either; it seems that Japanese companies perceive that the knowledge base will be the key to competitive advantage. Against that, in the example you used, DRAM manufacture, the cost of investment is going up, which is why so many companies are dropping out in the UK. We've seen two of our big three go in the past year; there is only one left that can keep up with the scale-ups. It will be interesting to see whether they are just waiting to apply that knowledge and capital investment will increase again.

Kodama: That is a big question—I don't know.

Weinberg: Do you have comparable figures for other countries?

Kodama: No; I think some US companies may have R&D investments larger than their capital investments—Lockheed, or pharmaceuticals. The phenomenon that I described, that R&D investment surpasses capital investment, is general to all Japanese companies from electronics to pharmaceuticals.

Irvine: Did you obtain your expenditure statistics from the annual survey of R&D published by the Statistics Bureau?

Kodama: Data on capital investment were compiled directly from the companies.

Irvine: To understand your figures we probably need more information. To what extent are the trends the result of increased investment in basic research or of changing structures of development expenditure? Have changes in tax concessions in R&D had any effect? To what extent is the difference between investment and R&D accounted for by the introduction of flexible manufacturing plant which can be re-used? The shortening of product life-times may also mean that more investment is put into design, which is included in the R&D figures.

Kodama: Capital requirements might be less if flexible technology was used so that trend might certainly continue. The new phenomenon is as follows. We had a phase of establishing 'central research institutes' in the early 1970s. Sometimes this was interpreted as basic research, but in many cases it was not. We are now having a second boom of establishing what is called fundamental research, which is very basic research. We are talking about who is the next candidate for a Nobel Prize for the Japanese; he might be from a Japanese company.

Irvine: Japanese companies are devoting a lot of effort to the question of R&D evaluation, especially with respect to basic research. Could you comment on current corporate evaluation activities?

Kodama: There are said to be two kinds of evaluation or two types of research—bottom-up and top-down. 'Bottom-up' means that researchers submit a proposal but 'top-down' means that the president of a company says which areas should be explored. Twenty per cent of R&D expenditure is of the top-down type, in Japan.

Hill: It's a great pleasure to hear that Japanese companies will now begin to chase Nobel Prizes. Perhaps we in the USA shall have a chance against you in the commercial market!

The matrix of manufacturing sectors, product fields, and R&D expenditures (not shown), demonstrated a lot of R&D expenditure in product fields that are not obviously in the manufacturing sector, which is part of the idea of technology fusion (Kodama 1986a). Is that a result of the fact that you have a large number of highly diversified companies? Thus an electronics company might report R&D spending on paint products because it owns a paint company, not because it is exploring new opportunities to use paints in electronics.

Kodama: These are the statistics about R&D expenses and the minimum unit is a company. For example, Hitachi was asked to disaggregate its R&D investment in 32 product fields, but Hitachi belongs to the electrical machinery industrial sector (Kodama 1986b).

Narin: Does that include the elevator work and other lower technology work that Hitachi does? Is it all within that one group? It's a vast company.

Kodama: Hitachi metal is a separate company.

Blume: It would be interesting to know how much companies invest in relation to their profits. Are there any international statistics that show what share of total profit is invested? Do Japanese firms invest most of their profits because they are not under pressure to pay big dividends?

Kodama: Perhaps.

Kruytbosch: In the USA, industrial decision making on research is influenced by the company structure in which there is a competing set of vice-presidents. The members of the Industrial Research Institute (the vice-presidents for research of the top 250 research-performing companies in the USA) are constantly discussing how the vice-presidents for research can get the attention of the Chief Executive Officer, who historically has paid much more attention to marketing, production and finance. This has changed somewhat in recent years. You spoke of 20% of research coming 'top-down' because the Chief Executive Officer has identified a good strategic area to enter. Do you have this type of structure in Japan, where the research decision makers are 'low men on the totem pole' among the top executives of the company?

Kodama: I'm not from business school, so I am not familiar with that. Many of the presidents of the Japanese high-tech companies are engineers. The top five electronics companies all have engineers as presidents and one of these presidents has a PhD in basic science. In the past we had presidents whose backgrounds were in production engineering, but now more and more presidents have backgrounds in research or as managers of research design sections rather than production. That implies that presidents themselves are able to judge R&D investment, and are interested in doing so.

Narin: That's a very major difference from US companies.

Kodama: We don't have a tradition of business schools.

Anderson: We have heard a lot about the evaluation techniques that can be used for basic science. Obviously, techniques with which to evaluate applied science will be different. In relation to the 'bottom-up' support of research within high-tech firms, are there any techniques that you have heard about in this conference which you see as being useful within Japanese industry? For example, do any Japanese firms use quantitative approaches to the internal evaluation of performance for making decisions on resource allocation?

Kodama: In textbooks of research evaluation, there are many fine 'operations research' methods for decision making, such as the return ratio. Through interviews with people in industry, I have the impression that those methods are rarely used. More usual are simple formats with five or six criteria and scored in terms of, say, a three-point system.

In his book on research evaluation in Japanese companies, John Irvine (1988) describes the procedure in NTT where a researcher has to submit a proposal including milestones with dates for reaching particular goals. So the proposal involves automatic evaluation. If you miss that milestone, you have to give up.

Irvine: My understanding is that the approach to evaluation in Japan varies with different types of research. With very specific applied research, Japanese companies generally set up technical targets and monitor progress in meeting them. These sorts of techniques are starting to be used in government agencies like AIST (Agency of Industrial Science and Technology). For very basic research, however, the techniques used in industry have necessarily included the evaluation of papers, looking at their quality and innovativeness, especially those presented at international conferences.

Turning to your data on corporate R&D expenditure, your aim is to identify changed patterns of spending and use this to develop indicators for measuring corporate diversification and technology fusion. Have you not also been approaching these questions using other methods, such as analysis of bibliometric abstracting services? For example, one might take *Chemical Abstracts* and use various technological keywords to generate 'hits' (cross-impacts) across different research categories. I thought you were doing research along these lines for the forthcoming AIST White Paper.

Kodama: No, I haven't done that. However, to further study technology fusion, I am looking at joint applications for patents by different companies belonging to different industrial sectors.

Small: What is the attitude of management towards publication in Japanese firms? Do they encourage their scientists to publish? Do they want them to publish in international or national journals, or perhaps to write reports or keep results confidential?

Wald: The Japanese patent system encourages publication by scientists, including those in industry, through a 'grace period' which allows scientists to publish or to speak about their discoveries without forfeiting the patent rights. Apart from Japan, only the United States and Canada now have grace periods; Europe has unfortunately abolished them.

Kodama: Industrial scientists in Japan are encouraged to publish, especially in English, to enhance the company image. Of the papers presented at annual meetings of an international nature, the majority are presented by industry, not universities.

Garfield: Does that carry over to engineering publications? In the United States, UMI (University Microfilms International) launched a major effort to index and abstract Japanese science and technology publications, but it has been abandoned. It was thought that there were many important Japanese language publications, especially in technology and engineering, that were not covered by international abstracting services.

Kodama: Yes, that is the claim, but if you learn Japanese that will solve the problem! Many Japanese companies maintain that their scientists and engineers would like reputations as world scientists, and the best way is to publish in English. Therefore, they say, the top 10–15% of papers are automatically published in English, and the garbage might be written in Japanese.

Hill: I have been working for the US Congress on this translation problem. I would like some verification, or denial, using bibliometric techniques, of the belief that the top 15% or so of Japanese industrial research results are published in English. Is there a 'science citation index' for Japanese literature in Japan?

Kodama: The reason we write in Japanese is not that we have found some-thing important and want to keep it secret. Many Japanese academic journals require an English abstract for each paper.

Garfield: I don't think there is any doubt that the Japanese output has increased both in quantity and quality.

Hill: That is for the papers that you were able to access—the English language ones.

Garfield: Yes; but you would probably find similar changes for patents. Unfortunately, analyses based on the SCI omit citations in Japanese of other Japanese language articles. We can't afford to interpret Japanese language citations. We can only assume that the deletion of these citations is no less damaging than the failure to treat Japanese language journals, or others, as sources.

Kodama: Japanese scientists in various fields tell me that important papers are always submitted to international journals.

Narin: We attempted to test this seven or eight years ago when we were checking whether the SCI was a representative sample of the world literature. We compared the proportion of papers in *Chemical Abstracts* that were from Japan to the proportion of papers in the *Science Citation Index* from Japan. We did the same in six or seven fields, including biology with *Biological Abstracts* and physics with *Physics Abstracts*. There was no indication that the SCI was not a proportionate sample of the important work. If a Japanese publication is not represented by the SCI, it is also not being caught in any of the other services, some of which try to be exhaustive in their own fields. I suspect that much less is missed than is feared.

Hill: Scientific literature in general is largely a product of academic scientists. However, a much greater fraction of the Japanese literature that may be important to US industrial interests consists not of basic scientific papers in physics and chemistry written by academics, but of the more ephemeral pub-lications by industrial researchers in such fields as mechanical engineering or robotics.

References

Irvine J 1988 Evaluating applied research: lessons from Japan. Pinter, London
Kodama F 1986a Japanese innovation in mechatronics technology: a study of technolo-gical fusion. Science and Public Policy 13(1):44
Kodama F 1986b Technological diversification of Japanese industry. Science 233:291–296

General discussion II

Beyond bibliometrics

Phillips: I find myself thinking of an old story which is told in many contexts in science. A drunk is found looking for something under a street lamp and a passer-by asks him what the trouble is. The drunk replies that he is looking for his wallet, and the passer-by asks 'Did you lose it here?'. The drunk says 'Oh no, but this is where the light is'. In all our discussions we return to the issue of collecting bibliographies, counting papers and calculating citation index measures. Do we set about the evaluation of research in this way because there is a very strong light, provided by Eugene Garfield and others, on the numbers of publications and citations etc., or do these measures indeed reflect accurately what is happening in science and address relevant issues? It seems to me that we neglect many other approaches. Joe Anderson (this volume) raised the subject of research training, but that didn't lead to discussion of what sort of people are needed and whether trained people are an important output from the science industry; it led to discussion of how you judge those people according to the papers they publish. We are certainly looking where the light is, but is the light shining where we need it?

Lake: In deciding to fund a research grant, one thinks in terms of funding an activity that will produce research results. A quite different view is that one is funding the training of a graduate student to get a PhD and that he or she will become trained as a research scientist in rather general terms and may not pursue that exact discipline later, or that one is perhaps funding a postdoctoral worker to become more mature in his research activities. That the grant leads to some published and cited results then becomes almost a by-product.

We have not addressed here either this training element of research grants or the striking correlation between research excellence and clinical excellence in senior university physicians, which I think is paralleled by a general correlation between teaching excellence and research excellence. When a university is financed as a centre of excellence, far more is funded than some published and bibliometrically analysed papers. People receive training and their entrance into industry is just as important as the transfer of the research results. Both are associated with national wealth creation, which is an objective of science, or more generally with the social benefit of science for the nation.

Anderson: It is important to consider approaches other than simply bibliometrics. Perhaps we have so far focused on bibliometrics because these methods are now beginning to offer some interesting applications which must be discussed. But as I said earlier, such measures of output cannot stand on their own and they must be complemented with analyses of the process of research.

Many people would agree that a PhD course should train graduates to become research scientists in general terms so that they are equipped to move between scientific disciplines. But PhD graduates do not seem to be getting that kind of training. There is a lot of pressure on trainees to produce results; therefore they end up becoming specialists, not generalists. If we want generalists, what should their skills be? This is the question the Ciba Foundation is trying to answer in our national survey of PhD employers. Only when we know what the industrial, academic, civil service and other employment sectors require of a scientist can we begin to evaluate whether the PhD system is working.

Luukkonen-Gronow: We have talked about the role of the traditional method of evaluation, peer review, in the selection of proposals. Peer review has also been applied quite extensively in many countries to evaluate several aspects of scientific and other types of performances. In the Nordic countries, peer review panels have been used to evaluate research fields, institutions and programmes. The panels can address a wide range of questions, and the 'light' can be directed wherever seems most relevant. One can collect qualitative comments on the orientation of research and whether it seems fruitful; one can solicit opinions on the organization of the research; one can find out about contacts between researchers, whether there is enough collaboration at home or abroad; and one can study aspects of research training. Although we are all aware of the limitations of peer review, such as problems of bias, we cannot deny that it is a useful tool for evaluation. It is not cheap; like bibliometric studies, the use of peer evaluation teams is expensive and requires a commitment in time from all the parties involved.

Narin: There's an important point here about scale. When you are dealing with the Nordic countries you can do that kind of peer review. But the US National Institutes of Health support 40000 papers a year. It's very difficult to get a peer evaluation of that vast collection of research results. I agree that when you are dealing with relatively small numbers of papers, people, and departments peer review is a superior method of evaluation, but it does not work when you are dealing with 1000 or 10000 units. Then you have to use some other technique. The problem is, where do you make that transition? For large numbers, at least in the USA, the Congress will not accept the results. If you have 10000 projects and bring 100 experts in, who compares the value of the 100 they each review? You need a supplementary approach and are forced to the techniques largely based now on the *Science Citation Index* (SCI).

Luukkonen-Gronow: Even in Finland, there seems to be a size limitation; we have to define suitable units for evaluation so that peer review groups address a reasonable task.

Blume: The agenda for discussion on evaluation is largely set by the policy agenda, and policy makers are reaping the harvest for which they sowed. If people are looking where the light is, that's because policy makers have encouraged them to do that. If you want to shift resources from apparently ineffective universities to effective universities, or ineffective programmes to effective programmes, you necessarily ask different evaluative questions than, for example, in the famous Nordic approach when the Swedish Natural Science Research Council used international visitation panels not just to decide who was bad but, more importantly, to find a way of improving everyone. That evaluation was highly valued by the scientists because it gave them the chance to talk at length with international experts in their field about their problems.

John Irvine referred earlier to the split between professional evaluators and philosophers and sociologists of science. The concept of sophistication was coined in the 1960s with the suggestion that instrumentation, and therefore expenditure, had to advance if anything worthwhile was to be done. Mike Moravcsik (this volume) describes the same sort of view. But there is nothing inevitable about it. Later the meaning of sophistication was discussed, and many in the social studies of science community persuaded themselves that it means little more than how many resources governments had been prepared to make available. Not many people want to hear that: it conflicts with all existing interests! If you look at science in the ways that sociologists do, the consensus that instrumentation advances are essential to scientific advance is found in only a few fields. In many fields, there's no consensus about what the priorities are, but you see a process by which, for perfectly understandable social reasons, scientists reformulate the questions in terms of some new, up-and-coming and interesting apparatus. It's a social process; there's nothing inevitable about it. But who wants to hear that? It just makes life difficult for the scientists who want to get the money, for the policy makers who want to make the decisions, and for the evaluators who want to do a good, efficient and business-like job.

Montigny: We have spoken mostly about bibliometrics because we have concentrated on evaluation of basic research. For the evaluation of applied research, the discussion would have been different. Peer review is also important in applied research, but it can be used with other techniques. I have been working for the European Commission on the evaluation of some programmes carried out by the Directorate General XII (Science, Research and Development). For example, for the 'non-nuclear energy research programme', we have set up a panel of experts from that field and added to them someone representing a consulting group. Before the evaluation, the private consulting group and the panel developed a questionnaire to be sent to all the subcontractors working on the programme. Also, the consulting group was to conduct studies in each of the EEC countries. The consulting group was responsible for putting data into the evaluation process and asking the experts to react to it. Finally, the panel, the consulting group and also the programme managers meet to discuss the data. That is a way to develop other relevant indicators.

A new set of indicators, called 'network indicators', has been developed by the laboratory of the French School of Mines, the 'Centre de sociologie de l'innovation' (CSI). In this approach, an R&D field is thought of as a network in which the innovative capacity depends on the quality of the relationships between its members. An R&D programme is aimed at improving the communication process within this network and in particular is intended to have a positive action on any bottlenecks. The network indicators allow the measurement of the state of the network before and after the programme. This is done by four steps: (1) description of the network, i.e. the partners involved in a given R&D field (research institution, professional organization, company); (2) identification of bottlenecks, e.g. lack of communication between university and company, or professional organization expecting more or different basic research. This step must be characterized by *ad hoc* indicators; (3) action of the R&D programme to improve these difficulties; and (4) evaluation, using the same tools as in step 2 to measure the differences that have occurred after step 3. This approach has been implemented within the 'Agence Française pour la maîtrise de l'energie' (see Monnier & Montigny 1988).

Collins: I would say that the useful agenda has moved on from the particular lamp posts under which we have been standing during this conference, to look under different lamps as well. If you like, it's not a wallet we are looking for but money scattered all over the floor. We have focused on indicators of output— published work, products, or people—but we have looked much less at how these products are obtained using process indicators. In the UK, the political agenda, defined by what the University Grants Committee and the Committee of Vice-Chancellors and Principals are considering, and the discussions between the Treasury, government departments and their client bodies, now appears to be more concerned with process. Key words such as selectivity, concentration, flexibility, directed-funding, management efficiency, and interdisciplinarity are now occupying the centre of the political stage where output and value-for-money had the stage to themselves before.

Dixon: I would like to link peer review and citation analysis together and ask about citation analysis in relation to journal refereeing practices. By implication, high-impact journals have been almost equated with high-quality journals; there have been two comments to that effect during this conference. I can see the point, but, as we all know, there are journals that are conservatively or fastidiously refereed and there are those that are loosely refereed. There are great disparities in the standards applied to the acceptance or rejection of papers. Is this seen as a non-issue in relation to citation analysis? The appearance of a paper in each of those three sorts of journals and citations to them obviously mean quite different things.

Narin: That has been explored fairly extensively (Narin 1976). Several studies have looked at general correlations between peer reviews of papers, of people, of journals, of papers that were given different ratings before publication, and they all tend to show correlations in the order of 0.5, 0.6, 0.8 or 0.9. That's really not something that anyone argues about in the aggregate.

Garfield: Recently, I presented a series of co-citation maps of worldwide research to a conference in a small country, selecting a topic in which that country excelled. The audience included most of the leading research figures in that country as well as leading university administrators, but not one of them knew the person we identified as core author from that country. Perhaps I am expecting too much, but that incident symbolizes an important feature of the era of big science. Whether we call it the 'old boy network' or attribute it to information overload, we should be concerned about all the people who seem to get lost in the cracks. When I first came to the UK, certain individuals and the scientific press seemed quite affronted, even resentful, of the suggestion that 'mere' citation counting could perform as well as peer review. There was considerable scepticism about our ability to identify scientists of Nobel Prize class, including those who would be Nobel Prize winners. However, the SCI is not needed to identify candidates for the Nobel Prize—the committee manages nicely without us. But we are interested in helping to identify the larger number of less-recognized individuals who, for personality and other reasons, don't get through the peer review process as well as they might. I don't hesitate to discuss the potential misuse of citation data. But many scientists feel that the research councils don't treat them fairly and that the citation record would support their claim for continued funding or recognition.

Hills: Contrasting peer review and bibliometric techniques is perhaps mistaken because they are both varieties of the same process. When they give different answers, I fear some methodological problem might be the cause. In principle, they should come up with very similar answers. For basic research, peer review in its broadest sense is probably, if not the only light, the strongest light. We haven't discussed extensively the development end of the R&D spectrum. At the Department of Trade and Industry, we have studied a particular mechanism of collaborative research. Among other things, we looked not so much for peer review as for what might be called customer review. You can, in some cases, follow through into the area of products. This is similar to what Dr Lake is talking about. It is a pity that we have neglected that, particularly when we are under pressure to consider the wealth-creation objective of science.

van Raan: At Leiden we are working on an improvement of co-citation analysis (Braam et al 1988). We have defined a field called 'agricultural biochemistry' which contains much applied research. In *Chemical Abstracts* there are eight sections relating to this subject area. First, we obtained all 3500 papers from these sections and collected the reference lists, which gave about 60000 references. We performed co-citation analysis with these references and found that only about 14% of the original source papers were in the 'clouds' around the co-cited pairs, providing a much better picture of the relations between many different subfields in the rather complicated agriculture-related biochemistry field. This demonstrates the potential usefulness of sophisticated bibliometric methods.

Georghiou: Most of the methods we have discussed involve scientists as the consumers of research and may therefore be useful in directing where to place resources within science. The 'process' methods, looking at issues such as whether you should have industrial research centres, concern how you should use the resources you already have. The pressing question for science, certainly in the UK, is how to argue for having those resources at all. For this you have got to go beyond the scientist as consumer and consider the wider general population as the consumer. We cannot avoid economic and social evaluation, however weak the present methods are. Patents and other technological indicators have something to offer—that's another lamp to stand under. But there are also methods which do not have the elegance and statistical sophistication of the ones we have talked about. Evaluation also involves doing interviews, making surveys, putting together a picture. The model is perhaps a novel by John le Carré, rather than the work of a statistician, but it is still evaluation.

References

Anderson J 1989 The evaluation of research training. In: The evaluation of scientific research. Wiley, Chichester (Ciba Foundation Conference) p 93–119

Braam RR, Moed HF, van Raan AFJ 1988 Mapping of science: critical elaboration and new approaches. A case study in agricultural biochemistry. In: Egghe L, Rousseau R (eds) Informetrics 87/88. Elsevier Science Publishers, Amsterdam, p 15–28

Monnier E, Montigny P 1988 Evaluating R&D programmes—lessons from French evaluations in the non-nuclear energy field. CCE-DGXII, Brussels

Moravcsik MJ 1989 The contemporaneous assessment of a big science discipline. In: The evaluation of scientific research. Wiley, Chichester (Ciba Foundation Conference) p 188–200

Narin F 1976 Evaluative bibliometrics: the use of publication and citation analysis in the evaluation of scientific activity. Monograph, 31 March 1976, p 456

How science policies are determined in the United States

Christopher T. Hill*

Congressional Research Service, The Library of Congress, Washington, DC 20540, USA

Abstract. In the United States, policies for the Federal funding of scientific research are established through an increasingly complex interplay of interests and agencies including: scientific societies; organizations representing universities, industries, or both; executive branch agencies; and Congressional committees. Interest has been slowly growing in using objective methods for deciding on priorities for funding research, such as cost–benefit analysis, bibliometric analysis, and systematic assessments of scientific fields and projects by peer experts. Scientists are being asked by policy makers to document the expected outcomes of science programmes, and appeals to past successes are less and less convincing. There have also been calls for the scientific community to advise government on priorities across fields and projects, in addition to the better established tradition of advising within fields. This has been precipitated by a combination of very tight Federal budgets and the high costs of several new, big science projects. This paper describes the evolving landscape in some detail. It addresses the differences of process and substance between policy for science and policy for other areas of public concern, and examines how these differences are reflected in the special challenges faced by evaluators and analysts of science policy.

1989 The evaluation of scientific research. Wiley, Chichester (Ciba Foundation Conference) p 221–233

Public policies for science are determined, just as they are for any other area, by profoundly political processes. However, the history of public policy making for science, at least since the end of World War II, reveals a continuing tension over the degree to which politics should be modulated by expertise (Levine & Benda 1986). The argument is that to decide about science, one must *know* science. On the other hand, even as war is too important to be left to the generals, the centrality of science and scientific knowledge to modern life means that science is too important to be left to the scientists.

---

*The views expressed herein are those of the author and not of the Congressional Research Service or other unit of the US Library of Congress.

I sense the emergence of a paradox in US science policy making. Public policy makers, from the schoolhouse to the White House, express a new recognition of the importance of science in human affairs, and they wish to take a firm hand in guiding the choices made about which kind of science gets how much support. They know the choices matter. But they're often not quite sure how. At the same time, scientists are reacting to this new interest on the part of the government by becoming ever more bold in their requests for public support for many and expensive projects. They want to do it all, now. Science itself seems to offer opportunity in unprecedented variety. And the audacity of proposals like the superconducting supercollider and the space station have given courage to scientists in other fields to make new demands on the Treasury in return for promised better life.

Here is the paradox. Even as policy makers have taken greater interest in science policy, they have come face to face with their own limited expertise, and they are asking scientists for more and more help in deciding what to support. And, after many years of denying such advice, scientists are beginning to respond.

The scope of science policy choice

The balance of politics and expertise differs among the different kinds and levels of choice encountered in making science policy. In describing these categories of choice, I shall try to limit my discussion to issues involving the promotion of basic research by public bodies. But we should keep in mind that public bodies usually only fund a significant amount of basic science because they expect it to yield results that will ultimately prove useful.

Levels of choice

Without necessarily being exhaustive of the possibilities, the levels of choice frequently encountered in science policy making include:

Which *sort* of science (discipline, field, 'big' or 'small') to support, toward which *ends*?

How much public *money* should be spent on each sort of science, and on science in total?

Which *projects* would best advance each sort of science?

Who should be selected to perform each project?

What *mechanisms* should be used to distribute the funds?

What *rules* should govern the processes of choice?

In the domain of basic science, including basic research performed under the banner of engineering, a relatively stable consensus seems to have prevailed until recently regarding which levels of decision should be reserved to policy makers and which to the scientists. The consensus goes like this. Policy makers decide the *ends* to be served by science, how much *money* should be spent on science in total, the *mechanisms* to be used, and the *rules* that govern the processes of choice. Scientists decide what *sort* of science would best help to reach the determined ends, the specific *projects* that would best advance each sort, and *who* should carry out each project. The two cultures interact most vigorously in deciding how much money should be spent on each sort of science. On matters clearly in the policy domain, scientists hope to be asked for advice; on matters clearly in the scientific domain, policy makers expect to be kept informed.

We are in a time of transition. The consensus is breaking down, and the shape of the new reality has yet to be agreed. The breakdown has come, not because either side is displeased with the consensus, but because external forces have intervened. Let me illustrate this.

Since the early 1980s, the United States has experienced a wave of 'pork-barrel' science — the allocation of Federal government money without scientific peer review to specific science facilities and activities by the appropriations subcommittees of Congress in response to demands by state and local officials on behalf of constituent groups, primarily universities and colleges. Here is why it is called pork-barrel science.

The responsibility for Congressional decision making on Federal spending is divided between authorization committees (which initiate, oversee, and set ceilings on spending for legislated programmes) and appropriations committees (which decide how much money each programme actually gets each year). The new practice of allocating Federal funds to specific science projects and institutions by the appropriations committees is consistent with a long tradition of Congressional funding of specific projects for the constituents at home in a variety of other domains (ports and harbours, water supply and flood control projects, highways, military bases, hospitals, and so on) through the appropriations process. In the United States, this practice has been referred to for decades, pejoratively, as 'bringing home the bacon' or 'pork-barrel' legislation. The pressure to fund science projects outside the consensus (under which such allocations would have been made by scientists, not Congress) comes from the belief that scientific research can contribute to the economic development of the place in which it is carried out, just as ports and harbours do. Widespread acceptance of this belief is new, and it has led to the 'intrusion' of policy makers into what the scientists consider their domain of choice.

Another illustration of an external intervention in the consensus on how to decide about science policy is the pressure to regulate the conduct of science in order to avoid the harm that scientific research itself — and not just its application — might cause. Motivated by religious beliefs, ethical precepts, and environmental concerns, activists not historically party to the consensus have called for restrictions on a variety of scientific activities, including research using fetal tissue, research using nuclear materials, research on altering the genetic make-up of species, and research on crop varieties that would facilitate the replacement of agricultural workers with machines. These interventions have led to greater involvement of policy makers in deciding, whether they wish to or not, what kinds of research should be done, where, and by whom.

The most powerful external factor that has led to the breakdown in the consensus is the Federal budget deficit. The availability of Federal funds for support of scientific research is constrained by the high public debt, by the lack of agreement on means to reduce the annual deficit sufficiently to release 'new money' for science, and by the inexorable growth in other demands on the public treasury. Increasingly, Congress is asking for help not only in deciding how much to spend in total but also in deciding what the priorities ought to be for public funding of science. And, the traditional formulation of the old consensus, in which each discipline and sort of science asked for as much public money as it could get, is proving less and less functional as hard choices have to be made.

The effect of the budget deficit in forcing a realignment of the roles of policy makers, especially those in Congress, and scientists is exacerbated by two other factors. First, an uncommonly large number of unusually expensive scientific projects has been proposed for Federal funding, with total price tags of several tens of billions of dollars over the next decade. Second, the Reagan administration has tended to endorse each new expensive proposal as it has come along, leaving the hard work of setting the priorities to the Congress. (In fairness, it should be noted that the administration has typically proposed cuts in other categories of Federal spending large enough to pay for the proposed increases in science funding, but those cuts have tended to be focused on politically popular programmes in other areas such as community economic development assistance.)

Early in 1988, calls went out to the American scientific community from the highest levels for help in setting priorities for Federal funding *among* fields and sorts of science. This represents a new departure. Previously, the organized scientific community has been more than willing to offer advice on priorities and opportunities *within* fields but quite reluctant to offer such advice *across* fields. Examples of the former include the Pimentel Report on chemistry (National Research Council 1985), the Amundson Report on chemical engineering (National Research Council 1988), and the Seitz–Eastman Report on major facilities for materials research (National Research Council 1984). In a report of the Congressional Research Service (Baldwin & Hill 1988), we noted that, 'Without such advice the Congress will have little choice but to make these decisions without formal guidance on priorities from experts in the scientific community, and the scientific community will have no choice but to accept the results'. The report of the US Senate Budget Committee on the fiscal year 1989 budget (set to begin on 1 October 1988) asked that the National Academy of

Sciences advise the Congress on mechanisms for setting priorities for science (Committee on the Budget 1988). At the 1988 annual R&D Colloquium of the American Association for the Advancement of Science in mid-April, such speakers as Erich Bloch, the Director of the National Science Foundation; Congressman Doug Walgren, Chairman of the House Subcommittee on Science, Research, and Technology; and Robert Rosenzweig, the President of the Association of American Universities, called for greater involvement of scientists in advising the government on priorities for science (Long 1988). And, in his presidential address to the 125th annual meeting of the National Academy of Sciences on April 27, Frank Press called for a constructive response by the scientific community to the requests for help (Press 1988). Press revealed his own list of priorities, discussed below. Whether his priorities are viable has not yet been tested, but they have received considerable attention (Boffey 1988).

Some additional considerations in science policy making

Before I turn to the question of how US government science priorities might be set in the future, I should like to discuss some other considerations that arise in determining science policy.

First, there is a sense in which policy making for science is different from policy making in many other areas of public policy. Typical issues in public policy have to do with allocating scarce public resources among policy alternatives whose outcomes are reasonably well understood. However, scientific activity, by its very nature, attempts to redefine what is known; that is, the outcomes of funding science, especially basic science, are highly uncertain. We often don't know what to expect. This part of the science policy problem can't be completely solved by bringing in more experts, although they may be able to help. Thus, the unease that many policy makers experience about science funding priorities arises not only from their lack of expert knowledge, but from the fact that not even the experts know for certain what the outcomes might be. Economic analysis can't help much either, because the uncertainties in the costs and the benefits of any particular scientific endeavour result from scientific, not economic unknowns. These uncertainties frustrate attempts to employ techniques like cost–benefit analysis in the prospective examination of science priorities.

There was some hope in the 1960s and early 1970s that technology assessment might represent a reasoned approach to projecting the outcomes of science, especially the outcomes of its applications, so as to guide policy makers in deciding whether to support certain R&D programmes. Even though the US Congressional Office of Technology Assessment is widely regarded as a highly successful organization, it has had quite limited success in attempting to anticipate scientific outcomes.

The second, and a closely related issue, is that the American system of public policy making is best suited to making decisions incrementally (Lindblom 1968). Science, on the other hand, often causes revolutions; revolutions in social possibilities as well as revolutions in understanding. The possibility of causing revolutions through supporting scientific activity, or the possibility of having to cope with their consequences, puts most American policy makers in a tough spot. It challenges their instinctive preferences for making small interventions and for revisiting issues as need arises. Very few political leaders have understood how to mobilize the power of scientific revolutions to redefine the terms of policy debate—four that come to mind are Roosevelt's decision to go ahead with the atomic bomb, Kennedy's decision to put a man on the moon by 1969, Nixon's war on cancer, and Reagan's Strategic Defense Initiative. Yet, each of these decisions has come under its share of criticism. Each has been criticized because the action taken was stronger than was needed or because it was taken without due regard for its consequences. The message for most policy makers is probably 'Watch out for scientific revolutions'.

While ultimate policy making authority in the United States is vested in the Congress, that body frequently delegates limited policy making authorities by law to executive branch departments and agencies. To maintain accountability to the public for the decision making that occurs pursuant to such delegation of authority, executive officials must usually make their policy decisions based on a public record and only after giving the public an opportunity to be heard on the issue. Furthermore, such decisions must be defensible on their merits, as well as in terms of appropriate procedures, if they are challenged in court. One consequence of these requirements is that policy analysis plays a significantly larger role in public decision making in the United States than it appears to play in other Western democracies. Retrospective evaluation of past policies is essential to creation of the database used in prospective analysis of proposed policies. Thus, there is a strong 'home market' for evaluation and analysis in the United States.

Another factor that strengthens the market for analysis and evaluation in the US is the pragmatic nature of most public policy making—American leaders are typically more interested in knowing what works than in following particular ideologies or party lines. The Reagan administration is regarded as having been somewhat more ideological than typical administrations, and I sense that there has been a decline in the number and scope of science policy analyses and evaluation studies done within and for government agencies in the last few years.

Finally, because science continually creates new possibilities in widely divergent areas of public concern, the authority for decision making over scientific priorities and resources has become widely distributed throughout both the Congress and the executive branch. From time to time, efforts have been made to centralize control over science decision making, but such efforts have typically been transitory or have had only limited success. The major rationale for such centralization has been that priorities for science could be better set if a single body were responsible for deciding about all of them at once. This is the main argument underlying the coordination functions of the Office of Science and Technology Policy in the Executive Office of the President, as established under the National Science and Technology Policy and Priorities Act of 1976. This desire to centralize control over scientific priorities has also been at the heart of the concept of a Department of Science and Technology, which has been proposed by, among others, the President's Commission on Industrial Competitiveness (1985).

Possibilities for reform of science policy making in the United States

There has been a surge of interest in reforming the institutions and mechanisms of science decision making in the Federal government in the past two to three years. The reasons for this new interest include the challenge of priority setting discussed above, dissatisfaction in some quarters with the effectiveness of the current White House Office of Science and Technology Policy (OSTP) (Committee on Science, Space, and Technology 1988), and the prospect that a new administration in January 1989 will offer an opportunity to renew the science advisory apparatus. Also, the series of hearings held by the Science Policy Task Force of the US House Committee on Science, Space, and Technology in 1985 and 1986 caused a number of students of, and participants in, science policy making to refresh their knowledge and concern about scientific decision making in the United States.

Reform generally has three aspects: organizational, procedural, and substantive. First, regarding organization, a compilation by William Golden of over 80 commissioned articles shows that there is much sentiment for strengthening the OSTP (Golden 1988). Increased strength would presumably derive from actions such as selecting a visible and distinguished director for the office, reestablishing a high-level committee of scientific expert advisers to the President, and building up the OSTP staff so that it can play a major role in budget decisions for science in conjunction with the Office of Management and Budget. Some people with close understanding of the operations of the White House advocate that the science adviser should be made a formal member of the Cabinet, or at least a special assistant to the President, so that he can have free access to the President. For the most part, these admonitions are addressed to the current group of candidates for President and to their top advisers, since it is widely noted that the President ultimately decides how to organize his science advisory mechanism and how he uses it.

Procedural reform for science decision making in the United States is only beginning to emerge as an issue. As noted above, there is a rapidly growing interest in devising new mechanisms for tapping the scientific community for advice to the government on science priorities (Greenberg 1988). As yet, it is unclear what impacts the speeches by Frank Press, Robert Rosenzweig, Doug Walgren, and others, as well as the request by the Senate Budget Committee for advice on priorities, will have on either the scientific community or the government. Whatever happens, it is likely to be obscured in character and significance by the arrival on the scene of a new President, along with a new cast of advisers and a new set of priorities. Regardless of who is elected in November 1988, I expect to see several experiments over the next year or two with formalized advising on science priorities.

Finally, what constitutes appropriate substantive reform in science policy making depends, of course, on the preferences of the commentator. Clearly, many issues are before us. These include determining the balance of defence versus civilian-related R&D support, determining the level of support for very large 'big science' projects — both individually and collectively — versus smaller 'individual investigator' projects, and determining the appropriate Federal role in the direct support of R&D that is of interest to industry and international competitiveness.

Frank Press's speech on priorities in science (Press 1988) presented not only his call to seek processes for priority setting, but also his own set of broad science priorities, in three categories:

(1) Highest priority to training and research grants that reach large numbers of investigators and graduate students, programmes to deal with national crises, such as AIDS and the loss of access to space, and research to exploit extraordinary breakthroughs like high-temperature superconductivity;

(2) Second priority to large projects like the superconducting supercollider and sequencing the human genome;

(3) A third, 'political' category including research related to such subjects as national security, the space station, regional economic development, manned space flight, and industrial competitiveness.

These three categories would not please everyone, certainly not in this order. Also, the fact that Press laid out his own preferences in a speech that otherwise called for a response by the scientific community to the requests from policy makers for help on *processes* of priority setting raises the question of whether his speech was motivated by interest in advisory processes, by disagreement with current priorities, or by the hope of stimulating debate on the entire issue.

Concluding remarks

Despite the complexity of the processes of decision making for science, and despite the procedural requirements imposed on US policy makers in general to make decisions in apparently rational and defensible ways, the actual use of formal evaluation in science policy making has been limited. This has been especially true at the highest levels of decision making, where leaders must truly make trade-offs between apples and oranges—between science and housing for the poor, for example. We have established none of the institutions or mechanisms adopted in the UK in the past few years that put formal evaluation at the core of major decisions on the futures of laboratories, universities, or entire fields of scientific endeavour.

The British experience with evaluation-driven science policy making has not gone unnoticed in the United States, although most attentive observers are probably more worried than uplifted by British actions. The next few years will be interesting ones for both nations.

References

Baldwin E, Hill CT 1988 The budget process and large-scale science funding. Congressional Research Service Review 9:(2)13–16

Boffey PM 1988 Two leaders challenge the 'big science' trend. New York Times, May 3 C1

Committee on the Budget 1988 Concurrent resolution on the budget 1989. US Senate Report 100–311, March 31, p 22

Committee on Science, Space, and Technology 1988 Oversight hearings on Office of Science and Technology policy. Report No. 106, February 17

Golden WT (ed) 1988 Science and technology advice to the President, Congress and judiciary. Pergamon Press, New York

Greenberg D 1988 Carnegie creates commission on science policy. Science and Government Report April 15, p 8

Levine CH, Benda PM 1986 Expertise and democratic decisionmaking: a reader. Science Policy Background Report No. 7, Committee on Science and Technology, US House of Representatives

Lindblom CE 1968 The policy making process. Prentice Hall, New Jersey

Long JR 1988 Priority-setting urged in funding of major science initiatives. Chemical and Engineering News, May 2, p 25–27

National Research Council 1984 Major facilities for materials research and related disciplines. National Academy Press, Washington, DC

National Research Council 1985 Opportunities in chemistry. National Academy Press, Washington, DC

National Research Council 1988 Frontiers in chemical engineering: research needs and opportunities. National Academy Press, Washington, DC

President's Commission on Industrial Competitiveness 1985 Global competition: the new reality.

Press F 1988 The dilemma of the golden age. Address to 125th annual meeting of the National Academy of Sciences, April 26

DISCUSSION

Moravcsik: Dr Hill, you mentioned that determining science policy is particularly difficult because science is esoteric. I agree with you in some respects, but it would be interesting to analyse what knowledge is needed by policy makers for science. They do not need to know about the solutions of the Schrödinger equation but there is some general understanding of science—perhaps of methodology, for example—that is necessary for policy makers to deal with issues such as contradictory peer reviews. What qualifications does one need to be able to direct the traffic in this area?

Hill: There are some areas in which it is necessary to understand the potential of science. For example, what is the human genome sequencing project about and what do we hope to learn from it? I saw a piece on British television that said this project offers the hope of curing heart disease and cancer. However, what we are really likely to get out of the project is one kind of basic knowledge.

An understanding of the social process is more important. Policy makers need to understand the tendency on the part of the advocates of any science or scientific project to overstate the claims for what they are likely to be able to contribute in the short run. I wrote an article in the 'Science and the budget' report called 'Considerations in funding large-scale science' (Hill 1988). We suggested 43 questions that Congress might want to consider in examining big science programmes. They ranged from broad issues, such as what are the scientific, technical and social goals and are they clearly defined, to what is the probability of major cost over-runs and how might they be paid for. Congress is very alert to the possibility that scientific institutions make proposals for new projects because old projects are about to be finished; NASA (National Aeronautics and Space Administration) is particularly susceptible to that syndrome.

Irvine: It will be a major task to develop effective priority setting procedures in the USA, and, in particular, to persuade the scientific community to take such activities seriously. Attempts have been made previously to encourage researchers to become more strategic and selective in planning how to use public funds for R&D. However, the history of previous initiatives—such as the 'five-year outlook', the National Academy of Sciences field reviews and the more recent 'research briefings' exercise—shows that the scientific community generally turns them to their own advantage (using the opportunity to argue for more money) and refuses to participate in selecting priorities.

One of the main problems is the stress the US system puts on disciplines and on specific field committees. For example, the National Academy of Engineering report on engineering priorities focused on opportunities in existing fields, whereas in Sweden a similar study used a holistic approach to identify emerging cross-disciplinary areas (like micronics). US science policy structures are not in a state where they can handle the important decisions that need to be made in a research environment where fields are converging and technologies fusing.

A second problem in identifying funding priorities across research areas is the way 'big science' debates in the US are always phrased in terms of needing to beat the rest of the world. Thus discussion of the superconducting supercollider (SSC) emphasizes regaining the international lead and the negative consequences if the facility is not funded. Yet US physicists fail to mention that the SSC proposal arose from international discussions about a world accelerator. When the Brookhaven machine was terminated, high-energy physicists were essentially promised a new facility and they decided upon the SSC. The rational choice would have been to invest in a higher energy Stanford linear collider, which uses a novel and cheap technology. It is also an area where the USA has a comparative advantage. However, that type of technology caters for fewer scientific users than the SSC, and the Stanford proposal was outvoted by the research communities linked to the Fermi Lab and Brookhaven. Politically the correct choice was impossible and yet at the same time it duplicated plans at CERN (Centre Européen pour Recherche Nucleaire) to build a similar facility. This illustrates the difficulty of introducing an element of international collaboration in US science policy. It also shows how difficult it will be to introduce systematic procedures for priority setting when decisions are essentially based on adversarial politics.

Hill: If I can interrupt your comments about American public policy, we would all probably agree with you, John. The struggle that we face is indeed to develop mechanisms to bring a different kind of rationality to bear. A political scientist might argue that there is nothing irrational in political terms about any of the choices made in the US, but they often don't make sense to scientists.

Blume: It seem to me that apart from xenophobia and ideology there are at least two problems connected with the rational development of science policy. First, looking back over the development of public policy making in the last 40 years, one sees that belief in the possibility of rational policy on the part of policy makers goes through waves. In the 1960s it was thought to be possible; cost–benefit analysis, and planning, programming and budgeting systems (PPBS) were developed. In the 1970s faith in rational policy disappeared, partly because inflation made thinking about the future difficult, partly because it just went out of fashion. We are now in a new phase when people again want to believe in rational policy making, though the constraints are different from those in the 1960s. That's why some of the techniques that we are hearing about seem to be carrying weight. I think that time will also pass; we shall return to pork-barrel allocations. This may mean that one ought to try to get a few things in place while the going is good!

Second, the way in which problems arise structures the questions that have to be asked. Priority setting in a system such as the Congressional Appropriations Committee is a different sort of business from setting priorities within a science budget. Having to make a case for a certain amount of expenditure on health research with regard to the total national expenditure on health is different from doing so for a given amount of health research expenditure in relation to that for physics, chemistry or road research. There are many subtle gradations in between. There isn't a single class of question which lends itself to a particular model of rationality. The questions emerge in a variety of ways, depending upon political traditions and organizations.

Perhaps the scientific community has to think more carefully about the way in which the questions it's being forced to confront arise, and to consider the nature of the political arena in which the questions arise. Perhaps the *structures* of science policy making have to be more effectively problematized. Is a science budget an advantage? Under what conditions is it useful to have a science budget? Might it be better under certain circumstances to fight on various fronts? A science budget may mean that you can defend a declining level of expenditure, but you can also be forced to play one bit of science off against another. One has to think more about the structure of decision making; there's nothing obvious about priorities being set in one way or another.

Dixon: What are the problems peculiar to managing science in what's been called a 'steady state'? It can be argued that resource allocation between different sectors is more difficult in a 'steady state' than in both an expansion period, when there is plenty of money for everybody, or even a contracting period, when hard choices have to be made. In a steady state the rival claims of different sectors have to be looked at afresh. Are new mechanisms required for that situation?

Hill: You have done more thinking about that in the UK than we have in the USA. We had a so-called budget summit agreement between the President and the Congress after the 19th October 1987 stock market crash. It included essentially steady state, zero growth of domestic discretionary expenditures, within which all R&D outside defence falls. Yet within the context of a 2% real growth in that overall category, the President proposed a 29% increase for 'budget function 250', which includes the NSF (National Science Foundation), NASA and some of the R&D for the Department of Energy. So we have yet to face up to reality. I agree with you that it's going to be difficult. We only have a science budget in the USA as an *a posteriori* fiction. There is no such thing as a science budget in functional terms; we don't make decisions in the context of an overall pot of money for science and then chop it up. That's an important characteristic of our system.

Georghiou: There are some dangers in the concept of a steady-state model for science. The only thing that's steady is the total input of funds. Perhaps, at a political level, it's similar to the old 'limits-to-growth' debate. Underneath that particular thing being constrained everything else is not steady; the mix of science that is done, the relative costs of that science, and the costs of doing particular kinds of science are all changing. So the idea of the steady state can lead you into the same kind of arguments that limits-to-growth did in the 1960s where you assume that you are going to run out of particular resources. We think we shall run out of science resources, but a few years later things always look different.

Phillips: But a biochemist would understand that immediately as a dynamic steady state!

Braun: Christopher, you have done some work on Nobel prizes. Did you use the number of the Nobel prizes or the number of people to whom they were awarded?

Hill: Joan Winston and I examined the relationship of Nobel prize-winning in the sciences at a national level to other indicators of national scientific and technological performance (Hill & Winston 1986). For the period 1945–1984 we developed indicators of prize-winning in terms of the numbers of prizes in each field by decade and by country, as well as in terms of the numbers of prizes *per capita*. These were compared with indicators of factors such as national levels of R&D spending, scientific manpower, publication counts, citation ratios relative to the nation's literature, patent performance, high-technology trade, economic growth, and public health status. Nobel prize-winning correlated best with other measures of basic research quality, and least well with indicators of success in practical applications of science. All the data are based on the allocation of fractional prizes. When the prizes are shared, they are always allocated as a single prize, half a prize or a quarter of a prize.

Braun: And in the relative citation ratio did you use just the percentage of published papers with the percentage of citations?

Hill: We looked at percentage of citations. I also looked at numbers of publications but they do not correlate with Nobel prize indicators.

Braun: The use of other awards as indicators is also attractive. We are compiling a database of science awards and who wins them. This could be used to provide indicators that augment bibliometric studies.

Hill: I applaud your effort. We looked at the directories of science awards. My judgement was that every other prestigious award in science has serious problems of what, for our purposes, would be national bias. That is to say, there is either a clear historical pattern of awards to one nation or an explicit requirement for eligibility. There really are no other unbiased international awards, except perhaps the Fields Medal in mathematics.

References

Hill CT 1988 Considerations in funding large-scale science. Congressional Research Service Review 9(2):3–5

Hill CT, Winston JD 1986 The Nobel Prize awards in science as a measure of national strength in science. Science Policy Study Background Report No. 3, Committee on Science and Technology, US House of Representatives, Washington, DC

The impact of evaluation data on policy determination

Terttu Luukkonen-Gronow

The Academy of Finland, Hämeentie 68, SF-00550 Helsinki, Finland

Abstract. This paper discusses uses and impacts of evaluations of scientific research drawing from concepts and results obtained in studies of the utilization of research findings. Examples are derived from case histories, personal communications, and a study of evaluations in the Scandinavian countries in which the author is involved. The utilization of evaluations is analysed by three broad concepts—instrumental, conceptual, and persuasive use—and examples of each case are supplied. Attention is paid to the audiences of evaluations and their effects on utilization. The impacts of evaluations are assessed to be mainly piecemeal changes and small-scale modifications in programmes and policy. For evaluations to contribute to more dramatic changes there must be a special combination of circumstances. Evaluations are but one of the factors that affect policy. Three categories of factors that enhance utilization and impacts are discussed: relevance, credibility, and communication.

1989 The evaluation of scientific research. Wiley, Chichester (Ciba Foundation Conference) p 234–246

This paper deals with systematic evaluations of past and present performance of scientific research. Systematic evaluations of scientific research that concern levels of aggregation that are higher than individual scientists, research proposals, or articles, are a relatively new phenomenon, and studies of their uses and impacts are virtually non-existent. Therefore, I shall draw from the results obtained in research that studies to what extent research findings are utilized, the so-called evaluation research (see e.g. Leviton & Hughes 1981). Most of this research, however, relates to social programmes and policy. A few studies also deal with programmes to promote innovation or other issues of research and technology policies (e.g. Gray et al 1986, Eveland 1986). My examples originate from both a study of evaluations in the Scandinavian countries (T. Luukkonen-Gronow & B. Ståhle, unpublished work 1988)* and other studies, case histories or personal communications about evaluations of scientific research.

---

*This study analyses functions and impacts of evaluations undertaken in the Scandinavian countries by the research councils or equivalent organizations. It is a cooperative project between the Academy of Finland and the Nordic Council of Ministers.

Use and impact: a conceptual clarification

The concepts *use*, (or *utilization*), and *impact* have nearly identical meanings. Nevertheless, they describe slightly different aspects of what is expected to happen after an evaluation has been completed. 'Use' (or utilization) is, at a minimum, an attempt to relate evaluation findings to policies, programmes or other issues (Leviton & Hughes 1981). 'Impact' refers to the actual change or modification of programmes, personnel deployment, funding or policy to which evaluations have contributed. Thus, 'use' emphasizes the intentions or efforts of those involved in a policy process whereas 'impact' refers to the end result of a policy process. Impacts may be unintended or even unrecognized: sometimes the most important impacts are both unintended and unrecognized.

Meanings of evaluation use

Evaluation researchers have attributed a diverse array of meanings to use. Attention has been drawn to the facts that in different situations, uses are of different kinds, and that there is more than one criterion by which to judge whether information is used. Three broad categories of use dominate the discussion: instrumental, conceptual, and persuasive (Leviton & Hughes 1981).

Instrumental use

Instrumental use was defined by Weiss (1977, p 11) as a situation in which information provides 'empirical evidence and/or conclusions that will help to solve a policy problem'. This is a conventional view of use which, however, has proved too narrow to suit all situations.

An approach used by the Japanese Agency of Industrial Science and Technology, at the Ministry of International Trade and Industry, provides an example of instrumental use. Within a programme that aims to develop 'revolutionary basic technology', projects are evaluated at three stages during their execution. According to Irvine, most important are the mid-term assessments to choose the most promising options among candidate prototype technologies (Irvine 1988, p 38–39). The achievement of technical aims is the main assessment criterion. Evaluations are built into the decision process and have a direct effect on whether the projects are continued.

A more dramatic example of instrumental use is provided by the evaluation of hydrobiology undertaken by the Danish Natural Science Research Council. The Ministry of Education requested the University of Copenhagen to reduce the number of personnel in natural sciences and medicine. The University decided that some of the decrease was to be in biological sciences. Even though the evaluation was intended to have other purposes, it was used as a tool to identify

where a decrease in personnel was justified; it prevented the dismissal of one
of the proposed persons in hydrobiology, and it warranted the strengthening
of the scientific capacity and resources of the institute that was to be hit hardest
(T. Luukkonen-Gronow & B. Ståhle, unpublished work 1988).

Bibliometric indicators have been reported to be in instrumental use in the
allocation of resources in universities in The Netherlands (Moed et al 1985) and
as a management tool to keep a balance between basic and applied activities
in a research institute of the Hungarian Academy of Sciences (Vinkler 1986).

Conceptual use

Conceptual use implies that an evaluation is not used concretely to formulate
decisions, but that it provides information that 'enlightens' decision makers
about the scope of problems and it influences their thinking about an issue (see
Rich 1977, p 200). Such information might not be applied immediately, but it
may serve as a basis for revising policies in the future.

The Academy of Finland commissioned peer review panels to evaluate
performance in research fields. These evaluations reported about structural
problems in academia in Finland, such as inbreeding and inflexible career
structures. These observations led to new forms of funding, researcher education
and exchange programmes. Some of these problems had been discovered before,
but the results of the evaluations highlighted their significance. It should be
noted that this impact was achieved because several consecutive evaluations
produced convergent comments.

Persuasive use

When evaluation results are used to advocate a stance that was taken earlier,
they are used in a *persuasive* or partisan way. Research information is said to
have become 'ammunition for the side that finds its conclusions congenial and
supportive' (Weiss 1979, p 429). In fields which require large investments in
equipment, evaluations tend to result in persuasive use. A frequently cited
criticism of peer review is that researchers in a given field regard their own area
to be important and stress the urgent financial requirements, sometimes even
recommending a multiple increase in funding (see Rekstad 1987). In such cases,
the representatives of the field lend their authority to a persuasive use.

An important category of persuasive use is the 'legitimation' of activities.
The European Community started an evaluation activity to obtain 'a simple
judgement on the quality of the execution of a programme' (i.e. legitimation),
but their evaluations are evolving into 'an essential tool in the selection of the
activities and mechanisms which are best suited to the attainment of the goals
of the European Community', that is they are being put to instrumental use

(L. Massimo, unpublished paper, Economic Commission for Europe, Ad Hoc Meeting, 22–26 June 1987).

Roessner analysed four evaluations of US Government innovation programmes, and concluded that an advocative behaviour, or use as ammunition, was an important precondition for evaluations to have impacts (J. D. Roessner, unpublished paper, Organization for Economic Cooperation and Development (OECD) Meeting, 16–18 December 1987). The concept that the information itself is so compelling or authoritative that it will inevitably drive toward implementation (the so-called knowledge-driven model of utilization, see Weiss 1979) is not usually realistic, especially if the issues have a strong political dimension.

Audiences of evaluations

Evaluations are intended for various audiences. A basic distinction can be made between internal and external audiences. Internal evaluations provide the research-sponsoring organizations with feedback on their decisions and an assessment of their strengths and weaknesses (see Cozzens 1987). They also provide information for future planning and decisions. IBM, the US National Science Foundation and the Japanese Agency of Industrial Science and Technology, are examples of organizations that carry out continuous review of their research programmes for internal use (Cozzens 1987, Irvine 1988). The use of evaluations for budget allocations or to improve the efficiency of the organization corresponds to instrumental use. Internal budget review processes may also involve partisan use of evaluation data (cf. Roessner 1985). As the example of the Academy of Finland indicated, internal use may also be conceptual.

Assessments for external audiences are carried out mainly by government agencies, because they rely on external bodies for their resources (Department of Treasury/Finance and the Parliament/Congress/Diet). Government agencies that fund and perform scientific research also have to justify their activities to the public because of their reliance on budget procedures for finances. The growing need to legitimate activities to external audiences is behind the increased demand for evaluations in research funding and performing organizations in the past few years (cf Phillips & Turney 1988). This 'legitimation' corresponds to partisan use. It is apparent that most external use is of the partisan type.

Evaluations are often carried out for both types of audiences. In such cases, the uses are different. Roessner (1985) discovered that in the US Department of Energy formal, quantitative decision aids were used internally in an instrumental way (for R&D project selection), but externally in a partisan way (to legitimate the project selection process). The Swedish Natural Science Research Council uses evaluations of research fields in a similar way—internally for project selection, and externally to provide a justification for successful activities. The external justification has contributed to increased funding for the Council (T. Luukkonen-Gronow & B. Ståhle, unpublished work 1988).

This differentiation of audiences applies to decision making bodies. In evaluations of scientific research, the scientists who do the research studied are an important audience. Many evaluations recommend that researchers reorient their work. Whether the recommendations will be followed is, therefore, also dependent on the behaviour of this group. Some impacts arise as a reaction of the research community to an evaluation, e.g. researchers may get frustrated if an evaluation raises unrealistic hopes of an increase in research funding and these hopes are not fulfilled (see Rekstad 1987).

Piecemeal impacts

No comprehensive information is available on how frequently evaluations are used and have impacts. First, let me make a methodological observation. It is hard to study the impacts of evaluations, because the application of an evaluation to a problem or the usefulness of an evaluation in redefining a problem is not always documented. It is also difficult to prove that a decision was taken because of an evaluation, as many other factors affect the decision process; at best, evaluations contribute an additional element.

When we study impacts we have to remember that the use of an evaluation does not always produce observable impacts. If an evaluation is positive—that is, it regards projects as of high quality or leads to the conclusion that the present allocation of funds or state of affairs is the best option—it is not conducive to change. This was referred to as a 'legitimation' of activities. In exceptional cases, too positive a result may be the reason for a change. Irvine (1988, p 39) described an evaluation at the Japanese Agency of Industrial Science and Technology which warranted termination of a project just over half-way through its planned duration because it had surpassed its technical goals.

Evaluations for internal audiences are usually carefully read and the information is taken into account inside the organization. For example, assessments of research units, such as projects or teams, are used in funding decisions. These evaluations tend to have impacts, if not directly and immediately, then on future decisions. The impacts of evaluations for external audiences are much more difficult to detect and the factors that affect the end results are more complicated. Here we enter a more political arena in which the role of evaluations is to a great extent to provide ammunition to the parties involved.

My experience with evaluations is that they often have some impacts, but seldom result in drastic changes in the allocation of funds or organization of personnel or policy: most impacts are piecemeal. For example, they involve decisions concerning the start, continuation or discontinuation of projects, small adjustments in the present allocation of funds, a modification of researcher exchange programmes, or a modification in the size and organization of projects. If a thorough reorganization of a research institution or a decision concerning the acquisition of expensive equipment follows an evaluation, these options must have received strong support before. The evaluation was only a contributing factor and perhaps gave evidence to support the arguments of the advocates of change. We may even assume that the evaluation was undertaken to gain such support for a planned or desired change (i.e. persuasive use). There are concrete examples of more dramatic change. The Scandinavian Institute of Asian Studies will be reorganized as a consequence of an evaluation completed in 1985. The evaluation, however, was only one phase in a long process of change that had started many years earlier. The evaluation did not cause a reorganization immediately, but a heated debate and a special committee for reorganization preceded the final decision in autumn 1987 to implement change (B. Ståhle, personal communication 1987). In Finland, an evaluation of experimental particle and nuclear physics contributed to a decision to acquire a new medium-size accelerator, and although the evaluation was an important factor in the process, its role was not straightforward.

Factors influencing use and impacts

Relevance

Case histories of successful evaluations illustrate the importance of relevance of the questions that the evaluation addresses (Jones 1983, J. D. Roessner, unpublished paper, OECD Meeting, 16–18 December 1987). To be relevant, an evaluation must meet the needs of the managers of the programmes in question or the decision makers on the pertinent issues. There are several factors that contribute to relevance. One is that evaluations are not undertaken as an academic exercise, but have a specific purpose. If evaluations are not built into the decision process or do not systematically concern all scientific areas or units, there should be an answer to the questions of why this area, this institute or this programme is evaluated, and why it is evaluated now, and not in a few years time. Research evaluations are now fashionable, and this entails the possibility that they are initiated without any clear aims.

Relevant questions cannot be asked without sufficient interaction between those in charge of an evaluation and the decision makers. If evaluations are done routinely in a special evaluation unit, there is a danger that the evaluation evolves 'a life of its own' — that is, it becomes too detached from the concerns of the organization and does not address relevant questions (J. Freamo, personal communication 1987).

Credibility

The credibility of an evaluation depends on several factors. One precondition for credibility is that the methodology should be of high quality. The expertise of those in charge of an evaluation or the scientific reputation of a peer review panel affects the credibility of the results. Another aspect of the quality of the methodology is its objectivity. This implies that those who conduct the evaluation should be external to the evaluated activities. Quantitative methods surpass peer review methods in this aspect. Quantitative methods are not, however, credible in all fields. Formal, quantitative methods may require an unobtainable degree of specification, they may not be easily understood by potential users, or such methods might not be able to address the questions facing decision makers (cf. Roessner 1985, Office of Technology Assessment 1986, Phillips & Turney 1988).

Cozzens (1987) found that evaluation for internal audiences tends to be done 'informally, without great attention to procedural detail', whereas for an evaluation in which the validity of the assessment must be demonstrated to an outside group, the evaluation procedure tends to be more formal and rely on external experts.

Methodological rigour is not sufficient for credibility to be established. How well an evaluation corresponds to the preconceptions of users and how well other information corroborates the evaluation results are also important (Leviton & Hughes 1981, p 539–540, Jones 1983, p 180). Methodological questions gain importance if the evaluation data are unexpected and disappointing from the point of view of potential users (Patton et al 1977). Users are more likely to act upon an evaluation if it confirms their expectations or intuition (cf. persuasive use; see Roessner 1985).

Communication

Interaction and communication between the evaluators and the users is important both before and after an evaluation. Without sufficient efforts at the dissemination of the results to the audience, they tend to be unused (see Leviton & Hughes 1981, p 536–7, Jones 1983, p 182). Even in such cases, an evaluation may have impacts.

Dissemination of results is most effective when there exists a network or 'an invisible college' of specialists or 'an evaluation champion' within the user organization. This means that an individual or a group of people has to make a special effort to use the evaluation to formulate decision options (E. Ormala, unpublished paper, Nordforsk meeting on evaluation of technological R&D, 10–12 November 1986). This is also referred to as the 'personal factor', i.e. the personal energy, interests, abilities and contacts of specific individuals are important for impacts (Patton et al 1977). If evaluations are built into the decision process, this problem is not as acute (cf. the example of the Japanese Agency of Industrial Science and Technology). The interaction between the evaluators and the users is most effective if the users are actively involved during early phases of the evaluation, e.g. in formulating the questions that the evaluation addresses.

Costs and benefits of evaluations

One of my conclusions has been that the impacts of evaluations tend to be piecemeal and are not always noticeable. It takes a special combination of circumstances for an evaluation to contribute to dramatic changes. Evaluations do not address the most important questions concerning the allocation of resources among fields. This might give rise to the impression that the costs outweigh the benefits of evaluations. Before we come to any such conclusion, we must remember that evaluations also have effects other than those considered. Evaluations stress the importance of quality and productivity. That an evaluation is imminent may have a positive impact on the research communities and may orient scientists' work into desirable directions. Evaluations may also have negative and unexpected impacts, such as the creation of too competitive an atmosphere, emphasis on quick results and creation of conflicts (cf. Rekstad 1987).

Irrespective of our judgement of the cost-effectiveness of evaluations, they seem to be here to stay. As I said earlier, the interest in evaluations is to a large extent due to a need in recent years to provide data for external audiences, i.e. to justify scientific research activities in the eyes of the public and the holders of public purse-strings. In an era of increasing costs of scientific research and stronger demands for selectivity in which directions will be funded, evaluations serve a multiple purpose: they legitimize activities, provide a tool to select targets and help to identify problems that hinder the effectiveness of the system. Even if the evaluations do not produce sizeable impacts, they supply a useful tool that is difficult to replace.

Acknowledgements

I am greatly indebted to Erik Allardt, Joe Freamo, J. David Roessner and Bertel Ståhle for comments and to J. David Roessner for his help in search of pertinent evaluation literature.

References

Cozzens SE 1987 Expert review in evaluating programs. Science and Public Policy 14:71–81
Eveland JD 1986 Small business innovation research programs: solutions seeking problems. In: Gray DO et al (eds) Technological innovation: strategies for a new partnership. Elsevier Science Publisher, Amsterdam, p 195–206

Gray DO, Hetzner W, Eveland JD, Gidley T 1986 NSF's Industry–University Cooperative Research Centers Program and the innovation process: evaluation-based lessons. In: Gray DO et al (eds) Technological innovation: strategies for a new partnership. Elsevier Science Publisher, Amsterdam, p 175–193

Irvine J 1988 Evaluating applied research: lessons from Japan. Pinter, London

Jones WJ 1983 Can evaluations influence programs? The case of compensatory education. Journal of Policy Analysis and Management 2:174–184

Leviton LC, Hughes EFX 1981 Research on the utilization of evaluations: a review and synthesis. Evaluation Review 5:525–548

Moed HF, Burger WJM, Frankfort JG, van Raan AFJ 1985 The use of bibliometric data for the measurement of university research performance. Research Policy 14:131–149

Office of Technology Assessment 1986 Research funding as an investment: can we measure the returns? Science Policy Study Background Report No. 12. Prepared by OTA, transmitted to the Task Force on Science Policy. Committee on Science and Technology, US House of Representatives. US Government Printing Office, Washington

Patton MQ, Grimes PS, Guthrie KM, Brennan NJ, French BD, Blyth DA 1977 In search of impact: an analysis of the utilization of federal health evaluation research. In: Weiss CH (ed) Using social research in public policy making. Lexington Books, Lexington, Massachusetts, p 141–163

Phillips DC, Turney J 1988 Bibliometrics and UK science policy. Scientometrics 14:185–200

Redkstad J 1987 NAVF evaluates research disciplines—why? In: Ståhle B (ed) Evaluation of research: Nordic experiences. Nordic Science Policy Council, Copenhagen (Proc Nordic Workshop, Saltsjöbaden, 1986) p 35–44

Rich RF 1977 Uses of social science information by federal bureaucrats: knowledge for action versus knowledge for understanding. In: Weiss CH (ed) Using social research in public policy making. Lexington Books, Lexington, Massachusetts, p 199–211

Roessner JD 1985 The multiple functions of formal aids to decision making in public agencies. IEEE Transactions in Engineering Management, EM-32:124–128

Vinkler P 1986 Management system for a scientific research institute based on the assessment of scientific publications. Research Policy 15:77–87

Weiss CH 1977 Introduction. In: Weiss CH (ed) Using social research in public policy making. Lexington Books, Lexington, Massachusetts, p 1–22

Weiss CH 1979 The many meanings of research utilization. Public Administration Review, 35:426–431

DISCUSSION

Pavitt: Even before evaluation was formalized and quantified, decisions were made by what might be called the 'informed judgements of wise men'. One has to ask whether recent methods and quantification improve on the previous evaluations.

Terttu, you classify the impacts of evaluations as instrumental, conceptual and persuasive. At the Science Policy Research Unit (SPRU) most of our impact has, in my judgement, been in the category you describe as conceptual. By publishing our work, we influence the way that decision makers behave, or change their perceptions. You are right that these impacts are piecemeal, small-scale modifications, and one wouldn't want it otherwise in a democracy. On the other hand, they are quite important in aggregate. For example, in the UK, Britain was widely perceived to be a great technological power in the early 1970s. Over the next ten years that perception changed considerably, because of information published by the government and research done at such places as Manchester and Sussex. Another example is the growth of Japan as a technological power. Policy research institutes were well ahead of public opinion and practitioners when they reported the explosive growth of Japanese patenting in the USA from the mid 1960s onwards.

Anderson: As Keith says, an important feature of science policy research is its ability to influence policy making by changing public opinion. Therefore it is important for at least the main conclusions of policy research to be published in the general scientific literature and the lay press.

Bernard Dixon suggested earlier that we might need a new journal to improve dissemination of the results of research evaluation. But science policy researchers already have their own set of journals and professional societies. I am worried that the field is becoming too isolated as an academic discipline. As well as good communication between policy researchers and policy makers, we also need better communication of important results to the general population.

Kodama: I mentioned earlier that evaluation is one part of the social process and that the mobility of scientists is an important aspect. Terttu referred to some mid-term evaluations by the Japanese Agency for Industrial Science and Technology (AIST). Japanese society is generally very immobile but some sectors are mobile. AIST organizes several research projects and does many evaluations. Many of the researchers for these projects come from industry or from national research institutes and their previous positions are secured. Therefore if evaluation leads to a decision against a project, the researchers have jobs to which they can return. However, for in-house evaluations in national research institutes the scientists continue to work there. When the results of the evaluation are announced there is no way of putting the decision into effect.

Many breakthroughs in Japan come from international pressure. For example, using the argument of symmetrical access, the United States is demanding that we bring their researchers to Japanese laboratories. The USA is claiming that our society is closed to foreigners, but an immobile society is also closed to us, the Japanese! The importance of mobility for the implementation of an evaluation cannot be overstated. I am surprised that Dr Hill complains about gradualism of budgeting for the science projects in the USA; I thought the USA was dynamic in putting the money into NASA and similar enterprises. It is difficult in Japan to think about a brand new science frontier. Our budgeting system is really based on incrementalism; we put in some money and then see whether there are results. This feedback system works well in industry, but for science projects in a brand new area there is a critical mass that must be reached before anything can be produced. Thus the incremental system has an intrinsic deficiency: there is no chance to catch the bus.

Weinberg: I recently reviewed energy policy in the USA and the world. Over the past fifteen years none of our forecasts of energy demand has been right. The response has been incrementalism with respect to new sources of energy: don't build big plants, do build a succession of small plants. Incrementalism is a fundamental human reaction. Professor C.E. Lindblom called it the 'science of muddling through'. and said that in some sense it is inevitable and perhaps more efficient. With respect to the superconducting supercollider (SSC), Frank Press (President of the US National Academy of Sciences) has suggested a kind of incrementalism; we should spend a reasonable amount of money on studying the SSC, but we should not invest large amounts until we can afford to do so, even if this means waiting a very long time.

Occasionally we do make hard decisions,such as the decision in the late 1960s between higher energy and higher current in high-energy physics experiments. A committee headed by Professor H.A. Bethe recommended high energy and that project went ahead. The other project was disbanded even though 50 or 100 people had already been employed and had to find other jobs.

Hill: Our perceptions of each other's countries on some of these matters are interesting. For example, the standard view in the USA about high-temperature superconductivity is that Japan moved extremely quickly to reallocate resources, create a consortium, and establish a central direction for the field, and that the USA was hopelessly behind. Yet if we look beyond the official figures, many of our government agencies—such as the National Science Foundation and the Departments of Defense and Energy—immediately reallocated money quite independently of any change in Congressional policy.

Kodama: This kind of drastic decision is not made by understanding the dynamics of the science process; it depends on international relations and diplomacy. Because Japan has become the country with the highest *per capita* income, we have to do something which is highly visible for reasons of international diplomacy. Superconductivity and, in my opinion, the Human Frontiers Project are examples of this. As I said, the symmetrical access argument provides a major breakthrough in solving our intrinsic problem of immobility. Those kinds of international expectations or obligations break the 'vicious circle'.

van Raan: Did you reach any specific opinions about the environment in which research is performed from your evaluations, Terttu? For example, what about the problems scientists have with bureaucracy? What was learnt about the role of young people in research? What's the role of mediocre research? The latter is an important question because we still have the famous Ortega hypothesis that the giants in science stand on the shoulders of the dwarfs. The opposite of this hypothesis is that mediocre research can be abandoned; you just need top research. Do the results of the studies in Scandinavian countries have any bearing on these topics?

Luukkonen-Gronow: In some evaluations it has been pointed out that the periods of financing are too short; researchers are having to write new proposals too frequently. The research funding organizations now tend to award longer term grants.

The problems for young researchers have been noted. The evaluations may have had some influence on the formulation of exchange programmes for training abroad. This impact does not affect large numbers of researchers, but it does represent an intervention brought about by the evaluations.

As for the problems of the elite versus the rest of the research community, the essence of evaluations is that they stress the importance of the quality of research. Nevertheless, it is acknowledged, at least in smaller countries, that one cannot be at the forefront in many fields. However, it is important to be able to follow developments over a broad range of scientific fields so as to be able to make a special effort in promising areas. Researchers who do mediocre work might have functions other than advancing international science, for example in training and in the transfer of knowledge. This is not talked about, but it's understood.

Phillips: I'm reminded of a remark by P.M.S. Blackett that a first-class laboratory is one in which mediocre scientists do outstanding work.

Garfield: I originally thought that this conference would be focused on bibliometrics and citation analysis. I didn't interpret the charter of evaluation research as being to answer the question 'how do we prove the economic impact of basic research?' However, Dr Hugh Fudenberg of the University of South Carolina analysed the economic impact of the polio vaccine (Fudenberg 1972). Hundreds of millions of dollars are saved every year because we now have a polio vaccine; we no longer need to treat the disease by spending millions on high-technology iron lungs. We need more investigations like that if we wish to address the question of economic impact.

A logical scientist can think beyond his basic research and estimate what it could mean economically. You get reflections of that in the TRACES study (see Narin, this volume), but those results were not packaged for consumption by Congressmen or other legislators and funding groups. Intuitively, Congressmen support the National Institutes of Health without the slightest reservation because they recognize the political and economic benefit for themselves and their constituents; they don't have trouble convincing ageing people that we should do research on Alzheimer's disease. But we should make retrospective analyses of such fields to trace the basic research that has contributed to progress in that area. A mixture of historical bibliometric and economic analysis is required. When Henry Small and I suggested using co-citation maps, we didn't interpret our mission as being to provide the economic argument for basic research. However, using these maps, you can trace the impact of basic discoveries, where they are being applied, and so on, and you can then attach appropriate financial data.

Let me add that if we can make the economic case for basic research in the USA, smaller countries might argue they can simply sit back and reap the benefits of using the literature wisely. But that leads to the subsidiary question—can a country like the UK, or even Finland, apply the basic discoveries if it doesn't maintain a research infrastructure capable of exploiting them? This in turn leads to the relationship between research and science education.

References

Fudenberg HH 1972 The dollar benefits of biomedical research: a cost analysis. Journal of Laboratory and Clinical Medicine 79:353–363
Narin F 1989 The impact of different modes of research funding. In: The evaluation of scientific research. Wiley, Chichester (Ciba Foundation Conference) p 120–140

The Cassandra paradox relating to the effectiveness of evaluation and forecasting methods

Philippe Montigny*

Directorate for Science, Technology and Industry, The Organization for Economic Cooperation and Development, 2 rue André-Pascal, Paris 75016, France

Abstract. Because many forecasts have no impact on the decision-making process, although they are based on precise data and made using recognized and improved methods, it seems that forecasting is affected by the 'Paradox of Cassandra': 'the effectiveness of forecasting techniques is independent of the vigorous methods by which they have been formulated'. In Greek mythology, Cassandra received from Apollo the gift of being able to predict the future and she foresaw the fall of Troy. However, she could never make her father, King Priam, believe her predictions: to him she had no *competence*, no *legitimacy* and no *authority*. The question of forecasting is located at the interface of the scientific community on the one hand, and the political one on the other, and this paradox is very up-to-date. Evaluation and forecasting are two aspects of the same question: what conclusion for the future can be drawn from what is happening now? Evaluation is focused on specific programmes and oriented on short-term decisions, whereas the field of forecasting is wide open and is oriented on long-term decisions. Evaluation and forecasting require their own methods and processes. However, similar factors are involved, such as the scientific community and the political authorities. To make evaluation and forecasting techniques effective, it is essential to know how they can acquire the *expertise*, *legitimacy* and *authority* necessary to escape from the 'Paradox of Cassandra'.

1989 The evaluation of scientific research. Wiley, Chichester (Ciba Foundation Conference) p 247–264

Appraisal of the effectiveness of forecasting techniques used by strategic planners may be approached in two ways. The first approach is to review systematically the different forecasting methods and place them in broad categories—mathematical models, scenario methods, etc. There is no shortage of

---

*This paper represents the views of the author and does not necessarily represent the views of the Organization for Economic Cooperation and Development.

documentation in this respect. Articles published in periodicals such as *Futures* and the *Journal of Forecasting* provide impressive bibliographies. This approach is amply justified by the fact that forecasting has a long history and that some forecasts have already had to face the test of time and therefore are available for systematic experimental investigation. The second approach is based on a method diametrically opposed to the first, and consists of tackling the question of forecasting techniques on an *a priori* rather than an *a posteriori* basis by focusing on the prerequisites for discussion.

This paper will pursue the second line of enquiry, because it highlights a concept that is referred to as the 'Cassandra paradox'. Analysis of this concept, based on the relationship between the political community and science, raises the question of the use of evaluation and forecasting exercises as instruments to aid decision making.

Forecasting and the Cassandra paradox

Cassandra and the curse of Apollo

At a recent international conference, André Piatier spoke of the danger of an international monetary crisis. His paper made it clear that this topic was commonly held to be 'old hat' (A. Piatier, unpublished paper, Int Conf Fr Speaking Econ, Freiburg, June 1987). The date on which he gave his paper was 3rd June 1987, just a few weeks before the financial crash that stunned observers by its suddenness! Forecasts therefore must not merely be accurate, they must also be heeded by those to whom they are addressed.

This is by no means a new development. In Greek mythology, Apollo accorded Cassandra, the daughter of Priam and Hecuba, the gift of prophecy but accompanied it by a curse to the effect that nobody would believe her predictions. It was therefore to no avail that she forewarned her father of the fall of Troy! It would seem that Apollo's curse is still in force today and that many of our forecasters have unwittingly become the spiritual heirs of Cassandra.

The sophistication of techniques and tools (mathematical models and statistics, information technology, etc.) seems to have no effect on the way in which forecasts are received. To take the analogy further, it is worth noting that oracles in Ancient Greece, despite their use of irrational logic (observation of birds in flight, etc.), were believed by princes and populace alike. In those days a prediction could instigate political action. Modern politicians, however, have been caught napping by events such as the student revolt in 1968, the oil crisis of the 1970s, and the stockmarket crash in 1987, despite the fact that the number of centres specializing in forecasting and prospective analysis techniques has been steadily increasing.

This has prompted me to formulate a concept that I refer to as the Cassandra paradox: 'the effectiveness of forecasting techniques is independent of the rigour of the method used'. This paradox illustrates a principle of the theory of knowledge, dear to the English-speaking school of philosophy, whereby it is not enough for something to be thinkable, there has to be a theory for it to fit into. By changing the terms of reference, it could be said with respect to forecasting that it is not enough for a forecast to be accurate, it must also be acceptable. This concept of acceptability will serve as a starting point for our analysis.

The explanation of the Cassandra paradox lies in the personality of Cassandra. Despite the divine source of her inspiration (Apollo), her prophecies were not heeded by Priam for three major reasons. Firstly, as his daughter, she was supposed to learn from her father and not the other way around. Her words therefore had no *legitimacy* in her father's eyes. Secondly, as a woman she had no say in military affairs. Presumably the words of Hector, son of Priam and Commander of the army, would have carried greater weight. Cassandra therefore was not considered *competent* to speak. Finally, were Cassandra to have been a priestess practising her craft at Delphi, then, despite the fact that she was a woman and the daughter of Priam, her words would have been heeded by the King, her father. She did not have the *authority* of the sibyl at Delphi.

Legitimacy, competence and authority therefore seem to be the three prerequisites for account to be taken of prospective analyses. Consequently, rather than reviewing the scientific bases of long-term forecasting techniques, I shall address the factors that determine their credibility in the eyes of public decision makers, with particular reference to public policies for science and technology.

Priam and Cassandra, or the relationship between policy makers and science

The issue of public policies for science and technology concerns two communities which differ in many respects; the scientific community on the one hand, and the policy-making community on the other (Montigny & Meyer-Krahmer 1987).

The legitimacy of the scientific community is founded upon international recognition. The scientific community acknowledges sectoral boundaries between biology and physics, for example, but is relatively unfettered by territorial or national frontiers. The way in which the Nobel Academies are run is highly significant in this respect. Admittedly, the degree to which frontiers are taken into account has increased during the past 50 years in areas of applied science.

In contrast, the policy-making community, which finances a large part of the scientific community, bases its legitimacy on other principles, namely those conferred by its territorial ascendancy at regional, national or supranational level (e.g. the European Economic Community). As a result, the scientific and policy-making communities adopt different rationales in that they do not share the same space–time frame of reference. The funding of public R&D stops short at political boundaries, whereas scientific activity crosses over them. The existence of set terms of office in political life imposes a different time-scale to that imposed by constraints of a strictly scientific nature.

The problem of communication becomes crucial when the policy-making community has to obtain information from the scientific community to formulate and implement policies for science and technology. This is what happens when an R&D programme has to be evaluated or a strategic prospective analysis carried out (Montigny & Restier-Melleray 1987b).

As there are similar difficulties in establishing the credibility of either evaluation or forecasting, the two exercises will be discussed in parallel (see Chabbal 1987). This approach also has the merit of highlighting the similarities and differences between the two activities.

Evaluation and forecasting

The purpose of evaluation and the purpose of forecasting

In this paper the term 'research evaluation' refers to the evaluation of research operators, i.e. the appraisal of structures (programmes, organizations) set up by governments. This evaluation is fundamentally different from assessment by peers, which is carried out by researchers themselves in accordance with their own rules and which addresses the quality of research. In contrast, the evaluation of an operator addresses *added value*: in other words, is a given operator the best means to achieve a specific goal? This type of evaluation is carried out by scientists in collaboration with others who offer a variety of skills (economists, industrialists, etc.).

When viewed in this light, evaluation, in the same way as forecasting, is one of the methods used by public decision makers in preparing their action.

> 'Program evaluation and forecasting . . . are at first glance quite different and unrelated approaches . . . One is focused on knowing and understanding the past, whereas the other . . . seeks to "peer deep into the veil of the future". . . . These differences in focus logically lead to different interpretations of reality . . . However, . . . together they make up a natural continuum for examining programs and policies. In practice, they depend upon each other; they overlap.' (Chelimsky 1987)

This natural affinity between evaluation and forecasting is even closer in practice since the two activities address the same person (the public decision maker), require the same degree of professionalism (even if the methods represent specific disciplines), both involve committee work (even if the committees are made up in different ways), and both must be based on established authority, regardless of whether the latter is institutional (high authority) or moral (ethical codes of practice).

Customer and addressee

As the name suggests, the addressee is the end-user for whom the evaluation or forecasting exercise is intended, and as such represents a kind of 'Priam' whose ear must be attuned to a certain type of discourse. It is important to establish who the addressee is. If he is to take account of the results of an evaluation or prospective analysis, it is necessary to determine his identity, expectations and reactions, and gain an understanding of what he will listen to. To use the language of signals theory, this amounts to saying that it is necessary to understand how the receiver works to ensure that the message sent is perceived as a signal and not as noise.

The addressee is first and foremost the customer, i.e. the party who 'buys' or finances an evaluation or a prospective analysis. For public R&D, the customers are the directorates of Ministries, agencies or large scientific organizations. For evaluation of public scientific research, the customer is a readily identifiable group of people consisting of research administration managers, mainly from the scientific community, who are familiar with the R&D area. Nevertheless, their tasks in research administration have been assigned by some other agency, less specifically scientific and more political in nature, which is either a government or a parliament and to whom they report.

The party designated as the customer is therefore merely a proxy, and the real end-user of the evaluation and forecasting work is the policy-making community. At this point the issue becomes more complicated. The policy-making community is eminently varied, by virtue of the democratic process, and is made up of a variety of addressees including politicians, economists, industrialists, and also the media, whose action is of considerable importance in that they are a major channel for conveying information to the rest of society.

The objective is therefore to set up machinery to ensure that any message relating to evaluation or prospective analysis is fully credible to the entire policy-making community, i.e. there must be no possible doubt regarding the competence, legitimacy or authority of the analysis.

The competence of evaluation and forecasting specialists

With regard to evaluation and forecasting, the policy-making community (Priam) has to recognize the competence of the scientific community (Cassandra) before it will listen to the latter; not the scientific competence, which it accepts unreservedly, but the competence to make valid statements outside a strictly scientific frame of reference in the grey area mid-way between science and policy. This raises the question of the methods and techniques used for evaluation and forecasting, because recognition of competence is based on the rigour and comprehensiveness of these methods and techniques. It so happens that the techniques used in evaluation and forecasting are based on different principles.

In the evaluation of a research operator (organization or programme), the crux of the matter is to acquire quantitative and qualitative data that describe the operator to be assessed. Such data range from available input–output indicators to documents such as reports by decision-making bodies, and those that describe the follow-up of actions and the way in which the operator functions. Techniques are chosen on the basis of the type of research operators to be assessed (large-scale programmes, incentive programmes, research organizations, etc.). It would be inappropriate to describe these techniques in this paper, although it should be stressed that they should only be dealt with by specialists ('evaluologues', to use the term coined by R. Chabbal) — organizations that have acquired real competence in methods of investigating the R&D process.

In forecasting, the problem is similar, but the area for analysis is far greater than in the case of evaluation. The scope of evaluation is fairly well-defined while that of long-range forecasting is virtually unlimited. Again, forecasting methods vary considerably and range from the use of panels of experts (Delphi) to very specific methods like the Micmac methods developed by the French nuclear agency (see Godet 1987); there is no shortage of instruments, and the choice of instrument will depend upon the forecasting exercise.

Given that evaluation and forecasting must meet different criteria, the methods used must also be different. However, these two activities have one fundamental point in common in that the use of evaluation and forecasting methods must be left in the hands of professionals. Depending upon circumstances, these professionals may belong to:

(a) An independent organization, e.g. the Deutsches Institut für Wirtschafforschung in Berlin, the Science Policy Research Unit in Sussex, or the Gruppen for Resursstudier in Oslo;

(b) A specialized department in a research administration, e.g. the Evaluation Unit of the Directorate General XII and the EEC's Forecasting and Assessment in the Fields of Science and Technology (FAST) programme, or the Centre de Prospective et d'Evaluation at the French Ministry of Research in Paris;

(c) A consultancy, large numbers of which have been set up over the past few years, e.g. Bossard for the EEC, Hayek Engineering for the Swiss federal polytechnic schools (Montigny & Restier-Melleray 1987a).

What they all have in common is a real mastery of retrospective and prospective analysis techniques applicable to R&D. It is worth noting that in such organizations evaluation specialists and forecasting specialists work alongside each other. It is essential for these organizations to have a professional approach, since the prerequisite for effective retrospective or prospective analysis is *competence*.

Legitimacy of evaluation and forecasting analyses

The fact that retrospective or prospective analyses are carried out by professionals is not in itself a sufficient guarantee of effectiveness; the analyses must still acquire legitimacy. Because this type of analysis involves two separate communities (the policy-making community and the scientific community), each of which bases its legitimacy on different principles, committees are called upon to play a major role in this area.

The committee has the specific task of presenting the data collected by evaluation and forecasting professionals in a form that both meets the expectations of the addressee and faithfully reflects the concerns of the scientific community. It is probably in the composition of these committees that the difference between evaluation and forecasting is most apparent.

The distinguishing feature of a committee entrusted with the task of evaluating a research operator will be its independence with regard to both the source of financing and the operator itself. It is precisely this independence that lends credibility to its comments; it allows the committee to distance itself from the data on the research operator being evaluated. By virtue of its neutrality, an evaluation committee can act as a real bridge between the policy-making community (to whom the evaluation is addressed) and the scientific community (the target of the evaluation).

In contrast, with regard to predictions, a committee asked to carry out a prospective analysis must involve all protagonists, i.e. representatives of both the policy-making community and the scientific community, to the greatest extent possible. The purpose of such an analysis is twofold: firstly, to be as wide-ranging or all-encompassing as possible; and secondly, to establish a common basis for agreement among the various actors. Whereas an evaluation committee has only a few members, a forecasting committee may have up to fifty. Furthermore, the work of the evaluation committee is not only discreet, to ensure that it has full control over the evaluation process until the latter is completed, but also intensive so that it can swiftly satisfy the expectations of end-users. Conversely, a forecasting committee proceeds by wide-ranging consultation (seminars, symposia, etc.), and considers its findings for a period of one or even two years. For example, whereas the evaluation of a large European programme costs in the region of $100 000, a comparable strategic analysis will cost up to $1 million (Chabbal 1987).

Authority: the basis for the effectiveness of
evaluation and forecasting analyses

The legitimacy of evaluation or forecasting committees does not yet have enough currency for their proposals to have any impact on the decision-making process; this legitimacy must still be founded upon an authority which reflects a general consensus. Such agreement is fundamental in that it confers a prescriptive role on the recommendations resulting from the evaluation or forecasting exercises. This authority may take one of two forms; it may be either an institutional authority (academies, for example) or a moral authority (ethical codes of practice).

In some research organizations there are institutions that have a universally recognized reputation. For example, the National Academy of Sciences in the USA has two distinctive attributes: firstly, all scientific fields are covered by top-level specialists; and secondly, its reputation at national and international level carries undisputed weight with policy makers. The Academy is also proof that it is possible for the scientific community and policy makers to speak a common language, a prerequisite for any type of consensual approach to research. Because the Academy never makes rash commitments, is mindful that it should remain above any suspicion of bias, and only issues an opinion after wide-ranging consultation with the representatives of different schools of thought, its comments have a wide audience and are often heeded.

These considerations prompted Professor R. Chabbal to propose that the Commission of the European Communities set up, in place of an Academy, a High Council which would invest evaluation and forecasting exercises with the authority they need to be truly effective. He suggested that two main authorities be set up, a 'Conseil Européen de l'Evaluation et de la Prospective' (European Evaluation and Forecasting Council) and a 'Conseil de l'Analyse Stratégique Scientifique' (Council for Scientific Strategic Analysis). Such bodies could accommodate in their composition and procedures the specific disciplines of evaluation and forecasting.

Nonetheless, the idea behind the setting up of these two committees is the same; the principle is to provide a guarantor to underpin the entire organization of the evaluation and forecasting system.

Another way that forecasting and evaluation gains authority is by agreement between policy makers and the scientific community upon a set of 'ground rules' guaranteeing the effectiveness of retrospective and prospective analyses. This is what happens in Scandinavian countries (Montigny 1987a,b). A consensus is reached by asking such questions as: What is the subject? How should the analysis be carried out? With whom?

The approach of establishing ground rules is being investigated by a group of government experts from OECD member countries (OECD joint workshop on Evaluation of Technological Innovation Programmes, December 1987, unpublished work). Admittedly, this group studies mainly evaluation, but, given the relationship that we have established between evaluation and forecasting, the basic principles apply to both. The experts recommend the adoption of a code of ethics for policy makers, experts, and the parties being assessed. Some principles have already been established, although the code is still at an early stage of development.

Public decision makers must:
(a) Be aware of the potential consequences of an evaluation exercise;
(b) Clearly define their goals, i.e. establish whether the objective is to improve a programme, terminate a programme, redefine an existing policy or develop a new policy;
(c) Respect the independence of evaluators;
(d) Refrain from improvising deadlines and means;
(e) Choose suitable evaluators, i.e. if the objective is to improve a programme, experienced 'technical' teams should be chosen; conversely, if the aim is to refine policy, 'credible' individuals should be chosen. In both cases, and as a general rule, multidisciplinary groups will be set up.
(f) Choose the right moment for evaluation.

Experts must:
(a) Only accept the job if they are sure that they have the requisite skills, and either have, or can acquire, the means needed for the task (experts);
(b) Verify the reliability of results (control groups);
(c) Work in concert with decision makers;
(d) Avoid disturbing the parties being evaluated, respect the requests of the latter with regard to confidentiality, gain their confidence and inform them of results;
(e) Offer alternative recommendations;
(f) Maintain their level of competence (coaching, training, exchanges).

Scientists must:
(a) Accept evaluation as a tool;
(b) Respect the evaluation process;
(c) Participate in the evaluation process.

At the conclusion of their meeting, the OECD experts recommended that three lines of action should be taken:

Improvement of evaluation techniques should continue, i.e. the *competence* of evaluators should be improved still further;
The possibility should be investigated of setting up an international association to include the different partners involved in the evaluation procedure (public decision makers, scientists, experts), i.e. the scope of *legitimacy* should be widened;

Finally, a proper charter should be drawn up on the basis of the principles referred to above; this charter would act as a *guarantee*, i.e. it would confer *authority* on recommendations ensuing from evaluation exercises.

It is necessary to study further the scope of application of forecasting exercises to determine which aspects of these recommendations for evaluations would also be pertinent to forecasts. However, these proposals are particularly interesting in that they clearly demonstrate the close relationship between *competence, legitimacy* and *authority*. Without competence, authority and legitimacy lose their credibility. Without legitimacy, competence is merely a formal technique and authority a hollow prescription. Without authority, competence and legitimacy have only limited *effectiveness*. These comments are equally applicable to both evaluation and forecasting.

Conclusion: evaluation, forecasting and policy making — from Greek mythology to contemporary democracy

Broadly speaking, the mechanics of policy making in the heroic age of Ancient Greece had three basic components: the King, who decided which action to take; the Oracle, who determined, by divination, whether a given action was feasible and, if so, under what conditions; the People, for whom the words of the King, supported by those of the Oracle, had the force of prescription.

The mechanism is simple, linear and, to a certain extent, effective because it elicits the consent of both the civil and policy-making segments of society. Nowadays, Delphic oracles no longer hold sway and the power of the public decision maker is vested in the citizens he or she represents. Power is matched by reactive power in the science policy arena. Consensus is rare, takes time to achieve and is hard to maintain. Yet only consensus has any real prescriptive force, because its effectiveness is contingent upon the consent of all parties.

Consequently, the only objective for evaluation and forecasting is to achieve this consensus, even if the latter is essentially provisional. This is the price that must be paid for effective evaluation and forecasting. Perhaps it is also the price to be paid for democracy.

References

Chabbal R 1987 Reorganisation of research evaluation in the Commission of the European Communities, CEC, Brussels
Chelimsky E 1987 Retrospective and prospective analysis — linking program evaluation and forecasting. Evaluation Review vol 11, Sage Publications, Washington
Godet M 1987 Scenarios and Strategic Management. Butterworth, London
Montigny P 1987a L'organisation de la R&D en Suède et en Norvège. CPE, Paris
Montigny P 1987b L'organisation de la R&D en Finlande. CPE, Paris

Montigny P, Meyer-Krahmer F 1987 Sample of evaluations of measures in favour of innovation in selected European Countries of the OECD. OECD document DSTI/SPR/87.52

Montigny P, Restier-Melleray C 1987a L'audit d'un grand organisme de recherche et d'enseignement public par un cabinet privé: le cas des écoles polytechniques fédérales hélvétiques. CPE, Paris

Montigny P, Restier-Melleray C 1987b Utilization of evaluation in defining scientific policy. France: overview and perspectives. UNO document SC.TECH/AC.24/R.6

DISCUSSION

Hill: Philippe, I would like to be provocative and disagree with you strongly in several respects. It seems to me that there's no particular obligation on the part of the public official, the King, to listen to the evaluators or to engage in a consensus process of evaluation. The King is in control: he has the money, the power and the authority.

You present a list of things decision makers should do. I suppose they must be aware of the consequences of evaluation or they wouldn't have asked for it, but they don't have to define their goals; in fact, they rarely do. There's a great premium on public decision makers *not* defining their goals!

Montigny: That's why I refer to the necessity for accepted professional ethics.

Hill: In the political world, defining one's goals clearly is not necessarily an ethical perspective. It may be unethical to do that. Respecting the independence of the evaluators is not something politicians necessarily want to do; it may be in their interest to interfere in what the evaluators are doing. Deadlines are not in their control—there may be a crisis. Rather than saying that decision makers must refrain from imposing deadlines I would say that evaluators must learn to work to whatever deadline decision makers face in their political world. The Congressional Research Service, for example, often has to respond with an evaluation while the debate is happening on the floor of the Congress. We get a telephone call asking for data immediately. The OTA (Office of Technology Assessment) may take two years; we are allowed five minutes. You must work within the framework. The OECD exercise seems to incorporate a scientist's view of what ethics in public policy making ought to be, and it's not very realistic.

Luukkonen-Gronow: I find the idea of setting norms for evaluations strange. I acknowledge that professional ethics are necessary, but it is unrealistic to define strict rules. In my paper (this volume), I referred to 'relevance' as one of the factors that influence impact, but I did not mean to imply that evaluations must have predetermined goals. The process of evaluation incorporates surprise. If an evaluation does not produce something that is unexpected we have set the goals too narrowly. In addition, I do not accept that researchers must acknowledge the results. Evaluators are not infallible and the researchers have a right to contest the assessment given.

Montigny: Luke Georghiou (this volume) spoke about the importance of the first phase of evaluation. When I design evaluations I emphasize the initial negotiation between everyone involved in the evaluation process. The policy makers must be aware of the consequences of what they do and these issues should be discussed before the evaluation is initiated. One third of the time allocated to the evaluation should be spent on this preliminary negotiation phase.

Hills: On the issue of consensus, I agree with you, Philippe, rather more strongly than I agree with Christopher Hill. Perhaps 'consensus' is not the right word. What is required for an evaluation to be effective is mutual understanding. If the evaluator doesn't know the objectives and interests of the policy maker, the evaluation will lack an important dimension. Equally, if the policy maker doesn't understand, for example, the importance of citation analysis and whether or not there is fractional counting, he will misunderstand the significance of the evaluation. The evaluator must know what kind of presentation and analysis will be taken seriously and must appreciate the broad policy framework within which he is drawing his conclusions.

In my experience in the Department of Trade and Industry I find that in the early stages of setting up the evaluation it is important to ensure that those who are being evaluated understand the process. Then they cooperate with the evaluation, and, rather than viewing it as a threat, see it as an opportunity to learn. From an academic point of view, the mechanisms of evaluation may appear to be relatively unimportant but, in the real world in which we work, they matter. The setting up and acceptance of an evaluative mechanism within government and within the scientific community is essential if evaluation results are to be taken seriously. Evaluators ignore such matters at their peril, and policy makers who do not understand evaluation methods exclude an important area of information.

Lake: Philippe, you said that evaluators should be neutral whereas forecasters must be involved in the field. I would remind you of the role of Hector, Cassandra's brother, from whom we get the term 'hectoring', because he had a strong capacity for putting her down! He said that as she had no understanding of the subject her forecast was not valid. Evaluations must be based on facts that are gathered impartially about the topic, but unless the evaluators have some grasp of the subject they will not be recognized by those being evaluated as having authority.

Montigny: When I said that evaluators should be neutral I meant that they are the go-between for the scientific community and the policy-making community. They must be aware of the dynamics of science and also of the dynamics of the political system. My background is in philosophy but perhaps the most interesting evaluation I have done was for a French engineering school concerned with public works. Everyone in that school was aware that I had no competence in public works, but it was assumed that I was impartial between those who want to build bridges and those who want to build roads! That perceived neutrality was helpful.

Lake: There is a general problem of timing associated with evaluations. Many of the techniques discussed here must be applied long after the research was funded. We look at the third year after publication for citations, but publication took place 18 months after the paper was submitted, which was three years after the grant was awarded. So one is looking back seven or eight years, long after decisions were taken. Yet you now speak about evaluation after 18 months, part way through a research programme; somehow one must bring these two extremes together realistically.

Montigny: I was referring to applied research, particularly the R&D programme within the European Commission. The impact of such research is relatively rapid in comparison to that of programmes in basic research.

Wald: One problem is that you never clearly define who you mean by 'policy makers'. This gives rise to Chris Hill's objections. The beautiful logic that you present is valid up to a medium level of decision makers, but not for higher levels. To include those, you would have to re-write your paper and refer to the Jeremiah paradox rather than the Cassandra paradox! The prophets of the Old Testament had everything that Cassandra lacked: complete legitimacy, because they spoke for God; great authority, more than that of the kings of Israel; everyone knew they spoke the truth. However, the Kings of Israel did not listen to the prophets but threw them into pits or killed them. The top level of decision making, to which Chris Hill referred, poses a problem which differs from the Cassandra paradox and should be analysed differently. What do you do when you have a chief ruler who is as competent, or believes that he is as competent, in science policy, as the best science policy experts?

Montigny: I recognize that my concept of policy makers is not very well defined. Do we know how decisions are taken? Who is the policy maker? Is it only the Head of State, or is it also the government and the assembly? What sort of roles are most important? What rights do academics have? I tried to include a variety of people in my definition but I need another concept if I want to discuss the top-level decision makers.

Irvine: I thought your presentation was very skilful and firmly in the French tradition of Colbertist state planning.

Montigny: Is that a compliment or not?

Irvine: That is your decision! I want to draw attention to the cultural specificity of the way evaluation is organized. What Christopher Hill said brought this out clearly. I would caution against trying to implement your proposed framework within the OECD without taking into account the different cultural and political environments for evaluation in member countries.

I was interested in your strongly Cartesian dualism of means and objectives, but I found it difficult to appreciate the role of the scientific community in your evaluation framework. The bureaucrat seems to be preeminent.

In addition, the state planning orientation of your framework leads to evaluation techniques being accorded little importance. The emphasis is rather upon politics, consultation and consensus. I would strongly disagree with you when you say that the effectiveness of forecasting is independent of the techniques employed. However, I would agree that the converse holds, in that rigour and technique are no guarantee of success.

Montigny: That is why it is a paradox. I tried to show the importance of techniques by emphasizing the expertise of those doing an evaluation. In the OECD we certainly must be aware that we have 24 cultures. Yet we are asked to establish a common 'language'. The common set of rules was not my idea, but was proposed by a group of governmental experts. I have always maintained that we should respect certain ethics in the evaluation process. That's why I thought that the OECD was a good institution in which to do this sort of study.

Weinberg: I am not sure whether the President's Science Advisory Committee (PSAC) under President Kennedy was Cassandra or Jeremiah, but in 1960 I was a member and we were all but ignored in the most important scientific decision of that decade—the decision to go to the moon. The PSAC was ignored because President Kennedy had decided to go to the moon and he knew that every one of the members was against the project. So the only deliberation that the committee participated in was a very brief announcement by the President's Science Advisor, just as we were all ready to leave, that the decision had already been made. Everybody was dumbstruck, but nothing could be done. Therefore scientists should have a certain degree of humility in thinking that anything they do will affect the political process. I don't think matters have changed all that much. I would not be surprised if the next President of the USA decides to go ahead with the superconducting supercollider whatever the scientists recommend.

Hill: The same happened with the Strategic Defense Initiative (SDI). When President Reagan announced his decision to develop SDI at a meeting of his White House Science Council they were not consulted as to 'whether', but only as to 'how'.

We have indulged here in generalizations about evaluators, policy makers and programmes, but the truth of what we have said depends greatly on circumstance. As Keith Pavitt suggested earlier, a lot of evaluation research is most useful, not for the evaluated programme, but as a basis for thinking about the next initiative or policy. Thus timeliness is not as important as technical adequacy. If I am advising the Congress on changes in tax policy towards research, I need to know what happened the last time we changed that policy, or in Canada, Sweden or the UK when similar policy changes were made. It's the use of earlier evaluation in anticipation of new policy change that I find most interesting and important. Frankly, I am frustrated by my own government's lack of attention to *ex post* evaluation for this purpose.

Pavitt: The interesting thing about the Apollo decision is that President Kennedy didn't listen to the PSAC and was perhaps fortunate not to have done so, in the sense that the technology was ready and it worked. The same is not necessarily true of SDI—a report by the OTA has questioned that. Expertise can be important in setting the bounds of what is feasible.

What is the nature of that expertise? We define it very loosely as science although we are sometimes talking more about technology. That was certainly the case for the moon shot and is the case for SDI. I have grave doubts about the ability of scientists to evaluate technology. For example, one of the greatest failings of the British nuclear energy programme was its dominance by physicists. Chemical engineers knew more about the problems of mucky processes, or what happens to wastes when they get into water. On these issues, nuclear physicists have no more legitimacy or authority to make predictions then anyone else.

Chris Hill talked about learning from the past for the next decision. I am uncomfortable about putting together forecasting and evaluation, as Philippe Montigny does. I know that 'prospective' has a great and legitimate tradition in France but, especially at the level of programmes that he is dealing with, forecasting techniques do not work. Industrial decision makers do not routinely use a sophisticated algorithm to make decisions; if they do they give it up after a few years because they make silly mistakes.

Montigny: I was speaking about the evaluation of a research operator (programme or research organization), and not the assessment of the quality of a scientific field or a programme. Thus, for me, evaluation and forecasting are very close because they have the same objective (see Chelimsky 1987). Unfortunately, we lack quantitative data about the future! Michel Godet developed a computerized method called Micmac which was used by the French nuclear energy agency. You gather five or six experts together and ask them to choose the important variables for the field in question. In the 1970s a group of experts was asked to identify the main problems that the nuclear plants in France would face in the future. The experts made a list of variables, classified them and constructed a matrix. The group then had to find a consensus for the relationship between the individual variables—it can be strong or weak. They were not allowed to leave until they had agreed on a diagram showing these relationships. A computer was used to reorganize the variables. For example, each expert listed the issue of the location of nuclear plants between position 10 and

20, but the results of the computer programme suggested that it would be the second problem in the next decade, as it in fact was. This illustrates the sort of methods we can use to look both backward and forward.

Collins: We are used, as scientists, to dealing with a world that is more or less predictable; it's only a matter of getting the right techniques and staring hard enough. As evaluators, we take that rationality and try to talk to a world governed by a completely different set of premises. I would not call politicians irrational, but their behaviour and thought processes are governed quite differently from scientific processes. It was perfectly rational for the President to ignore his Scientific Advisory Committee because he didn't want to be told 'no'. Kennedy got away with it; Nixon didn't, because cancer couldn't be solved by the same sort of approach. We're finding out about Reagan and SDI at the moment.

Chris Hill said that decision makers don't have to lay out their objectives at the beginning: that is an example of these competing rationalities. It is perfectly reasonable for decision makers to move the goal-posts and say 'I gave you until the end of next month, but I am making my decision tomorrow'. Two different approaches to two different kinds of job are rubbing against each other.

Hill: Political rationality is just as understandable, and just as rational on the same terms, as the rationality of science, but the database of relevant parameters, constraints and forces is very different. It's hard for scientists and engineers, myself included, to admit the legitimacy of those other constraints and forces.

In deciding to go to the moon, President Kennedy felt under enormous political pressure to respond adequately to the Sputnik threat, and to show the world that the USA hadn't lost to the USSR. Interestingly, SDI is rather similar. President Reagan's decision, as I interpret it, was also in response to a threat he perceived, not from the USSR, but from the nuclear freeze movement, which in early 1983 showed every sign of destroying the political consensus that underlay the President's dominance of the American political system. In ten minutes and in one fell swoop he destroyed the nuclear freeze movement worldwide, and with that preemptive strike he achieved a rational objective for himself that was terribly important. These things can easily be understood in rational terms.

Hills: We are dealing with different approaches to rationality and we must therefore make explicit the different concepts of what is rational. For example, in the UK Department of Trade and Industry we have a system known as ROAME—rationale, objectives, appraisal, monitoring and evaluation. The theory is that before any technological programme is agreed and accepted, a broad rationale as to why government should consider funding the programme must be produced. Then the objectives have to be stated. Essentially one has to assess the initial validity of the programme against the same objectives that will be used for its evaluation. The scientists and technologists proposing a programme often say that we are being bureaucratic in asking them to state what is obvious to them. Equally, the considerations of the policy maker are rational within the context in which he works, but are not made clear. The process of evaluation involves making explicit the various perceptions of the parties involved of what is rational within their decision framework. Ultimately the policy maker's rationality dominates, but he has to act knowing that the other forms of rationality are made clear. A complex series of interactions is involved and easy answers aren't available.

Blume: This discussion suggests two important conclusions. First, one must go forward with humility and not expect to achieve too much. Second, the task and the behaviour that the professional evaluator is presented with and should adopt is structured by political organization and culture. That limits the extent to which a universal discourse on evaluation is possible. There are inevitably significant differences in national political cultures. Joe Anderson says that the activity of research evaluation shouldn't be integrated solely within a field of science policy research. I take the opposite view. The indicators with which evaluators may be inclined to work are sometimes not what they seem and the work of historians and sociologists of science provides a vital corrective. Indicators such as Nobel Prizes seem useful, and are easy to count. On the other hand, historical research on how Nobel prizes are awarded shows that questions of nationality, nationalism and politics play a role. Thus the variables are not really independent.

Although the connections with science and technology studies won't necessarily make evaluating easier, they ought to provide an intellectual critique and ensure an adequate professional standard. At the same time, there ought to be a critical dialogue on the meaning of the indicators and techniques that evaluators are driven to use.

Georghiou: I partly agree with Stuart Blume. Evaluation is essentially an interdisciplinary and multidisciplinary activity. To tackle it, we should understand the underpinnings of some of the activities of the scientific community in terms of the concepts that the science studies community offer. But also within an evaluation team you need a good understanding of economics, particularly innovation economics. It is useful to include scientists and engineers, not necessarily from the field concerned, who can talk the language and relate to those being evaluated. We need to keep this balance.

Lake: I would like to hark back to the opening paper by Dr Weinberg and consider the purpose of evaluation. We have heard that one objective might be to persuade politicians of something. Evaluation may have another quite separate intrinsic purpose in the context of the evolution of science. Evaluation enables one to identify areas where there is clear success, on which it seems valid to build further activity, and to identify other areas which had seemed promising but where there is no perceived success, and which could therefore be allowed to diminish. That system builds on what is already there; one should also take into account the possibility of surprise. One option is to seek rapidly emerging nodes of science, because a discovery is usually made in three or four laboratories across the world more or less simultaneously and independently. We should build on methods that are now being developed for detecting areas of rapid growth, where discovery is inevitable. More pragmatically, within the UK Agricultural and Food Research Council a good method for identifying possible nodes has been to bring together for an annual 'brainstorming' people who have had individual merit promotion at an early stage in their careers.

References

Chelimsky E 1987 Retrospective and prospective analysis — linking program evaluation and forecasting. Evaluation Review vol 11, Sage Publications, Washington DC

Luukkonen-Gronow T 1989 The impact of evaluation data on policy determination. In: The evaluation of scientific research. Wiley, Chichester (Ciba Foundation Conference) p 234–246

Georghiou L 1989 Organization of evaluation. In: The evaluation of scientific research. Wiley, Chichester (Ciba Foundation Conference) p 16–31

Weinberg A 1989 Criteria for evaluation, a generation later. In: The evaluation of scientific research. Wiley, Chichester (Ciba Foundation Conference) p 3–15

Chairman's summing-up

Sir David Phillips

Laboratory of Molecular Biophysics, Department of Zoology, University of Oxford, The Rex Richards Building, South Parks Road, Oxford OX1 3QU, UK

The evaluation of scientific research concerns not only narrow political and scientific communities but also a much broader international community with strong industrial, commercial and political pressures within it. At the end of this conference I am left with the conviction that we need a deeper understanding of the dynamics of scientific research in a broad cultural context, and I hope we all agree that activity on this seemingly academic front must continue and be intensified. Otherwise, the relationships between the inputs to and outputs from research, however they are measured, will remain a mystery and the prospect of optimizing them a dream.

Even so, the meeting has demonstrated that important advances are being made in the evaluation of research. We would all agree that we cannot evaluate anything without measures of success and that there has been dramatic progress in the production of data for the evaluation of research. Particularly important are the evidence of research activity, from the numbers of scientific papers produced, and the evidence of research quality, from the extent to which those papers are cited by subsequent authors. Here we acknowledge a great debt to Eugene Garfield for the provision of a database that underpins the development of bibliometric methods.

On the evidence of this conference, everyone must be impressed by the rapid development of bibliometrics and by the extent to which methods are being elaborated to address policy-relevant questions. Several papers have shown the kind of insights that are being obtained and we can look forward to further important advances on this front. Nevertheless it may be appropriate to sound a cautionary note or two.

First, we must remember that the scientific literature is only a vehicle for knowledge transfer and that publication and citation rates do not provide simple measures of success in achieving the extrinsic goals of science — not even the increase of understanding, let alone social and economic benefit — that I listed in

1989 The evaluation of scientific research. Wiley, Chichester (Ciba Foundation Conference) p 265–267

my introduction. This concern underlies the opening paragraph of this summing-up and I shall return to it.

Second, as the scientific community becomes increasingly aware that its performance may be judged by bibliometric methods, we must surely expect to see adjustments in behaviour calculated to maximize apparent performance. Some people have already discerned a trend towards the 'minimum publishable paper'. Is there a developing pressure against long-term research aimed at major objectives which leads only rarely to the publication of papers? We have certainly moved a long way from Niels Bohr's view that one paper a year may be worth reading but that any more, from any one author, will not.

Third, there is a danger that over-emphasis on numbers of publications, as if maintaining a high publication rate was the objective of the public support of science, will end by alienating both public and politicians. We should consider carefully a recent statement by a UK Government Minister, Mr Christopher Patten: 'Scientific achievements should be judged less by the numbers of quotations in learned journals and more by success in meeting perceived needs.'

Clearly, as I emphasized at the beginning of the meeting, the overall aims of governments are not primarily to maximize the number of scientific papers produced (or even those that are widely cited) but rather to maintain the economy, develop and sustain the most effective defence, and achieve popular social benefit. The relationship between the health of the science base and the achievement of these objectives is evidently very complex and tenuous. We have not given it much attention during the meeting and, given the difficulty of the problem, I am not likely to make good that deficiency in a brief summing-up. But it does seem clear that more effort should be devoted to finding additional measures of scientific performance and relating them to ultimate benefits. One rather neglected area is the provision of trained manpower (the primary university product) and the part that people play directly in the processes of knowledge transfer within and between universities, industry and society generally.

Such studies would necessarily involve the development of a wider range of indicators, related to a wider range of activities and involving diverse sectors of the community. In particular, we need to involve not only scientists and technologists, but also the industrial and commercial communities as well as politicians and civil servants. And we must remember that methods of evaluation will only have an impact on policy making if they can be easily understood by non-experts, are effectively communicated to the scientific and policy-making communities, and readily withstand the analyses and criticisms of those being evaluated.

Finally, interpretation of the results must be approached with great care. Nearly all evaluations are empirical in nature and cannot address the issue of causation. I still remember my surprise when, as Chairman of the Advisory

Board for the Research Councils, I first encountered the question 'are countries prosperous because they invest in research or do they invest in research because they are prosperous?'. There is that kind of problem in the interpretation of indicators of activity and we need a much better understanding of how quantitative measures of performance relate to the activities they are designed to evaluate. Here we see again the need for more emphasis on evaluating the processes and organization of science, rather than simply its products. Such an enterprise will certainly keep a developing international community busy for some time, and provide material for another fascinating conference in the future.

.

Index of Contributors

Non-participating co-authors are indicated by asterisks. Entries in bold type indicate papers; other entries refer to discussion contributors

Indexes compiled by John Rivers

Subject Index